DAVIES ON CONTRACT

by

ROBERT UPEX, M.A., LL.M., A.C.I.Arb, F.R.S.A.
of the Middle Temple, Barrister
Emeritus Professor of Law,
University of Surrey

GEOFFREY BENNETT, M.A., F.R.S.A.
of the Inner Temple, Barrister,
Professor of Law and Director,
University of Notre Dame, London Law Programme

with a contribution by

Jason Chuah LL.M. (Cantab.)
Professor of Law, Westminster University

TENTH EDITION

LONDON
SWEET & MAXWELL
2008

First Edition	1970
Second Impression	1972
Third Impression	1972
Second Edition	1973
Second Impression	1974
Third Impression	1975
Third Edition	1977
Second Impression	1978
Fourth Edition	1981
Second Impression	1983
Third Impression	1984
Fourth Impression	1985
Fifth Edition	1986
Sixth Edition	1991
Seventh Edition	1995
Eighth Edition	1999
Ninth Edition	2004
Tenth Edition	2008

Published by
Sweet & Maxwell Limited
100 Avenue Road, Swiss Cottage
London NW3 3PF
Computerset by YHT Ltd, London
Printed in the UK by CPI William Clowes Beccles NR34 7TL

No natural forests were destroyed to make this product; only farmed timber was used and replanted.

A CIP catalogue record
for this book is available
from the British Library

ISBN: 978-1-84703-447-2

All rights reserved. Crown copyright material is reproduced with the permission of the Controller of HMSO and the Queen's Printer for Scotland.

No part of this publication may be reproduced or transmitted in any form or by any means, or stored in any retrieval system of any nature without prior written permission, except for permitted fair dealing under the Copyright, Designs and Patents Act 1988, or in accordance with the terms of a licence issued by the Copyright Licensing Agency in respect of photocopying and/or reprographic reproduction. Application for permission for other use of copyright material including permission to reproduce extracts in other published works shall be made to the publishers. Full acknowledgment of author, publisher and source must be given.

©
Sweet & Maxwell
2008

PREFACE TO THE TENTH EDITION

In the first edition F.R. Davies stated, "this book tries to give a shorter and simpler account of the law of contract than is provided by the well-known textbooks". The tenth edition of this book seeks to attain the same object.

Developments in the general principles of the law of contract have been relatively modest since 2004 but there are a significant number of changes in detail that have been noted in this edition. A trend that has continued is the increasingly elaborate provisions made for consumer protection in areas which involve the law of contract. As in previous editions, we have incorporated reference to these developments where we thought it appropriate, but have concentrated on the basic principles of orthodox contract law. This reflects, we believe, the central thrust of most taught courses on the law of contract.

As ever, we are indebted to Professor Jason Chuah for his work on Chapters 13 and 14.

The law is as stated at June 1, 2008.

Robert Upex
Geoffrey Bennett
June 2008

CONTENTS

CONTENTS

TABLE OF CASES

ix

TABLE OF CASES

TABLE OF CASES

TABLE OF CASES

xiv

TABLE OF CASES

TABLE OF CASES

xix

TABLE OF CASES

TABLE OF CASES

TABLE OF CASES

TABLE OF CASES

TABLE OF STATUTES

INTRODUCTION

A CONTRACT is an agreement which binds the parties to it. Some agreements are not contracts; for example, an agreement to meet at Burger King: what distinguishes contractual agreements from other agreements is the feature of binding legal obligation. Some legal obligations (for example, in the law of torts) arise without agreement: what distinguishes contractual obligations from other obligations is the feature of agreement.

Although agreement is a basic element of every contract, it should be noted that the agreement is not always of such a kind that it would be so called in popular speech.

First, the courts take an objective, rather than a subjective, view of agreement, and if a person has so conducted himself as to give the appearance that he has agreed, then he may be held to have agreed, even though, in his own mind, he has not.

Secondly, where one of the parties holds a monopoly position the other party has no real choice, and can hardly be said, in a popular sense, to agree. For example, if a householder wants to have electricity in his home he has to take it from an electricity company, and his "agreement" to their terms of supply is more notional than real. The same absence of real choice arises where, although there is no monopoly position, one of the parties belongs to a group who have agreed together to put forward identical terms. Many trade associations have drawn up "standard form contracts" upon which alone their members are willing to contract. The impact of these standard form contracts is particularly felt where they contain exemption clauses (see Chapter 5).

Thirdly, the law sometimes imposes terms upon one or both of the parties. The courts have developed a doctrine of implied terms, holding that a term sometimes exists in a contract even though it has not been expressly stated by the parties. In theory an unexpressed term is only applied by the court where it arises from the presumed intention of the parties. If that is so, then the doctrine of

1

the implied term does not at all conflict with the idea that contract is based on agreement. But there are cases in which the courts seem to be imposing terms rather than merely deriving them from the intention of the parties. In some areas of the law implied terms which have become well settled by judicial decisions are later set out in an Act of Parliament. An example of this process is to be found in the implied terms incorporated into a contract for the sale of goods by the Sale of Goods Act 1893. That statute, however, expressly reserved to the contracting parties the right to exclude those statutory terms if they so wished, so the principle of agreement was not really infringed. But by subsequent Acts, including the Sale of Goods Act 1979 (which repealed the Sale of Goods Act 1893), that position has been altered. Some implied terms cannot ever be excluded by the parties, and others cannot be excluded in a "consumer sale", and only in certain circumstances in a non-consumer sale. At this point one can truly say that the agreement of the parties is being limited by law. Moreover, there are many fields of activity in which, without there being any preceding history of judicially implied terms, statute law restricts the freedom of persons to agree their own contractual terms. The letting of residential property is such a field.

Subject to these qualifications, it is still broadly true to say that agreement is a necessary feature of a contract.

The other necessary feature of a contract is binding obligation. To restate the opening proposition, a contract is an agreement which binds the parties to it. This is sometimes put in slightly different words, namely that "a contract is an agreement which is enforceable at law". That is a true statement, provided that the word "enforceable" is correctly understood. It might be thought that if a party can get his contract "enforced" that means that he can necessarily get from the court an order compelling the other party to perform his part of the contract. This is not so. Whilst the court will sometimes make such an order, called an order of specific performance, it will not always do so. Indeed, by far the most usual remedy for breach of contract is an order for damages. That means that the party in fault is not ordered to perform the contract, but is ordered to make a money payment to the claimant for not having performed it. In lawyers' language an order for damages is as much "enforcement" as is an order of specific performance.

A more fundamental point about lawyers' language is that the word "law" itself has several meanings. It can mean a law, or it can mean common law as distinct from equity, or it can mean the whole body of legal rules, including both common law and equity.

There are some topics in this book which can only be fully understood by reference to history, and the history reveals the different contributions that have been made by common law and equity. But it is important to understand that by a process beginning with the Supreme Court of Judicature Act 1873 the systems of common law and equity have been fused. Professor Ashburner, writing in 1902 and referring to the Judicature Act, said: "the two streams of jurisdiction [law and equity], though they run in the same channel, run side by side and do not mingle their waters". In *United Scientific Holdings Ltd v Burnley Borough Council* (1978, HL) Lord Diplock said:

> "This metaphor has in my view become both mischievous and deceptive ... As at the confluence of the Rhône and Saône, it may be possible for a short distance to discern the source from which each part of the combined stream came, but there comes a point at which this ceases to be possible. If Professor Ashburner's fluvial metaphor is to be retained at all, the waters of the confluent streams of law and equity have surely mingled now."

In any discussion of the nature of a contract it is necessary to emphasise the feature of obligation. An agreement which does not bind the parties—an agreement, that is to say, which is not a legal obligation—is not a contract. A study of the law of contract is largely a study of actual cases which have been decided in the courts. The law is the cases, the cases are the law. But students of contract law, though they must largely occupy themselves with a study of litigation, should occasionally step back, as it were, and see the litigation in its true perspective. Contracts which give rise to litigation are a minute proportion of the vast numbers of contracts which are made every day. The overwhelming majority of contracts never give rise to any dispute whatever; where a dispute does arise, it is generally settled without recourse to the courts, or, indeed, without recourse to lawyers at all. The true importance of the law of contract is that its very existence in the background, with its principles and detailed rules, ensures that the activity of contracting runs smoothly on.

We all engage in the activity of contracting; in that sense we are all contractors. It would be a great mistake to think that it is only other people who make contracts. It would be a great mistake to think that a contract is necessarily an important and complicated transaction, such as an undertaking to build a power station. We all make contracts in the course of our everyday lives. Buying a packet of tea or a pint of bitter, renting a flat, buying a house, getting a job, even taking a bus—all these activities involve a contract. In all these activities, two (or more) persons agree and bind themselves.

So we come back to the opening proposition that a contract is an agreement which binds the parties to it.

This book examines the contractual agreement.

Part One

MAKING THE AGREEMENT

OFFER AND ACCEPTANCE

A CONTRACT is based on agreement, which arises from offer and acceptance. One person makes an offer; another person accepts that offer. When that has happened, and provided that the other necessary factors, consideration and intention to contract, are present, there is a contract. Consideration will be dealt with in Chapter 2; intention to contract in Chapter 3.

OFFER

An offer is a proposition put by one person (or persons) to another person (or persons) coupled with an indication that he is willing to be held to that proposition. The offeror (the person who makes the offer) may make the offer to a particular person, or to a group of persons or to people generally, as in a reward case. The offer may be in writing, or spoken or by conduct. Thus the offer may take any form between an elaborate document with numerous clauses and sub-clauses and an ordinary everyday act of conduct, such as a bus driver stopping at a bus stop. The indication that the offeror is willing to be bound need not be stated in words (written or spoken); it may be, and frequently is, inferred from the nature of the offeror's proposition or from the circumstances in which the proposition is made.

Offer distinguished from invitation to treat

It is necessary to distinguish an offer from an invitation to treat. The importance of the distinction is that, if an offer is made and accepted, the offeror is bound; on the other hand, if what the offeror said or did does not amount to an offer, the other person cannot create a contract by accepting it. The process leading to an agreement may be long. It may consist of requests for information, statements made to encourage interest and the like. When the negotiations have reached the point where one of the parties has made it clear that he is willing to contract on specific terms that need no further elaboration or clarification, and all that is required is acceptance by the other party, at that stage it can be said that an offer has been made.

It is not always easy to make the distinction between offers and invitations to treat, and there have been suggestions that the analysis of the existence of an agreement by means of offer and acceptance should be abandoned. In *Gibson v Manchester City Council* (1979, HL), however, Lord Diplock made it clear that offer and acceptance should remain the normal method of analysis.

Tenders

In the case of tenders the distinction between an offer and an invitation to treat is reasonably clear. If A asks a number of suppliers to put in tenders for supplying particular goods or services, he is not making an offer. This means that he is not bound to accept any of the tenders. The position is similar where A asks one supplier to put in an estimate for supplying particular goods or services. It is not A who makes the offer; the offer comes from the supplier in the form of the tender or estimate: see *Spencer v Harding* (1870).

On the other hand, there may be cases where the person inviting tenders may indicate his willingness to be bound by the highest or lowest bid, particularly in the case of competitive tendering. This is what happened in *Harvela Investments Ltd v Royal Trust Co of Canada (CI) Ltd* (1985, HL). The Royal Trust Company invited two parties to make sealed competitive bids for some property; they promised to accept the highest offer received, provided that other conditions were met. One of the parties made a bid of $2,175,000; the other made a referential bid of "$2,100,000 ... or $101,000 in excess of any other offer ...". The House of Lords held that this kind of bid was invalid. They said that the purpose of a sale by fixed bidding was to provoke the best price which the prospective purchasers were prepared to pay, regardless of what rival bidders were prepared to pay. It was inconsistent with this purpose to allow a referential bid, whose meaning could only be ascertained by looking at another bid. Lord Templeman said that the vendors could have decided on a process of bargaining by referential bids but that, in the absence of express words to that effect, such an interpretation could not be put upon a request for competitive tenders.

In the later case of *Blackpool and Fylde Aero Club Ltd v Blackpool Borough Council* (1990, CA), on the other hand, the Court of Appeal decided that there was an implied contract governing the tendering process by which the club bound itself to consider bids submitted before the deadline. This case was distinguished in the later case of *Fairclough Building Ltd v Port Talbot B.C.* (1993), although the Court of Appeal accepted the analysis of an implied contract regulating the tendering process.

Reference may also be made to *Walford v Miles* (1992) and *Pitt v PHH Asset Management Ltd* (1993), considered on pp.26 and 27.

Display of goods for sale

The displaying of goods for sale is not the making of an offer. In *Pharmaceutical Society of Great Britain v Boots Cash Chemists (Southern) Ltd* (1953, CA), for example, the Society brought an action against Boots alleging that Boots were breaking the Pharmacy and Poisons Act 1933, which requires the sale of any article containing any substance included in Part I of the poisons list to be made under the supervision of a registered pharmacist. Boots had a self-service shop in Edgware. A customer went in and selected articles from the shelves, put them in a wire basket, went up to the cash-desk and paid for them. There was a registered pharmacist standing by the cash-desk but not by the shelves. If the sale took place when the customer picked up the article, then (subject to another point in the case) Boots were in breach of the law; if the sale took place at the cash-desk, then they were not. The Court of Appeal held that the sale took place at the cash-desk. The display of articles on the shelves was not an offer, only an invitation to treat. The offer was made by the customer taking the article to the cash-desk. That offer could be, but need not be, accepted by Boots at the cash-desk. If it were accepted there, the contract of sale would arise at that point, and so would be under the supervision of the registered pharmacist.

The courts have taken the same view of goods displayed in a shop window. Indeed, in *Fisher v Bell* (1961) Lord Parker considered the point to be beyond argument. He said:

"It is perfectly clear that according to the ordinary law of contract the display of an article with a price on it in a shop window is merely an invitation to treat. It is in no sense an offer for sale, the acceptance of which constitutes a contract".

The law is the same if the article is displayed without a price on it.

Advertisements

The same rule applies to an advertisement by, for example, a trader stating that he is willing to sell goods. The advertisement is not an offer, merely an invitation to treat. In *Partridge v Crittenden* (1968), for example, Partridge was charged with the criminal offence of unlawfully offering for sale a wild live bird, after placing an advertisement stating that he had such birds for sale. It was held by the Divisional Court that the advertisement was an invitation to treat, not an offer for sale, and that therefore the offence charged was not established.

There are situations, however, where an advertisement will be held to be an offer, not a mere invitation to treat, for example, where an advertisement offers a reward for the return of lost property. If the finder returns the property, knowing of the reward offer, he is entitled to the reward. It is not open to the owner to say that he was not making an offer, but was merely inviting offers. This kind of situation is sometimes described as a unilateral contract. It is a one-sided contract in the sense that one party binds himself by a conditional promise leaving the other party free to perform the condition or not, as he pleases. In a unilateral contract the offeror will not know whether the contract is valid and effective until the other party has performed his part. An example of a unilateral contract is *Carlill v Carbolic Smoke Ball Co* (1893, CA). The defendants were the makers of a medicinal item called "The Carbolic Smoke Ball". They issued an advertisement in which they promised to pay £100 to anyone who caught influenza after having sniffed at the smoke ball for a specified period in a prescribed manner. They stated that they had deposited £1,000 with their bankers "to show their sincerity". Mrs Carlill saw the advertisement, bought a smoke ball, sniffed at it in the prescribed manner and then caught 'flu. She sued for the £100 and succeeded. The defence argued that the advertisement was not a true offer, but the Court of Appeal held that it was.

Doubts have sometimes been expressed as to whether unilateral contracts really constitute a separate category of contracts, but the Court of Appeal has held that there is such a category. See *United Dominions Trust (Commercial) Ltd v Eagle Aircraft Services Ltd* (1968, CA).

Auction sales

The analysis of auction sales in terms of offer and acceptance is not entirely easy. The bidder is the offeror; his bid (which may be by words or by conduct, such as waving a catalogue) is the offer. The auctioneer accepts the offer by striking the table with the hammer. It follows that the auctioneer can withdraw an item at any time provided he has not accepted a bid. Previous bids, it seems, lapse as offers as soon as a higher bid is made. In *Harris v Nickerson* (1873) it was decided that the advertising of an auction sale to be held at a particular time and place is not an offer. But it seems that an advertisement that a sale will be held "without reserve" is a definite offer, if the sale actually begins, that the auctioneer will accept the highest bid. According to *Warlow v Harrison* (1859) the auctioneer in such circumstances makes a contract with each bidder that he will sell to the highest bidder. This approach was followed by the Court of Appeal in *Barry v Heathcote Ball & Co* (2001). The facts were that auctioneers advertised that they would sell by auction without reserve two new engine-analyser machines, for each of which the manufacturers' list price was £14,521. The claimant made the only bid of £200 for each of the machines but the auctioneers purported to withdraw the machines from the sale. The Court of Appeal upheld the trial judge's decision in favour of the claimant. They said that the promise to hold the auction without reserve was an offer of a collateral contract which was accepted by the claimant making his bid. See p.64 where collateral contracts are discussed more fully.

11

Negotiations for the sale of land

In the case of sales of land there are so many points to be settled between the parties that the courts are inclined to treat as a mere step in the negotiations a communication which in other circumstances might be held to be a definite offer. A good example of this is to be found in *Harvey v Facey* (1893, PC). The plaintiffs telegraphed to the defendants: "Will you sell us Bumper Hall Pen? Telegraph lowest cash price". The defendants replied by telegraph: "Lowest price for Bumper Hall Pen £900". The plaintiffs telegraphed: "We agree to buy Bumper Hall Pen for £900 asked by you ...". It was held by the Privy Council that there was no contract. The second telegram was not an offer but merely an indication of the price the defendants would want if they eventually decided to sell.

Another example is to be found in *Clifton v Palumbo* (1944, CA). The plaintiff estate owner wrote to the defendant:

"I ... am prepared to offer you or your nominee my Lytham estate for £600,000 ... I also agree that a reasonable and sufficient time shall be granted to you for the examination and consideration of all the data and details necessary for the preparation of the Schedule of Completion."

It was held by the Court of Appeal that this letter was not a definite offer. Consequently, the defendant's "acceptance" was ineffective and there was no contract.

ACCEPTANCE

An offer will not ripen into a contract until it is accepted by the offeree and communicated to him. This is the necessary ingredient for turning an offer into an agreement. There may be questions, however, as to whether the offeree's action amounts to an acceptance. To do so, it must be made in response to the offer and must correspond to its terms. This means that if, for example, the offeree tries to introduce different terms, his action may be treated as a counter-offer which puts an end to the original offer.

Two questions are therefore involved here: (1) has there been an acceptance in fact; and (2) has there been communication of that acceptance to the offeror?

12

The fact of acceptance

Two questions have to be dealt with here: (1) how does one recognise that acceptance has occurred as a fact? and (2) what amounts to acceptance?

Negotiations

When parties carry on complex negotiations it is sometimes difficult to say when (if at all) an offer has been accepted. As in the case of *Clifton v Palumbo*, it is sometimes hard to determine whether or not an offer has been made. It is sometimes harder still to say whether an acceptance has been made. This is because it is necessary to find two things instead of only one; an acceptance as well as an offer. What is more, it is necessary to find an acceptance that exactly fits the offer: see below. As negotiations go on, each party may advance a new point or withdraw a former point, and in the end they may disagree as to whether they have ever agreed. The court must then look at the whole course of the negotiations and decide whether the parties ever did agree to the same terms.

An example of this type of problem is to be found in *Walford v Miles* (1992, HL). The defendants owned a photographic business, which they were interested in selling. After negotiations with the plaintiffs, they agreed in principle to sell the business to them "subject to contract". Soon after, it was further agreed that if the plaintiffs provided a comfort letter from their bank, the defendants would terminate negotiations with any third party and would not deal further with any third party. The comfort letter was duly provided, but the defendants sold the business to a third party. The plaintiffs argued that there was a binding "lock-out" agreement, under which they had been given an exclusive opportunity to try to come to terms with the defendants and which was collateral to the negotiations for the sale of the business. The House of Lords said that a lock-out agreement may be an enforceable agreement, but went on to say that an agreement to negotiate in good faith for an unspecified period is not enforceable. They therefore held that the agreement in question was unenforceable. On the other hand, in *Pitt v PHH Management Ltd* (1993, CA), the Court of Appeal found that there was a lock-out agreement, in the context of negotiations for the sale of land, and that the defendants were in breach of it. This case is considered more fully below: see p.26 ("Subject to contract").

Acceptance by conduct

Just as an offer may be made by conduct, so may an acceptance. This is clearly so in the case of a unilateral contract. Thus if A offers a reward for the return of his lost dog, Fido, then B, by taking Fido to A, both accepts the offer of the reward and performs the act necessary to gain it. It is more important to note that a bilateral contract can be made by means of an acceptance by conduct. In *Brogden v Metropolitan Railway Co* (1877, HL), Brogden had for years supplied the railway company with coal without a formal agreement. The company wished to regularise the situation, and so they sent a draft form of agreement to Brogden. He inserted a new term into the draft and returned it, marked "approved". The company's agent put it in his desk and it laid there for two years. For two years Brogden sent, and the company paid for, deliveries of coal in accordance with the terms of the draft. Then a dispute arose, and Brogden denied that any binding contract existed. The House of Lords held that a contract had been created by conduct, and that it came into existence either when the company ordered its first load of coal upon the terms of the draft or at least when Brogden supplied it. In *Jayaar Impex Ltd v Toaken Group Ltd* (1996) Rix J. said that such acceptance can only be established where the conduct is "only referable to the contract document".

Acceptance must exactly fit the offer

A reply to an offer is only effective as an acceptance if it accepts all the terms of the offer without qualification or addition. Thus, in *Brogden v Metropolitan Railway Co*, above, the return by Brogden of the draft marked "approved" did not amount to an acceptance because he had introduced a new term. In *Jones v Daniel* (1894) Daniel made a written offer to purchase Jones's property for £1,450. In reply Jones's solicitors wrote "accepting" the offer, and adding: "We enclose contract for your signature". The enclosed draft contract contained special terms not referred to in the offer, including the payment of a deposit of 10 per cent by the purchaser, a stipulation fixing the date for completion and a provision limiting the title to be shown by the vendor. Daniel returned the document unsigned. It was held that the letters did not constitute a contract; the solicitors' letter with its enclosure was not an acceptance but a counter-offer. Daniel was free to accept or reject this counter-offer; he chose to reject it, and so no contract came into existence.

Counter-offers

A counter-offer takes place where one party changes the terms contained in the other's offer. So, for example, if A offers to sell his compact disc player to C for £100, and C responds by offering £85, C's response is a counter-offer. Here, the response of the offeree shows that he wishes to contract on terms different from those proposed by the offeror. It puts an end to A's offer and itself amounts to an offer which may be accepted or rejected by A. If A rejects the counter-offer, C cannot then try to accept A's original offer, unless he expressly revives it.

A good example of this point is *Hyde v Wrench* (1840). Wrench offered to sell his farm for £1,000. Hyde responded by saying that he would give £950 for it. Wrench wrote rejecting this proposal. Hyde then wrote to say that he would give £1,000 after all. Hyde sued Wrench, trying to enforce a sale at £1,000. He failed. It was held that no contract came into existence. Hyde's response (£950) was a counter-offer, which put an end to the offer (£1,000). The counter-offer was refused, and so did not lead to a contract. The subsequent "acceptance" by Hyde of the original offer was not an acceptance at all; it could not be because there was no offer in existence. It was itself another offer (by Hyde) which Wrench was quite entitled to refuse. See also *Jones v Daniel*, above.

There are limits to the rule, however. It would be a mistake to think that every answer which does not exactly accept the offer is a counter-offer. It is quite possible for an offeree to respond to an offer by making an inquiry as to whether the offeror would be prepared to amend some term of his offer. Thus, in *Stevenson v McLean* (1880) the defendants offered to sell some iron to the plaintiffs for cash. The plaintiffs asked whether they could have four months' credit. That inquiry was held not to be a counter-offer, but only a request for information, with the result that later acceptance of the original offer created a binding contract. Another example is *Brogden v Metropolitan Railway Co*, above. The insertion of the term into the draft contract amounted to a counter-offer; the respondents accepted it when they started performance of the contract and ordered and took delivery of the coal consistently with the agreement. See also *Jayaar Impex Ltd v Toaken Group Ltd* (1996), above.

The battle of the forms

In some cases there occurs what has come to be called "the battle of the forms". A makes an offer on his own printed form containing certain terms, and B accepts on his printed form, which contains conflicting terms. A contract may well come into existence by conduct, but on which terms? Often the answer is that the party who fires the last shot wins.

In *Butler Machine Tool Co Ltd v Ex-Cell-O Corporation (England) Ltd* (1979, CA), the facts were that sellers offered to sell a machine to buyers, the offer being made in a document containing terms, including a price variation clause, which were to "prevail over any terms and conditions in the buyer's order". The buyers placed an order in a letter containing conflicting conditions and with no price variation clause. At the bottom of the order was a tear-off confirmation slip expressly subject to the buyers' terms; the sellers completed it and returned it. They later claimed to be entitled to vary the contract price. The Court of Appeal rejected their claim. For more recent examples, see *Rimeco Riggelsen & Metal Co v Queensborough Rolling Mill Co* (1994) and *Ignazio Messina & Co v Polskie Linie Oceaniczne* (1995).

The communication of acceptance

It is not enough for the offeree to decide that he accepts the offer; he must also communicate his acceptance to the offeror. Thus, in *Brogden*'s case, the fact that the agent of the railway company put the amended draft contract in his drawer did not amount to acceptance, even though in his own mind he did accept the amendments. It would still not have amounted to acceptance if the agent had written on the draft, before putting it in his drawer, "Amendments accepted".

If the parties are in each other's presence, there is no problem unless their words cannot be heard because of a loud noise. In that case, the words must be repeated. In *Entores Ltd v Miles Far East Corporation* (1955, CA) Lord Denning gave a number of graphic examples. Thus, if A shouts an offer to B across a river and A does not hear B's reply because of the noise of a passing aircraft, there is no effective acceptance; if C makes an offer to D by telephone, and D's favourable reply is lost because the line is so bad, there is no contract.

If the parties are not in each other's presence, different rules will apply, depending upon whether the method of communication used is instantaneous or not.

Acceptance by post

The general rule that acceptance takes effect only when it is communicated to the offeror, raises difficulties where the acceptance is sent by post. The acceptance may be delayed, or even permanently lost, in the post. The question in this case is whether the offeror or the offeree should bear the risk.

The rule is that an acceptance by post takes effect as soon as it is posted. This special rule relating to the post was laid down in *Adams v Lindsell* (1818). On September 2, 1817, the defendants wrote to the plaintiffs offering to sell some wool and requiring an answer "in course of post". The letter of offer had been wrongly addressed, and it did not reach the plaintiffs until the evening of September 5. That same day the plaintiffs posted a letter of acceptance, which reached the defendants on September 9. The evidence was that if the letter of offer had been correctly addressed, a reply could have been expected "in course of post" by September 7.

On September 8 the defendants sold the wool to someone else. It was held that a contract came into existence on September 5, when the plaintiffs posted their letter of acceptance. The rule that postal acceptance dates from posting has been the rule ever since and applies even where the letter of acceptance is delayed in the post, and even where it is totally lost. This was laid down in *Household Fire (etc.) Insurance Co v Grant* (1879, CA).

It should not be thought that an offeree is always, in all circumstances, free to accept by letter and then claim that his acceptance took effect at the moment of posting. The principle is that this special rule only applies where postal acceptance is prescribed by the offeror, or is indicated by the manner or terms of the offer, or is the common sense mode of acceptance in the circumstances. The overriding consideration is reasonableness. If the offer comes by post, it is reasonable to use the post for acceptance, unless, of course, the offer says otherwise. If the offer does not come by post it is a question of fact whether it is reasonable to accept by post. The principle is fully discussed in *Henthorn v Fraser* (1892, CA).

The postal rule does not apply if, having regard to all the circumstances, including the nature of the subject-matter, the negotiating parties cannot have intended that there should be a binding agreement until the acceptance was received. This point was established by *Holwell Securities Ltd v Hughes* (1974, CA). In that case the defendant gave the plaintiff an option to purchase some land, the option to be exercisable by notice in writing to a given address within a specified period. A letter accepting the offer was posted by the plaintiff but failed to arrive. The Court of Appeal said that the requirement that the notice should be in writing to a given address was sufficient to override the postal rule and apply the general rule of communication of acceptance.

A final problem in cases where the postal rule applies concerns the withdrawal of his acceptance by the offeree. If B, in the presence of A, accepts A's offer, B cannot withdraw his acceptance. But if A and B are not in each other's presence, and B accepts A's offer by posting a letter to him, it is not clear whether his withdrawal of his acceptance before the offeror receives it (for example, by telephone) is legally effective. There is no English decision on this point. A Scottish case, *Dunmore v Alexander* (1830), suggests that the offeree can withdraw his acceptance. But there is a New Zealand case which goes the other way: *Wenkheim v Arndt* (1873). That case suggests that the effect of a letter of acceptance cannot be altered once it has been put into the post. Principle requires that the offeree, having posted a letter of acceptance, should not be free to withdraw it. Acceptance takes effect from posting, thus binding the offeror; it should equally bind the offeree.

Other types of communication

A telegram is treated in the same way as a letter: a telegram of acceptance takes effect when it is handed in at a post office; see, e.g. *Cowan v O'Connor* (1888). But an acceptance by telex has been distinguished from an acceptance by telegram. In *Entores Ltd v Miles Far East Corporation* (1955, CA), it was held by the Court of Appeal that an acceptance took effect when it was received, not when it was sent. The evidence was that dispatch and receipt were not completely instantaneous, but the court took the view that they were so nearly so that the situation should be equated with a conversation face to face or by telephone, and should be distinguished from correspondence.

In the light of developments in modern communication technology, however, particularly the use of fax machines and emails, which may enable communications to be stored out of business hours until the next working day, the continuing relevance of this decision must be in doubt. In *Brinkibon Ltd v StahagStahl und Stahlwarenhandels GmbH* (1983, HL), Lord Wilberforce suggested that in cases where communication is not instantaneous the general principle that acceptance is effective when communicated would not apply. It is not clear, though, what principle would apply. He said that in such cases the problem must be resolved by considering the facts of each case, particularly the intention of the parties, sound business practice and (in some cases) a judgment where the risk should lie. In *JSC Zestafoni v Ronly Holdings Ltd* (2004) Colman J. applied the rule in *Entores* to a communication by fax and held that an agreement was made when and in the place where the fax was received. See also *Apple Corps Ltd v Apple Computer Inc* (2004).

In *Mondial Shipping and Chartering B.V. v Astarte Shipping Ltd* (1996), Gatehouse J. suggested that receipt of a contractual notice should be deemed to take place at the start of the next working day if it was received and stored outside normal working hours. The difficulty is, however, that that is a different issue from the issue of communication of acceptance of a contract.

Exceptions to the rule

Acceptance in unilateral contracts

The terms of an offer may be such that the requirement of communication of acceptance is waived by the offeror. This is commonly the case in unilateral contracts. In *Carlill v Carbolic Smoke Ball Co* the court rejected the argument that Mrs Carlill should have notified the defendants of her intention to put their medicament to the test. Bowen L.J. said:

"If I advertise to the world that my dog is lost and that anybody who brings the dog to a particular place will be paid some money, are all the police or other persons whose business it is to find lost dogs to be expected to sit down and write me a note saying that they have accepted my proposal?"

In such a case acceptance does not require communication in the ordinary sense. But, of course, there is a kind of communication; the bringing along of the lost dog is, in a sense, a communication.

In *Carlill*'s case it did not matter when acceptance took place; it was sufficient for the court to decide that acceptance had at some time taken place. But in some unilateral contract situations it is of

great importance to decide when acceptance takes place. A difficulty arises from the coming together in one situation of fact of two
rules: (1) that an offer can be withdrawn at any time before
acceptance; and (2) that acceptance need not be communicated. If
A promises £10 to anyone who returns his dog, can he withdraw his
offer when he sees the dog being brought back by the person who
found it? To put the question in another way, at what point in time
does B accept the offer of a reward? In *Daulia Ltd v Four Millbank
Nominees Ltd* (1978, CA), Goff L.J. answered this question in the
following terms:

> "Whilst I think that the true view of a unilateral contract must in
> general be that the offeror is entitled to require full performance
> of the condition which he has imposed and short of that he is not
> bound, that must be subject to one important qualification,
> which stems from the fact that there must be an implied obliga-
> tion on the part of the offeror not to prevent the condition
> becoming satisfied, which obligation ... must arise as soon as the
> offeree starts to perform."

An example of this is *Errington v Errington* (1952, CA). A father
allowed his son and daughter-in-law to live in a house which he had
bought for £750, of which he borrowed £500 on mortgage from a
building society. He told them that if they paid the mortgage
instalments the house would be theirs when the mortgage was paid
off. The couple did not bind themselves to continue paying the
mortgage instalments, but they began to pay them and did not fail
to pay any instalment that was due. At this point of time the father
died and his personal representatives purported to withdraw his
offer. It was held by the Court of Appeal that it was too late to
withdraw the offer. Denning L.J. said:

> "The father's promise was a unilateral contract—a promise of the
> house in return for their act of paying the instalments. It could
> not be revoked by him once the couple entered on performance of
> the act, but it would cease to bind him if they left it incomplete
> and unperformed, which they have not done."

In most unilateral contracts the same act is both the acceptance and
the consideration. On this view, however, given proper facts, the
two may be separated, in that partial performance can amount to

acceptance, while complete performance remains necessary to constitute consideration.

Silence and acceptance

The offeror may waive the requirement for acceptance to be communicated, as was mentioned earlier. He may not waive the requirement of communication in the sense of stating that silence is to amount to acceptance. In *Felthouse v Bindley* (1862) the facts were that Felthouse discussed with his nephew, John, the possibility of buying a horse belonging to John. A few days after the oral discussion, John wrote to his uncle that he gathered there had been a misunderstanding: the uncle apparently believed that he had bought the horse for £30; the nephew believed that he had sold it for 30 guineas. The uncle then wrote in reply to his nephew proposing to split the difference and adding that if he heard no more about it he would assume that the nephew agreed. John did not reply to that letter, the uncle did not pay any money, and the horse remained in John's possession. Eight weeks later, John held an auction sale of his farming stock. He told the auctioneer, Bindley, not to sell this particular horse, as it had already been sold. By mistake the auctioneer sold the horse. Felthouse sued Bindley in conversion; he could only succeed in conversion if the horse was his at the time. His action failed; the court held that the horse was not his at the time, there having been no effective acceptance of his offer. The case shows that even where acceptance is by conduct, that conduct requires to be communicated; it was clear from the nephew's conduct that he mentally accepted his uncle's offer, but that conduct was not revealed to the uncle.

An important application of the principle in *Felthouse v Bindley* is that if a trader sends goods to a householder by post, without request, he cannot claim later that the householder has contracted to buy them because he has remained silent in the face of the implied offer to sell. This matter is now to some extent governed by statute: see the Unsolicited Goods and Services Acts 1971 and 1975.

Cross-offers

The general rule that acceptance, to be effective, must be communicated, stems from the basic principle that contract is based on agreement. If acceptance is not communicated the agreement is not, or is not seen to be, complete.

A similar point arises in connection with cross-offers as with

21

unilateral contracts. (Cross-offers are offers that cross with each other in the post.) If A writes to B offering to sell his car for £1,300, and B, before he has received that letter, writes to A offering to buy the same car for £1,300, is there a contract? In form there is no acceptance; both letters are offers. Can it be said that in substance B is accepting A's offer, or A is accepting B's offer? Again, on principle the answer should be "No." But the principle is not so strong as in the case of B's doing an act which, unknown to him, has been the subject of A's offer of a reward. In the case of cross-offers, although there is no acceptance, there is a kind of agreement; both A and B want to make an exchange of a car for £1,300. This point has never been decided in England, but it has been stated, obiter, in *Tinn v Hoffman* (1873) that in such a situation there is no contract.

Unauthorised communications

The general rule that acceptance, to be effective, must be communicated to the offeror is established beyond doubt. But the question is whether the communication of acceptance is valid if made by someone without the authority to make it. In *Powell v Lee* (1908) the plaintiff applied for the headmastership of a school. The managers of the school decided, by a narrow majority, to appoint him. One of the majority, without being authorised to do so, sent a telegram to the plaintiff telling him that he had been appointed. At a later meeting the managers rescinded their former resolution and appointed someone else. The plaintiff sued for damages for breach of contract. The court rejected his claim.

In the light of this case, it must follow that the acceptor is not bound until communication has taken place. It would be strange if the acceptor could be deprived of his freedom to change his mind by the act of an unauthorised person.

TERMINATION OF THE OFFER

There are four ways in which an offer may terminate without ripening into a contract. The fifth, a counter-offer, has been considered above: see p.15.

Revocation

An offer can be revoked or withdrawn at any time before it is accepted. Revocation, to be effective, must be communicated to the offeree. Unlike an acceptance, however, a revocation need not be communicated by the party himself. It is sufficient if the offeree learns from a third party that the offer has been revoked. Thus, in *Dickinson v Dodds* (1876, CA), Dodds offered to sell a house to Dickinson for £800, the offer "to be left over until Friday, June 12, 9am". On Thursday, June 11, Dodds sold the house to one Allan, and that same evening Dickinson was told of the sale by a man called Berry. Before 9am on June 12, Dickinson handed to Dodds a letter of acceptance. The Court of Appeal held that there was no contract; Dodds's offer had been withdrawn before acceptance.

The revocation must be actually communicated to the offeree. This is so even though the post is used as the channel of communication. The rule that an acceptance by post takes effect from the moment of posting does not apply to a revocation of offer. This point is well illustrated by *Byrne v Van Tienhoven* (1880). On October 1, the defendants posted a letter in Cardiff to the plaintiffs in New York, offering to sell 1,000 boxes of tinplates. On October 8 they posted a letter revoking the offer. On October 11 the plaintiffs received the offer letter and telegraphed their acceptance. On October 20 the letter of revocation reached the plaintiffs. It was held that the revocation took effect only on October 20, and that, that was too late, as the plaintiffs had already accepted. This is a clear instance of how the law prefers an objective to a subjective view of agreement. Subjectively viewed, there was no agreement here; at the moment of acceptance, on October 11, the offeror was not willing to contract. But because the offeree did not know of this unwillingness he was held entitled to accept.

In some cases, the offeror promises to keep the offer open for a stated period of time. This kind of promise is sometimes called a firm offer. The question is whether such a firm offer may be revoked before the expiry of the stated period. In *Routledge v Grant* (1828) the defendant offered to take a lease of premises belonging to the plaintiff and promised to keep the offer open for six weeks. After three weeks he revoked the offer; the plaintiff waited until the end of the six weeks and then accepted it. The court held that there was no contract. If the promise to keep the offer open had been supported by consideration, it would have been enforceable, but, in the absence of consideration, it could be withdrawn at any time with impunity. A promise to keep an offer open which is supported by consideration is called an option contract.

Lapse of time

If an offer is stated to be open for a fixed time, then it cannot be accepted after that time. If it is revoked before the end of the stated period, the offeree can do nothing about it: see above. If no time is stated in the offer, then the offer lapses after a reasonable time. What is a reasonable time is a question of fact, depending on the means and the subject-matter of the offer. Thus, if an offer is sent by telegram, an acceptance by letter might well be held to be too late: see *Quenerduaine v Cole* (1883). Similarly, an offer to sell perishable goods, or an offer to sell something (such as a block of shares) that fluctuates rapidly in market value, would lapse after quite a short time. It is not possible to lay down detailed rules; the whole circumstances of the offer must be looked at.

It is not entirely clear whether lapse of time causes the offer to lapse in the sense that the offeror is deemed to withdraw the offer or in the sense that the offeree is deemed to refuse the offer. *In Manchester Diocesan Council of Education v Commercial & General Investments Ltd* (1970) Buckley J. preferred the latter view.

Non-occurrence of condition

An offer which is expressly or impliedly made subject to some condition cannot be accepted if the condition fails. A very important practical application of this principle is that an offer to buy goods (or to take goods on hire-purchase) is subject to an implied condition that they will continue, until acceptance, in substantially the same state as they were in at the time of offer. In *Financings Ltd v Stimson* (1962, CA), where this principle was applied, Donovan L.J. said:

> "Who would offer to purchase a car on terms that if it were severely damaged before the offer was accepted, he, the offeror, would pay the bill? ... The county court judge held that there must, therefore, be implied a term that until acceptance the goods would remain in substantially the same state as at the date of the offer; and I think this is both good sense and good law."

24

Death

In the case of the death of the offeror, it seems that, if the offeree does not know that the offeror has died, an acceptance will be valid if the nature of the contract is such that it can be performed by the offeror's personal representatives: see *Bradbury v Morgan* (1862). If the offeree is given notice of the offeror's death, the estate will not be bound.

There is no direct English authority on the converse situation, where the offeree dies. Probably the offer comes to an end, by operation of law, on the death of the offeree. A Canadian case, *Re Irvine* (1928), points that way.

It is important to note that the question whether death puts an end to an offer is quite separate from the question whether death puts an end (and with what effect) to a contract. The effect of death after acceptance will be dealt with in Chapters 13 and 17.

A contract may fail to come into existence, even though there is offer and acceptance, because of uncertainty as to what has been agreed. Thus in *Scammell v Ouston* (1941, HL), the parties agreed that Ouston should acquire from Scammell a new motor-van "on hire-purchase terms". The House of Lords held that the agreement was too vague to be enforced, since hire-purchase terms were many and various, and it was impossible to decide on which hire-purchase terms the parties intended to contract. But in *Hillas v Arcos* (1932, HL) the House of Lords upheld an agreement for the purchase of timber "of fair specification", holding that in the light of the previous course of dealing between the parties, and in the light of "the legal implication in contracts of what is reasonable", the words used were sufficiently certain. The House of Lords emphasised in *Scammell v Ouston* (which was later than *Hillas v Arcos*) that the court will, if possible, implement and not defeat reasonable expectations; they will, if possible, follow the example of *Hillas v Arcos*. This desire of the courts not to "incur the reproach of being the destroyer of bargains" (a phrase used by Lord Tomlin in *Hillas v Arcos*) was well shown in *Nicolene Ltd v Simmonds* (1953, CA). There was an agreement for the sale and purchase of a large quantity of steel bars. The terms were perfectly clear except for a statement that the transaction was to be subject to "the usual conditions of acceptance". The Court of Appeal held that, there being no "usual conditions of acceptance", the words were meaningless and must be ignored. Denning L.J. observed that if the court were to hold otherwise, "you would find defaulters all scanning their contracts to find some meaningless clause on which to ride free".

Problems of a similar sort may also arise where the contract provides for machinery to resolve disputes between the parties. In *Sudbrook Trading Estate Ltd v Eggleton* (1983, HL), for example, a lease gave lessees (tenants) an option to purchase premises at a price to be agreed upon by two valuers; one valuer was to be nominated by the lessor, the other by the lessees. In default of agreement, an umpire was to be appointed by the valuers. The lessees tried to exercise the option, but the lessors refused to appoint a valuer and claimed that the option clause was void for uncertainty. The House of Lords said that the question in such a case was whether the machinery agreed upon by the parties was an essential factor in determining the price to be paid or whether it was simply a means of ensuring that a fair price was paid. Only where the machinery was essential and had not been implemented would the agreement be held to be incomplete and not binding. On the facts, the House of Lords held that the machinery was not essential and ordered an inquiry into the fair value of the premises.

The lack of certainty was also an underlying reason for the House of Lords' refusal to uphold the "lock-out" agreement in *Walford v Miles* (1992). Lord Ackner said that the fundamental problem with the agreement was that its length was indefinite and it was therefore uncertain. If it had provided for a period of time during which the exclusive negotiations were to take place, it would have been enforceable. His approach was followed by the Court of Appeal in *Pitt v PHH Asset Management Ltd* (1993): see below.

SUBJECT TO CONTRACT

It is common practice in negotiations for the sale and purchase of land for the intending purchaser to make an offer which is expressed to be "subject to contract". In that event it is well settled that neither party is bound unless and until a formal contract is made between the parties. Authority for this is to be found in *Chillingworth v Esche* (1924, CA).

The clear general rule is that the phrase "subject to contract" is conditional, in that the condition to be fulfilled before a contract comes into existence is that there should be an exchange of contracts; before that event, either party can withdraw. The rule is not confined to agreements for the sale of land. In principle it could apply to any kind of agreement; it is only that in practice the phrase is most often used in agreements relating to land. Also, it is not always the purchaser who introduces the phrase "subject to contract". It may be introduced by the potential vendor. But even the offeree, whether vendor or purchaser, may be the one who introduces the phrase. If the offeree does so, saying that he accepts "subject to contract", is not a true acceptance, and he is not bound. On the other hand, such a statement does not amount to a refusal or a counter-offer.

The general rule may be displaced in exceptional circumstances which persuade the court not to give the words their usual meaning; for an example, see *Alpenstow Ltd v Regalian Properties Plc* (1985). The general rule may also be displaced if the court finds that there was a collateral agreement, such as a lock-out agreement. This is what happened in *Pitt v PHH Asset Management Ltd* (1993). The plaintiff and another would-be purchaser (B) were both trying to buy a property; both made an offer to buy for £200,000, but the plaintiff's was accepted subject to contract. B increased her offer to £210,000. When the selling agent told the plaintiff that the acceptance of his offer had been withdrawn, he threatened an injunction to prevent the sale. He and the selling agent then reached an oral agreement that the defendant would sell him the property for £200,000 and would not consider any other offers provided the plaintiff exchanged contracts within two weeks of exchange of a draft contract. The Court of Appeal held that this agreement was a lock-out agreement by which the defendant agreed not to consider any further offers for the sale of the property for a limited period. It was therefore capable of being a binding contract independently of the continuing negotiations and despite the fact that they were subject to contract.

Where some phrase other than the precise phrase "subject to contract" is used, it is often a difficult task for the courts to decide whether a provision in an agreement that some other normal document should subsequently be drawn up does or does not render the original agreement incomplete. An example of this difficulty is to be found in *Warrior Records v Hayes* (1966, CA).

The question of "subject to contract" is closely involved with the requirement that a contract for the sale of land must be in writing: see p.105, below.

THE LIMITS OF OFFER AND ACCEPTANCE

It is almost invariably possible to analyse agreement into offer and acceptance. But there are circumstances in which this analysis is impossible or highly artificial. A good example is to be found in *Clarke v Dunraven* (1897, HL). The owners of two yachts entered them for the Mudhook Yacht Club Regatta. Each owner undertook, in a letter to the club secretary, to obey all the rules of the Club. These rules included an obligation to pay "all damages" caused by fouling. While manoeuvring for the start, the Satanita fouled and sank the Valkyrie. The owner of the Valkyrie sued the owner of the Satanita for damages. By statute the liability of a colliding ship in such circumstances was limited to £8 per ton on the registered tonnage of that ship. The plaintiff argued that this general law was overridden by the defendant's contractual undertaking to pay "all damages". The question, therefore, was whether there was or was not a contract between the two owners. The difficulty was that their immediate relations were not with each other but with the Yacht Club. Despite this, it was held that a contract existed between them; it was created either when they entered their yachts for the race, or, at the latest, when they actually sailed.

NOTE ON MISTAKE

In this book "mistake" is dealt with in Chapter 9. It should be pointed out, however, that some (but not all) kinds of mistake amount to a failure by the offeror and offeree to reach agreement. Those kinds of mistake, therefore, could have been discussed in this chapter on offer and acceptance. They are more conveniently dealt with at a later stage.

CHAPTER TWO

CONSIDERATION

AN AGREEMENT does not, by itself, have legal effect so as to bind the parties at law. Two further elements are required: consideration and the intention to contract. The purpose of this chapter is to explain the meaning of consideration; intention to contract will be looked at in Chapter 3.

The Law of Property (Miscellaneous Provisions) Act 1989 has affected the legal requirements relating to seals in deeds. Before its enactment, it was sometimes said that a seal was an alternative to consideration and that a contract under seal did not need consideration. The present position is considered at the end of this chapter.

THE DEFINITION OF CONSIDERATION

In *Currie v Misa* (1875) consideration was defined as follows:

"A valuable consideration, in the sense of the law, may consist either in some right, interest, profit, or benefit accruing to the one party, or some forbearance, detriment, loss, or responsibility given, suffered or undertaken by the other."

That could be shortened into the statement that consideration is some benefit accruing to one party or some detriment suffered by

29

the other. Often the benefit and the detriment are the same thing looked at from different points of view.

Although the benefit/detriment analysis is still present in more recent case law, there has been a shift of emphasis to the notion of exchange. Sir Frederick Pollock said that consideration consists of "an act or forbearance of one party, or the promise thereof", which is "the price for which the promise of the other is bought". This statement emphasises the idea of exchange, whilst retaining the traditional elements of benefit and detriment. Such an approach may be seen in recent cases such as *Williams v Roffey Bros & Nicholls (Contractors) Ltd* (1990): see p.39, below.

Executory and executed consideration

Sir Frederick Pollock's definition of consideration talks in terms both of acts done or not done and promises of acts. It is thus possible that performance of the contract on both sides remains in the future. Executory consideration may thus be described as an exchange of promises; executed consideration consists of the exchange of a promise for an act. In both cases, the use of the term "exchange" should be noted.

An example of executed consideration is the delivery of goods by a supplier for which the customer has agreed to pay on delivery. If the supplier delivers the goods, he has given consideration in the form of the supply of goods. If the supplier agrees to deliver the goods in the future and the customer agrees to pay on delivery, the consideration on both sides is executory. If the supplier does not deliver the goods, the customer can sue him although he has not paid for the goods. When he sues the supplier the customer can point to his promise to pay as being the consideration for the supplier's promise to deliver the goods. The promise to pay is a detriment to the customer and a benefit to the supplier. The customer is relieved, in the events that have happened, from having to carry out his promise. It is enough that he was ready and willing to perform it at the due time.

Where, as in the last example, the consideration consists, on both sides, of a promise, each party is both promisor and promisee; he gives a promise and receives a promise. But if either party brings an action for breach of contract he will be suing as promisee. The plaintiff has to show that he gave something in return for the promise which was made to him, and that something may be either an act or a promise. Thus, consideration is one side of a bargain. The consideration given by the plaintiff, and the consideration given by the defendant, together make up a bargain. Neither party in a contract is making a free gift to the other; each is striking a bargain with the other. Hence the notion of exchange.

The doctrine of consideration requires that an agreement will only be enforceable as a contract if it contains consideration; that is, it will only be enforceable as a contract if it is a bargain. It need not be a good bargain, however.

Finally, the distinction between executed consideration and past consideration should be noted. Executed consideration consists of a promise followed by an act; past consideration consists of an act followed by a promise and is not good consideration. This topic is considered more fully at p.34, below.

Consideration must be sufficient but need not be adequate

In everyday speech the words "sufficient" and "adequate" mean much the same thing. In the law of contract "sufficient" consideration means such consideration as the law will recognise. "Adequate" consideration means something which is equal in value to that for which it is given in exchange. As long as some value has been given, the courts will not ask whether adequate value has been given. If A promises to sell his car to B for £100, the £100 is a sufficient consideration. The courts will not concern themselves with that; they will not investigate the condition of the car to see whether £100 is a fair price for it. The courts thus do not see it as their role to police agreements made freely between parties.

An example of this view is *Thomas v Thomas* (1842). The facts were that a dying man expressed the wish to his executors that his wife should live in his house for as long as she wished and so long as she remained a widow. Acting on this, they promised the house to the widow who, in exchange, promised to pay £1 a year as ground rent and to maintain the property in good repair. The court's view was that the executors' desire to satisfy the wishes of the dead man was not sufficient consideration. On the other hand, the widow's promise was of value and therefore amounted to sufficient consideration.

Thus, the statement that consideration must be sufficient only means that consideration must be of such a kind as has been accepted by the courts as being valid consideration. To assist an understanding of this question, various kinds of consideration that have been held to be not valid or sufficient will be examined. These are: (1) consideration which does not contribute to the bargain; (2) past consideration; and (3) consideration which does not move from the plaintiff.

Consideration which does not contribute to the bargain

Consideration which does not contribute to the bargain is not sufficient consideration. Of course, since consideration need not be adequate, the value of the consideration may be very small indeed. The bargain made between the promisor and the promisee may be, from the promisor's point of view, a very bad bargain. But so long as there is a bargain at all, and so long as there is some contribution, however small, coming from the promisee, the promisor can be held to his promise.

It is important to distinguish a situation where a promise is made for a very small consideration from a situation where a promise of gift is made in a conditional form. Three propositions may be stated: (1) a promise by A to give his car to B is not binding, as it is the promise of a gift; (2) a promise by A to transfer his car to B for £1 is binding, as it is supported by consideration (albeit very small) moving from B; (3) a promise by A to transfer his car to B if B will collect it from A's garage is (except in exceptional circumstances) a conditional gift, which, being a gift, is not binding. Of the three situations there is only one in which there is a bargain: situation (2). It is only in situation (2) that there is a contractual bond.

Trivial acts

A trivial act may make a contribution. In *Chappell & Co Ltd v Nestlé Co Ltd* (1960, HL) the plaintiffs owned the copyright in a piece of music called "Rockin' Shoes". The defendants (Nestlé) arranged for another company to make records of "Rockin' Shoes". Nestlé then offered the records to the public for 1s. 6d. (7.5p) plus three wrappers from their bars of chocolate. When the wrappers came in to Nestlé they were thrown away. Nestlé offered to pay Chappell a royalty at 6.5 per cent of 1s. 6d. per record. Chappell refused the offer. The relevant legislation permitted a person to make a record of a piece of music for retail sale if he gave notice to the copyright owner and paid him a royalty of 6.5 per cent of "the ordinary retail selling price". Chappell sued for breach of copyright. The issue was whether the ordinary retail selling price

32

was 1s. 6d. or something more. The House of Lords (by a majority) held that it was something more, on the grounds that the three wrappers were part of the consideration. Here too the more satisfactory analysis of the case is that the requirement for the wrappers amounted to part of the exchange; they could not be seen as a benefit or detriment in themselves.

Settlement of actions

If A has a right of action against B, but promises not to sue B, that promise is valid consideration for a promise by B. An example might be where B owes money to A and the money is now due. If A promises not to sue for the time being, and B promises to pay a higher rate of interest, A can enforce B's promise. A's forbearance to sue is consideration; it contributes to the bargain; the debtor gains extra time to pay, and the creditor suffers the detriment of being kept out of his money.

The rule is quite straightforward where the person who forbears has a clearly valid claim. It is less easy to identify the consideration where the claim which the promisee gives up is not a valid claim. It is a question of degree. If the claim is clearly invalid, and the promisee knows it is, giving it up is not consideration: *Wade v Simeon* (1846). Thus a promise by a bookmaker not to sue his client for a lost bet is no consideration for some promise made in return by the client. The bookmaker would not be giving up anything of value, and so he would not be making any contribution to the bargain. This is because a bookmaker cannot sue his client for the amount of a lost bet: see Chapter 10. If the claim is not clearly valid, nor clearly invalid, but is doubtful, a promise to give it up is consideration provided that the person making that promise is behaving honestly and reasonably: *Cook v Wright* (1861). So, for example, in *Horton v Horton* (1961) a husband agreed to pay his wife maintenance of £30 per month, in return for which she agreed not to bring an action for maintenance. He did not deduct income tax from the payments and later, when the issue of tax arose, agreed to pay an amount which would leave £30 after deduction of tax. After being presented by the Inland Revenue for a tax bill in respect of the tax notionally deducted he refused to make any further payments on the grounds that his second promise was not supported by fresh consideration. The consideration, if it existed, was to be found in the settlement of the wife's claim for rectification of the original agreement. (Rectification is an equitable remedy by which a document that is claimed not to represent the original agreement of the parties is altered to the correct version of their agreement.) Upjohn L.J. held that whether or not the wife's claim for rectification would have succeeded was irrelevant to the question provided that she had a genuine belief that she had a good claim.

A distinction should be made between the situation where a claim is settled and where a payment is made to meet an acknowledged liability but the payment is less than the amount owed. As will be seen, a lesser payment is not consideration for a promise not to pursue the balance of the claim: see p.42.

Past consideration

The general rule

Past consideration is not sufficient consideration. If A promises B £5 because B cleaned A's car last Tuesday, B cannot sue on that promise because the consideration furnished by B is past consideration. When A's promise was made B's act was already in the past. Past consideration can thus be identified by chronology. If a promise is made after the act in relation to which it is given, the act is past consideration.

A good example of the rule is *Roscorla v Thomas* (1842). Thomas sold a horse to Roscorla for £30. After the sale Thomas promised that it was sound and free from vice. It was not. Roscorla sued for damages for breach of warranty. He failed; the only consideration which he had given was the purchase price and clearly that was not given for the promise, since at the time of the promise that consideration was already past. Thus a guarantee given after a sale is past consideration and cannot be sued on.

Past consideration must be distinguished from executed consideration. If A offers a reward to anyone who finds and returns his lost dog, Fido, and B finds Fido and returns him to A and claims the reward, B has already performed his consideration when he makes his claim. That is executed consideration and is perfectly valid. When B made his claim his act was in the past, but it was not in the past when A made his promise. In other words, in this case, the promise was followed by the act. In the case of past consideration, the act is followed by the promise.

The question whether consideration is past or not is one of fact, and the wording of the contract is not decisive. In *Re McArdle*

(1951, CA) a man left a house by will to his widow for life and then to his children. During the widow's life her daughter-in-law (who lived in the house) made various improvements to the house. After this work had been done all the children signed a document addressed to the daughter-in-law promising to repay her £488 from the estate for the work she had done. The Court of Appeal held that this was past consideration.

On the other hand, in *Goldshede v Swan* (1847) a promise was made "in consideration of your having today advanced ... £750". The plaintiff proved in evidence that the advance was made at the same time as the promise, and the court held that this was not a case of past consideration. Although the wording was in the past tense, the evidence showed that the consideration was not in fact past. *Goldshede v Swan* also illustrates the point that the chronological test is not to be pressed to an extreme; if the act and the promise take place at substantially the same time, the act is not past consideration.

Exception to the general rule

A past act is outside the general rule if two conditions are satisfied: (1) that the act was done at the request of the promisor; and (2) that the parties all along contemplated that payment would be made.

In *Lampleigh v Braithwaite* (1615) Braithwaite had killed a man. He then asked Lampleigh to do all he could to get a pardon from the king. Lampleigh succeeded and Braithwaite then promised him £100. He broke his promise and Lampleigh sued him. The court gave judgment for the plaintiff. The judgment in *Lampleigh v Braithwaite* emphasises the point that the service was done at the request of the promisor. It does not expressly state that the parties all along contemplated that payment would be made; this is implicit in the judgment. It is clear now that such contemplation is essential if a past act is to be saved from invalidity. This was the view of Bowen L.J. in *Re Casey*'s Patents, *Stewart v Casey* (1892, CA). In that case, the owners of patent rights promised their manager a share in the rights in consideration for his past services to them. Bowen L.J. held that the promise was enforceable and found evidence on which to base the implication of a promise to pay. He said:

"The fact of a past service raises an implication that at the time it was rendered it was to be paid for, and, if it was a service which

35

was to be paid for, when you get in the subsequent document a promise to pay, that promise may be treated either as an admission which evidences or as a positive bargain which fixed the amount of that reasonable remuneration on the faith of which the service was originally rendered".

A similar view was taken by Lord Scarman in *Pao On v Lau Yiu Long* (1980, PC).

A possible explanation of the difference between the approach of the court in *Re McArdle* and the approach in *Re Casey's* Patents is that a court will be more willing to imply a promise to pay in the case of a commercial relationship than in the case of a domestic relationship, bearing in mind that in domestic relationships there is a presumption that there is no intention to create legal relations. Intention to create legal relations is discussed in the next chapter.

Consideration which does not move from the claimant

Consideration which does not move from the claimant is not sufficient consideration. The claimant is normally the promisee in contract cases. He has been given a promise by the defendant, and he is now suing to enforce that promise. He will fail in his action if consideration did not move from him, i.e. if he did not provide consideration. The basis of this rule is to be found in the judgment of Patteson J. in *Thomas v Thomas* (1842), when he said:

"Consideration means something which is of some value in the eye of the law, moving from the plaintiff; ... at all events it must be moving from the plaintiff."

The consequence of this rule is that, although there may have been a consideration, if it moved from or was provided by somebody else, it will not help the claimant. Thus, A may make a promise to B to put £10,000 into his business if X does the same. X does provide £10,000, but A does not. B cannot successfully sue A. The consideration has not moved from B, but from X, and that is not sufficient. B is the promisee but he has not provided consideration.

Nor can B sue A if the promise of A has not been made to B but to X. In *Tweddle v Atkinson* (1861) an agreement was made between William Guy and John Tweddle by which each promised the other that he would pay a sum of money to William Tweddle, who was the son of John Tweddle and the prospective son-in-law of William

Guy. William Guy died without having paid, and William
sued his executors. He failed. In this case, the plaintiff 1
merely not provided consideration; he was not even the pr\
(the person to whom the promise was given).

The fact that William Tweddle was not the promisee opens up
another ground on which a plaintiff in his position would fail in his
action. The doctrine of privity of contract says that a person who is
not a party to a contract cannot sue on it. This matter will be dealt
with later, in Chapter 12. It is relevant here, however, because the
rule that consideration must move from the promisee should not be
seen as being separate from the doctrine of privity. In fact, they may
be treated as being two ways of looking at the same thing. This is
because of the notion of contract as bargain. If a person gives no
consideration for a promise he cannot sue on that promise, whether
or not he is the person to whom the promise is made. If he is the
promisee he is a party to the agreement, but since a contract is a
bargain and he plays no part in the bargain, he is not a party to the
contract. It should be noted, however, that the rules relating to
privity of contract have been modified: see Chapter 12.

While consideration must move from the promisee, it need not
move to the promisor. Suppose that there is an agreement, as in
Tweddle v Atkinson, between X and A, that each will pay a sum of
money to B, and that X pays up and A does not. X can sue A, just
as John Tweddle could have sued William Guy (or his executors); it
does not matter that the consideration moving from X does not
move to A; it is a detriment to X, incurred at the request of A.

Performance of existing duty

If a person promises to do something which he is already under a
duty to do, the question is whether that promise can be valid
consideration for a promise made to him in return. The traditional
view has been that the performance of an existing duty cannot be
consideration for a further promise. This may be based on the view
that, if A promises B that he (A) will do something which he is
already bound to do, it cannot be said that his promise makes any
contribution to a bargain with B. Another way of looking at it is
that A's promise cannot be said to have been induced by the further
promise of B, since he was already under a legal duty.

This aspect of consideration is usually categorised into three
different types of situations: (1) where A makes a promise to B that
he will do something which he is already bound, by the general law,

to do; (2) where A makes a promise to B that he will do something which he is already bound, by a contract with B, to do; and (3) where A makes a promise to B that he will do something which he is already bound, by a contract with C, to do.

Duty imposed by the general law

The leading case is *Collins v Godefroy* (1831). Collins had attended on subpoena to give evidence for Godefroy in a case in which Godefroy was a litigant. Collins alleged that Godefroy promised to pay him six guineas for his loss of time. Collins failed in his action, on the ground that he was bound by the general law to attend the trial (because that is the effect of a subpoena). Consequently, in so attending he did not provide any consideration.

It is settled that if a person does his public duty and exceeds it, this does amount to consideration. In *Glasbrook Bros Ltd v Glamorgan CC* (1925, HL) a mine-owning company feared violence from strikers and asked for police protection for the mine.

They asked for more protection than the police authority reasonably considered necessary, and they agreed to pay for it. The House of Lords held that the police were only under a general duty to provide reasonably necessary protection, and that as they had provided more than that, the police authority had given valid consideration and were entitled to payment for the extra protection provided. See also *Harris v Sheffield United Football Club Ltd* (1987).

In *Ward v Byham* (1956, CA) the father of an illegitimate child promised the child's mother that he would pay her £1 a week allowance for the child, provided that she could prove that the child, was "well looked after and happy" and that she was allowed to decide for herself whether or not she wished to come and live with her mother. The Court of Appeal held that the mother could enforce the father's promise, although she was under a statutory duty to maintain the child. Morris and Parker L.JJ. based their decision on the view that the mother was undertaking to do more than her duty. Denning L.J. (as he then was) expressly reached his decision on the footing that the mother,

"In looking after the child, is only doing what she is legally bound to do. Even so, I think that there was sufficient consideration to support the promise. I have always thought that a promise to perform an existing duty, or the performance of it, should be regarded as good consideration, because it is a benefit to the person to whom it is given."

In *Williams v Williams* (1957, CA) Denning L.J. said:

"A promise to perform an existing duty is, I think, sufficient consideration to support a promise, so long as there is nothing in the transaction which is contrary to the public interest".

These statements by Lord Denning appear to be in conflict with *Collins v Godefroy*, above.

Existing duty imposed by contract with promisor

This is the situation where A is seeking to enforce a promise made to him by B, and is relying, as consideration, on his promise to do something (or his having done something) which he is already bound, by a contract with B, to do. In this situation A's promise is not valid consideration. A does not contribute anything to the new bargain with B. So, for example, in *Stilk v Myrick* (1809) the plaintiff, Stilk, was a seaman who had agreed to sail to the Baltic and back at £5 a month. There were 11 men in the crew. During the voyage two seamen deserted. The captain agreed to share the wages of the two deserters between the rest of the crew, if they would work the ship back to London. When the ship reached London, Stilk asked for his share, and was refused. He sued. He failed, on the ground that he was already bound by contract to work the ship back to London. Lord Ellenborough expressly said that he was reaching his decision on the ground of lack of consideration and not on public policy. In *Hartley v Ponsonby* (1857), on the other hand, a ship left England with a crew of 36. At Port Philip many of the crew deserted, so that only 19 were left, of whom only five were able seamen. The captain promised the plaintiff (and others) an extra £40 to work the ship to Bombay. In due course the plaintiff received his regular wages, but the £40 was refused him. He sued for it, and he won. The court said that the ship was so shorthanded that the voyage became a dangerous voyage. Consequently, the seamen were no longer bound to serve. Thus they were free of their original contract, and free also to make a new contract, in which their new promise to serve constituted valid consideration.

The rule in *Stilk v Myrick* has been examined and effectively overruled by the Court of Appeal in *Williams v Roffey Bros &*

Nicholls (Contractors) Ltd (1990). The plaintiff was sub-contracted to do carpentry work by the defendant building contractors on a block of flats they had contracted to refurbish. The plaintiff found himself in financial difficulties; the defendants were liable under a penalty clause in the main contract if it was not completed on time. So they agreed to pay him an extra £10,300 (£575 per flat) on completion to ensure that he continued with the work and completed on time. They paid him £1,500; he completed eight further flats. He then stopped work and brought an action against them. They denied that any part of the £10,300 could be claimed on the grounds that the agreement to pay was not supported by consideration. The Court of Appeal upheld the plaintiff's claim. They held that, where one party to a contract agrees to make a payment to the other over and above the contract price in order to secure the completion on time of the contract by that other, and by doing so obtains a benefit, such as the avoidance of a penalty payable to a third party, the obtaining of the benefit can amount to consideration for the payment of the additional sum. The agreement to pay the extra £10,300 was therefore supported by consideration. The Court of Appeal purported to distinguish *Stilk v Myrick*, but made it clear that they regarded the principle in that case as valid.

The decision was criticised by Colman J. in *South Caribbean Trading v Trafigura Beheer BV* (2004) on the grounds that it is inconsistent with the rule that consideration must move from the promise (or claimant).

Duty imposed by contract with third party

Where A makes a promise to B that he will do something which he is already bound, by a contract with C, to do, he can rely, as consideration, upon that promise (or upon his performance of that promise). In *Scotson v Pegg* (1861) the plaintiffs, A, had contracted to deliver a cargo of coal to B or "to the order of B" (i.e. to anyone nominated by B). B sold the cargo to the defendant, C, and, exercising his right under the contract, ordered A to deliver it to C. C then promised A that he would unload the coal at a stated rate. He did not unload the coal at the stated rate, and A sued him. They claimed that their delivery of the coal to C was consideration for C's promise. C (Pegg) argued that delivery of the coal was not consideration, because A were already bound by their contract with B to deliver it to him (Pegg). The court gave judgment for the plaintiffs, one judge saying that there was a benefit to the defendant, the other judge saying that there was a detriment to the plaintiffs.

Scotson v Pegg was expressly approved by the Privy Council in *New Zealand Shipping Co Ltd v A.M. Satterthwaite & Co Ltd*; *The Eurymedon* (1975, PC), which was followed in *Pao On v Lau Yiu Long* (1980, PC). In *The Eurymedon* Lord Wilberforce said:

"An agreement to do an act which the promisor is under an existing obligation to a third party to do may quite well amount to valid consideration and does so in the present case: the promisee obtains the benefit of a direct obligation which he can enforce."

Variations of contract

As may be seen from the facts of *Williams v Roffey*, the problem in a case of that kind is whether a contractual variation is supported by consideration and is thus enforceable. The plaintiff in that case agreed to provide the same performance as he had originally contracted to do, but the defendants, for sound commercial and contractual reasons, were prepared to pay more than they had originally agreed with him, to ensure that the contract was completed on time. The Court of Appeal's decision gave effect to the commercial sense of the transaction: from a commercial point of view it was in the defendants' interest to avoid the risk of breach by the plaintiff.

The other aspect of variations of contract arises from one party's inability to pay the full price for performance of the contract as originally agreed. If A pays, or promises to pay, part of a debt which he owes to B, and in return B promises to release A from the balance of the debt, the general rule is that B is not bound by such a promise; if B makes such a promise and then goes back on it and demands the balance of the debt, the law will see that he gets it. The reason is said to be that A has not given consideration for B's promise, and so B is not bound by his promise. A has not given consideration because he has only done, or promised to do, part of what he was already contractually bound to B to do. Logically this situation falls under the same principle as the situation considered above (*Williams v Roffey*, etc.), namely where A promises B that he will do something which he is already bound, by a contract with B, to do, and B in return promises extra remuneration. In that situation A will not be able to enforce B's promise, because he has not given consideration. In both situations A has not contributed anything to the new bargain. The earlier study of this principle showed that A could not succeed as claimant. Here the question is what will happen to A as defendant if he is sued by B for the balance of the debt.

A debt can only be discharged by "accord and satisfaction". Accord is agreement, and satisfaction is consideration. "Payment of a lesser sum on the day in satisfaction of a greater sum cannot be any satisfaction for the whole." This quotation from the judgment in *Pinnel*'s case (1602) is commonly called "the rule in *Pinnel*'s case".

The rule in *Pinnel*'s case was approved by the House of Lords in 1884 in the case of *Foakes v Beer*. Mrs Beer had obtained a judgment against Dr Foakes for £2,090. Dr Foakes wanted time to pay, and the parties entered into a written agreement that if he would pay £2,090 by stated instalments Mrs Beer would not take any proceedings on the judgment. Every judgment debt carries interest, but the agreement between the parties made no mention of interest. In course of time Dr Foakes paid, by instalments, the whole sum of £2,090. Mrs Beer then claimed a further £360 as interest. Dr Foakes refused to pay, and Mrs Beer applied to the court for leave to proceed on the judgment. Dr Foakes relied on the agreement; Mrs Beer argued that Dr Foakes had given no consideration in the agreement. The House of Lords upheld Mrs Beer's claim, applying the rule in *Pinnel*'s case.

Application of the Court of Appeal's decision in *Williams v Roffey* to this kind of situation would lead to the conclusion that a variation of the type found in *Foakes v Beer* was enforceable. In the later case of *Re Selectmove Ltd* (1995) the Court of Appeal reluctantly took the view that it was bound by *Foakes v Beer* and thus rejected the approach of *Williams v Roffey*. On the other hand, in *Anangel Atlas Compania Naviera S.A. v Ishikawajima-Harima Heavy Industries Co Ltd* (No.2) (1990), Hirst J. upheld an agreement between a client and a shipbuilder that, because of recession in the world shipping market, the client should pay less for the ship than originally agreed. The judge expressly relied on *Williams v Roffey*.

The final case to consider in this context is *Ferguson v Davies* (1997). The facts were that A sold goods to B and subsequently sued him in the county court. B sent a cheque for a sum less than that claimed by A enclosed in a letter stating that the cheque was in full settlement of A's claim. He completed the relevant county form admitting that he owed A money but disputing the am. claimed. A cashed the cheque but informed B that he was ˛ tinuing with the action. The county court judge held that the cashing of the cheque amounted to accord and satisfaction, but the Court of Appeal allowed his appeal. The case shows how fine a line there is between payment of a lesser sum in respect of an acknowledged liability and payment of a lesser sum by way of compromise of a contested claim. In the first case, the payment of the lesser sum will not be good consideration; in the second it will.

There is a number of qualifications to the rule in *Pinnel's* case at common law. Three qualifications appear in *Pinnel's* case itself. First, payment of a smaller sum before the due day, at the creditor's request, is valid consideration. Secondly, payment of a smaller sum at a different place, at the creditor's request, is valid consideration. Thirdly, payment of a smaller sum accompanied, at the creditor's request, by delivery of a chattel is valid consideration: "the gift of a horse, hawk or robe, etc. in satisfaction is good". A fourth qualification has been added by later judicial decisions, it says that the rule does not apply where the creditor's claim is unliquidated or disputed. The reason is that in such a case the value of the creditor's claim is unknown; the sum offered by the debtor may not be any less—it may even be more—than the true value of the creditor's claim.

There are two further qualifications to the rule in *Pinnel's* case. The first is where payment of part of a debt is made by a third party. If such payment is accepted by the creditor in full settlement, the payment is a good defence to a later action by the creditor against the debtor for the balance. In *Hirachand Punamchand v Temple* (1911, CA) the father of a young officer who was indebted to money-lenders sent them "in full settlement" a draft for a smaller amount. The money-lenders accepted the draft and then sued the son. The Court of Appeal rejected their claim. It is not easy to find a convincing consideration in this situation, but the result is justifiable, since to allow the money-lenders' claim would have been a fraud on the father.

The final qualification arises in the case of agreements between debtors and their creditors. These are called "individual voluntary arrangements", comprising a composition with the creditors. A "composition" is an agreement between a debtor and all his creditors that he will pay them, and that they will accept, a "dividend" (a division of his assets, but less than his full debts) in full settlement of their claims. A creditor who has received a dividend under such an agreement will fail if he sues the debtor for the balance of his original claim; the consideration supporting the agreement by each creditor is the mutual agreement of the other creditors to accept part payment as a discharge of the whole debt: see, for example, *Good v Cheesman* (1831). In addition, under s.260(2) of the Insolvency Act 1986, a composition approved in accordance with the provisions of that Act is legally binding on all creditors.

Estoppel

Estoppel and contractual variations

Until the decision of the Court of Appeal in *Williams v Roffey*, the previous state of the law meant that variations in a contract would run the risk of not being binding because they were unsupported by consideration. This was because, as has been seen, a variation which only benefits one party but not the other will only be binding if the other party provides additional consideration. The effect of *Williams v Roffey* is to modify that rule.

Another method by way which the courts have sometimes enforced contractual variations has been through the doctrine of estoppel, which was resorted to to prevent the kind of injustice which may arise if a variation which benefits one party is held to be unsupported by consideration. The most important example of this from the late nineteenth century is *Hughes v Metropolitan Railway Co* (1877, HL). The facts of the case were that a landlord gave his tenant six months' notice to repair the premises. If the tenant failed to comply the lease could be forfeited. A month after the notice, the landlord started negotiations with the tenant for the purchase by the landlord of the remainder of the lease. These negotiations were broken off two months later. During this time the defendant did nothing towards repairing the premises. When the notice had run for six months the landlord claimed to treat the lease as forfeited. The House of Lords held that he could not do so. The opening of negotiations amounted to a promise by the landlord that as long as they continued he would not enforce the notice. It was in reliance on this promise that the tenant had refrained from doing any repairs. The six months allowed for the repairs must run, therefore, only from the failure of the negotiations and the consequent withdrawal of the promise. The tenant was entitled in equity to relief from forfeiture. Lord Cairns said:

"It is the first principle upon which all Courts of Equity proceed, that if parties who have entered into definite and distinct terms involving certain legal results ... afterwards by their own act or with their own consent enter upon a course of negotiation which has the effect of leading one of the parties to suppose that the strict rights arising under the contract will not be enforced or will be kept in suspense or held in abeyance, the person who otherwise might have enforced those rights will not be allowed to enforce them where it would be inequitable, having regard to the dealings which have thus taken place between the parties."

As can be seen, the Hughes case itself concerned the forfeiture of a lease. It was made clear, however, by Bowen L.J. in *Birmingham & District Land Co v L. & N.W. Railway* (1888, CA), that the doctrine was not limited to forfeiture cases but extended to all variations of contractual rights.

This principle has been called "equitable estoppel" or "promissory estoppel". It is best to call it "promissory estoppel" because there is another kind of equitable estoppel, "proprietary estoppel", affecting owners of land (and, possibly, of other property). Promissory estoppel differs from estoppel strictly because estoppel strictly so called only operates to estop a person who has made a statement of present fact; it does not apply to a promise of future conduct.

The *High Trees House* case

The doctrine of promissory estoppel was given new life by Denning J. (as he then was) in 1947 in *Central London Property Trust Ltd v High Trees House Ltd*. In September 1939 the plaintiffs had let a block of flats to the defendants. In January 1940 they agreed to accept half rent, since many of the flats were unlet because of war conditions. In 1945 all the flats were let again and the plaintiffs claimed full rent for the last two quarters of 1945. Denning J. gave judgment for the plaintiffs on the grounds that the agreement of 1940 had, by the middle of 1945, ceased to operate by reason of change of circumstances. He said obiter that if the plaintiffs had sought to recover full rent for 1940 to 1945 they would have failed. The principle of the Hughes case would prevent them going back on their promise. He also said that, as a result of the doctrine "a promise to accept a smaller sum in discharge of a larger sum, if acted upon, is binding notwithstanding the absence of consideration".

Thus the effect of this decision is to extend the equitable doctrine established in *Hughes v Metropolitan Railway Co* from variations of contractual terms to the part payment of contractual debts. The effect of the rule in *Pinnel's* case, which was confirmed by the Court of Appeal in *Re Selectmove Ltd* (1995), is that consideration cannot consist of the performance of an existing duty. However, that rule is subject to modification where the conditions for the establishment of a promissory estoppel are satisfied.

In *Combe v Combe* (1951, CA) Lord Denning restated the doctrine in these words:

"The principle ... is that, where one party has, by his words or conduct, made to the other a promise or assurance which was intended to affect the legal relations between them and to be acted on accordingly, then, once the other party has taken him at his word and acted on it, the one who gave the promise or assurance cannot afterwards be allowed to revert to the previous legal relations as if no such promise or assurance had been made by him, but he must accept their legal relations subject to the qualification which he himself has so introduced, even though it is not supported in point of law by any consideration but only by his word."

He also made it clear that the doctrine cannot be used to found a cause of action; it may only be used to prevent someone from insisting on the enforcement of their strict rights. He stressed that the doctrine may not be used to create new causes of action where none existed before.

The promise must also be unequivocal. In *Northstar Land Ltd v Maitland Brooks* (2006) Ward L.J. stressed that the promise must be a "clear, unequivocal, unambiguous promise or assurance which was intended to affect the legal relationship between [the parties] or was reasonably understood by the [representee] to have that effect."

The doctrine only applies where it would be inequitable for the creditor to go back on his promise. This point is illustrated by *D.&C. Builders Ltd v Rees* (1966, CA). A firm of jobbing builders promised to accept £300 in full settlement of their claim for £482.

Lord Denning said that because this promise had been extr, from the plaintiff creditors by intimidation on the part of debtor, the debtor could not rely on the doctrine of promiss estoppel. This approach was also taken by Lord Scarman in *Pao On v Lau Yiu Long* (1979).

Enforcement of an estoppel

It is commonly said that the doctrine of promissory estoppel may be used as a shield, not as a sword: see *Combe v Combe*, above. In other words, it may not be used to found a cause of action, but only to prevent someone insisting on their strict legal rights. It does not mean, however, that it is available only to defendants and not claimants. A claimant may use the estoppel to support a cause of action which has an independent existence. Thus, in *Combe v Combe* (1951), a husband in the course of divorce proceedings promised to pay his wife a specified sum as maintenance. She gave no promise in return not to apply to the court for maintenance and later tried to enforce his promise on the basis of promissory estoppel. The Court of Appeal disallowed her claim.

What amounts to reliance

It is clear from both the *Hughes* case and the *High Trees House* case that for the doctrine of equitable or promissory estoppel to operate there must be an act of reliance by the promisee. But it is not clear whether the promisee must have relied on the promise to his detriment. In both the cases mentioned, it cannot be said that the promisees relied upon the promises made to their detriment. They did, however, rely upon the later promise rather than the original contract.

In *Alan (W.J.) & Co v El Nasr Export & Import Co* (1972, CA) Lord Denning said that, although it was essential to the doctrine of promissory estoppel that the debtor should have acted on the promise, it was not essential that he should have acted on it to his detriment. He said that all that was required was that the promisee should have "conducted his affairs on the basis" of the promise so that "it would not now be equitable to deprive him of" its benefit. Later, in *Brikom Investments Ltd v Carr* (1979, CA) Lord Denning said that it was not necessary that a party should have acted on the promise in the sense of acting differently from the way he would have done if the promise had not been made to him; it was enough that he had relied on the promise in any way. Subsequently, Robert

Goff J. said that the only requirement is that inequity should be shown: see *Société Italo-Belge pour le Commerce et l'Industrie S.A. v Palm and Vegetable Oils (Malaysia) Sdn Bhd* (1982). He said:

> "It does not follow that in every case in which the representee has acted, or failed to act, in reliance on the representation, it will be inequitable for the representor to enforce his rights, for the nature of the action, or inaction, may be insufficient to give rise to the equity, in which event a necessary requirement stated by Lord Cairns L.C. for the application of the doctrine would not have been fulfilled."

In the circumstances of that case, the judge found that it would not be inequitable for the promisors to enforce their strict rights.

The effect of an estoppel
The effect of an estoppel may well be to suspend the promisor's strict legal rights, as in *Hughes v Metropolitan Railway Co*, but it is not clear whether it will extinguish them. The effect of the Hughes case is that a promise to forgo payment of the balance of a debt is binding if the debtor has done something or not done something on the faith of the promise. It is only binding, however, to the extent of suspending the duty to pay: it is not binding for ever; the debt is not finally discharged. The duty to pay will revive if the creditor gives notice to the debtor that the suspension is at an end, or if the state of affairs that led to the promise comes to an end. Where the debtor's duty is to make periodic payments (as in the case of rent), to say that the doctrine is suspensory is ambiguous. It can either mean that after suspension has ended the debtor must make future payments in full but need not make up past lower payments to the full amount, or it can mean that he must do both. The latter view is preferable, because otherwise the periodic payer would be in a better position than the lump-sum payer. Events may happen, after the promise, which make the suspension permanent. But that does not invalidate the proposition that the doctrine itself is only suspensory.

Lord Denning clearly regarded the doctrine of promissory estoppel as being extinctive and not merely suspensory. He said in the *High Trees House* case (1947):

"The logical consequence, no doubt, is that a promise to ac\
smaller sum in discharge of a larger sum, if acted upon, is bin
notwithstanding the absence of consideration: and if the fusio.. ui
law and equity leads to this result, so much the better."

In the later case of *D.&C. Builders Ltd v Rees* (1966, CA) he said:

"It is worth noticing that the principle may be applied, not only
so as to suspend strict legal rights but also so as to preclude the
enforcement of them."

That view cannot be reconciled with *Foakes v Beer*.

There was perhaps a hint in his judgment in *Alan v El Nasr* (1972,
CA) that Lord Denning was there modifying his earlier view. He
said that:

"The creditor's strict rights are at any rate suspended ... He may
on occasion be able to revert to his strict legal rights for the
future by giving notice ... But there are cases where no withdrawal is possible. It may be too late to withdraw; or it cannot be
done without injustice to the other party."

It is clear from statements made by the Court of Appeal and the
House of Lords that there are limits to the doctrine of promissory
estoppel and that, although it may be useful in considering mod-
ifications or variations of contract, it should not be regarded as
abolishing the requirement for consideration, particularly in the
formation of a contract. The final point to make, however, is that if
the approach of the Court of Appeal in *Williams v Roffey Bros &
Nicholls (Contractors) Ltd* (1990) were to be widely adopted, that
would make the doctrine of promissory estoppel unnecessary.

In *Williams v Roffey*, the Court of Appeal made clear its view
that consideration remains a fundamental requirement for a valid
contract. Russell L.J. said:

"Consideration there must still be but, in my judgment, the
courts nowadays should be more ready to find its existence so as
to reflect the intention of the parties to the contract where the
bargaining powers are not unequal and where the finding of
consideration reflects the true intention of the parties."

CONSIDERATION AND DEEDS

Before the enactment of the Law of Property (Miscellaneous Provisions) Act 1989, a seal was sometimes said to be an alternative to consideration. A contract might be made "under seal" or "by deed". The seal was said to give a contract "form", and a contract under seal might be called a "formal contract". A contract not under seal was called a "simple contract". Before the 1989 Act, the rule was that a person might make a promise under seal which was enforceable even though there was no consideration. The 1989 Act has now abolished the requirement that a seal is necessary for the valid execution of an instrument as a deed by an individual: see s.1(1)(b). For an instrument to be a deed, it must make clear on its face that it is intended to be a deed and must be validly executed. Valid execution is a simplified procedure requiring the signature of the person making the deed, the attestation of the signature and delivery of the deed: see s.1(2) and (3). One of the requirements of s.1(3) is that the witness attesting the signature should sign the document in the presence of the signatories to it. In *Shah v Shah* (2001) the attesting witness signed the document after the defendants had signed it but not in their presence. This meant that the document did not comply with s.1(3). Nevertheless, the Court of Appeal held that the document was binding on the defendants because they were estopped from relying on the attestation defect. They had signed it and put it forward as a deed. The claimant had no knowledge or means of knowledge whether or not the signature was in the presence of the attesting witness. So the defendants were estopped from setting up the defect.

The effect of this change in the law is that validly executed deeds are enforceable without the need for a seal and without the need for consideration as explained in this chapter.

CHAPTER THREE

INTENTION TO CONTRACT

TWO ELEMENTS necessary for a valid contract have been looked at: offer and acceptance, and consideration. The third requirement—intention to contract—will be looked at in this chapter.

Some writers have argued that there is no separate requirement of intention to contract, and that if there is agreement and consideration—in other words, if there is a bargain—legal enforceability must follow. But the cases do not fit this theory. If A and B agree to lunch together, A promising to pay for the food and B promising to pay for the drink, there is a bargain (agreement plus consideration) but no legal obligations are created. The reason why no legal obligations are created is that none are intended. Thus, intention to contract is a necessary element for an enforceable contract. "Intention to contract" means in this context the readiness of each party to accept the legal consequences if they do not perform their contract.

Agreements are generally classified into commercial agreements and social and domestic agreements for the purposes of considering the requirement of intention to create legal relations. In both cases, presumptions are used: in the case of commercial agreements, the presumption is that there is an intention to create legal relations; in the case of social and domestic agreements the presumption is that there is no intention to create legal relations. The use of presumptions means that the party wishing to displace the presumption has the burden of persuading the court that it should be displaced. But it is clear from the cases that the court will not readily allow the presumptions to be displaced, particularly in social and domestic agreements. In the latter case, the courts have expressed their unwillingness to interfere. In *Balfour v Balfour* (1919), considered more fully below, Atkin L.J. said: "In respect of these promises each house is a domain into which the King's writ does not seek to run."

COMMERCIAL AGREEMENTS

The general rule

In commercial agreements there is a presumption that the parties do intend to make a legally enforceable contract. Thus it is not necessary, in the ordinary run of commercial transactions, for the claimant to give affirmative evidence that there was such an intention; but the defendant may defeat the presumption by reference to the words used by the parties and/or the circumstances in which they used them.

This matter was considered in *Esso Petroleum Co Ltd v Commissioners of Customs and Excise* (1976, HL). In that case, the facts were that the company organised a promotion together with the 1970 World Cup whose terms were that a person buying four gallons of petrol was also entitled to a free "World Cup Coin". The coins had no real value, but were intended for promotional effect. Customs and Excise tried to recover tax on the coins on the grounds that they had been produced for general use. One of the arguments in the House of Lords concerned the question whether there was an intention to create legal relations. The majority concluded that there was; the minority took the view that it was unlikely that any motorist who was denied a coin would believe that a legal remedy was available.

In a number of cases, the courts have been prepared to conclude that the presumption has been rebutted. Thus, if the parties have expressly declared that a transaction is not to be binding in law the courts will give effect to that declaration. Many football pool coupons contain the words "Binding in honour only", and it has been held that a dissatisfied punter (or "investor") cannot sue on a coupon containing those words. See, for example, *Appleson v Littlewood* (1939, CA).

There is one reported case where a similar form of words was inserted into what was otherwise an ordinary agreement for the sale of goods: see *Rose and Frank Co v Crompton* (1925, HL). The agreement contained the following clause:

"This arrangement is not entered into ... as a formal or legal agreement, and shall not be subject to legal jurisdiction in the Law Courts ... but it is only a definite expression and record of the purpose and intention of the ... parties concerned, to which they each honourably pledge themselves."

It was held by the House of Lords that the agreement could not be sued upon.

This question was considered again more recently in *Kleinwort Benson Ltd v Malaysia Mining Corporation Bhd* (1989, CA). The plaintiff bank agreed to make available a loan facility to a wholly-owned subsidiary of the defendants. During the negotiations, the parties had not been able to agree upon any security for the loan, but the defendants had provided a "letter of comfort". The relevant sentence read:

"It is our policy to ensure that the business of [the subsidiary] is at all times in the position to meet its liabilities to you under the above arrangements."

The subsidiary later went into liquidation without paying its debt to the plaintiffs. The Court of Appeal decided that the action should fail on the grounds that no contractual promise had been made. It said, however, that the case was not to be treated as turning on the question of intention to create legal relations but upon the correct construction of the sentence quoted. It concluded that it was without contractual force as it amounted only to a statement of present intention and not to a promise about the future conduct of the defendants. It also added that, in view of the approach it had taken, the burden lay on the plaintiffs to establish that the statement should be treated as a contractual promise rather than on the defendants to deny legal force. The decision thus reverses the general position set out above.

The other case to note in this area is another decision of the Court of Appeal in *Orion Insurance Co Plc v Sphere Drake Insurance Plc* (1992). In that case an agreement was reached orally and was later put in writing. The plaintiffs argued that the oral agreement had been agreed to be no more than a matter of goodwill, although there was no mention of this in the written record. The Court of Appeal upheld the trial judge's findings of fact which led him to conclude that there had been no intention to create legal relations.

If there is any ambiguity in a clause of this type, the courts will adjudicate upon it. In *Edwards v Skyways* (1964) an employee was dismissed as redundant. His employers promised to make him an ex gratia payment of a specified amount. It was held that the words "ex gratia" did not negative contractual intention; they simply meant that the employers did not admit any pre-existing liability on their part.

Although it is permissible for parties to agree that their agreement is not to have any legal effect at all (as in *Rose and Frank Co v Crompton*), an agreement which ousts the jurisdiction of the courts in favour of some other tribunal is treated by the courts as void as being contrary to public policy: see Chapter 10. It is surprising that the clause in *Rose and Frank* was not held to contravene this rule, since that seems to have been the intention behind it.

Collective agreements

Collective agreements are agreements entered into by trade unions and employers and govern the rates of pay and conditions of work of their members. If the terms of such agreements are then incorporated (as they frequently are) into the individual employment contract of each employee, those terms are legally binding on the parties, i.e. the employee and the employer. But that still leaves the question whether the collective bargain itself is an enforceable contract as between the parties to it, the trade union and the employer. Until 1969, there was a general belief amongst trade unionists, industrialists and lawyers that collective bargains were not enforceable at common law. That belief was given judicial backing in *Ford Motor Company v Amalgamated Union of Engineering and Foundry Workers* (1969). In that case it was held that a collective agreement is not intended to be legally enforceable, and accordingly the court will grant no relief for breach of such an agreement. This is an instance where an intention to contract is negatived, not by any actual words used by the parties, but by the circumstances surrounding their agreement.

The common law position has been affirmed by statute. Section 179 of the Trade Union and Labour Relations (Consolidation) Act

1992 states that a collective agreement is conclusively presumed not to have been intended by the parties to be a legally enforceable contract unless it is in writing and expressly provides that it is so intended.

SOCIAL AND DOMESTIC AGREEMENTS

Within the class of social and domestic agreements those between husband and wife are the most likely to be held not to be contractual.

In *Balfour v Balfour* (1919, CA) the defendant was a civil servant stationed in Ceylon. He and his wife (the plaintiff) came to England on leave. When his leave was over he went back to Ceylon alone, and his wife stayed in England on her doctor's advice. The husband promised to pay her £30 a month. He did not keep this promise and his wife sued him. She succeeded at first instance, but the Court of Appeal allowed the husband's appeal. Atkin L.J. said:

"One of the most usual forms of agreement which does not constitute a contract appears to me to be the arrangements which are made between husband and wife ... and they are not contracts because the parties did not intend that they should be attended by legal consequences".

A fact to note here is that the agreement was made when relations between the parties were amicable. There is no doubt, however, that, if the agreement had been made in the context of a breakdown of the marriage, it would have been enforceable, as may be seen from the later case of *Merritt v Merritt* (1970, CA). The Court of Appeal said that the principle of *Balfour v Balfour* does not apply to a husband and wife who are not living in amity.

The principle of *Balfour v Balfour* has been applied to an agreement between mother and daughter. In *Jones v Padavatton* (1969, CA) a mother agreed with her daughter, a secretary in the United States, that if she would give up her job and read for the Bar in England the mother would provide maintenance for her. The daughter came to England and began to read for the Bar. Later the agreement was varied, the mother agreeing to provide a house for the daughter. On the mother's claim for possession of the house the

Court of Appeal held that the arrangement was not intended to be legally binding and that the mother was entitled to possession.

The court reached the opposite conclusion, on the other hand, in *Parker v Clark* (1960). An elderly couple (the Clarks) invited the Parkers to share their house. This involved the younger couple (the Parkers) in selling their own house. The basis of the arrangement was that, if the Parkers moved in with the Clarks and shared the household expenses, the Clarks would leave them a sum of money on the death of Mr Clark. This arrangement was held to be legally binding. Devlin J. said:

"The question [whether or not there is a binding contract] must, of course, depend on the intention of the parties, to be inferred from the language they use and from the circumstances in which they use it."

PART Two

WHAT IS WITHIN THE AGREEMENT

THE TERMS OF THE CONTRACT

TERMS AND REPRESENTATIONS

BEFORE THEY enter into the contract, the parties are likely to be involved in negotiations, particularly if it is a complex commercial contract. During the course of the negotiations, the parties may say or write all kinds of things, but it does not follow that all they have said or written are terms of the contract. There is a distinction between terms—which do become part of the contract—and representations (i.e. statements of fact or opinion)—which do not. This distinction becomes important where a statement which has been made turns out to be untrue. In that case, the judge has to decide which statements are contractual terms and which are non-contractual representations, inducing the contract but forming no part of it.

It may help here to look at an example. A discusses with B selling him his television. During the course of the discussion, B asks A all about it—its age, how much A has used it, whether it has Teletext and so on. At the end of these negotiations, A agrees to sell him the television for £250. Clearly, the contract has more to it than the price. But not all A's answers will be classified as terms of the contract—some may be but some may be treated as representations.

The importance of the distinction between terms and representations arises where a statement is untrue; that is, where there is a misrepresentation. If a statement is a term of the contract its untruth is a breach of contract, for which the injured party may claim, amongst other remedies, damages. He is entitled to damages even though the misstatement was made entirely innocently; that is, without fraud or negligence. If a statement is not a term of the contract, the injured party will only be entitled to damages if the misrepresentor has acted fraudulently or negligently; if the misrepresentor has acted wholly innocently the injured party will be entitled only to rescission, though the court has a discretion to order damages instead. These matters are dealt with fully in Chapter 7: Misrepresentation.

Thus, it is important to be able to decide whether a statement is a contractual term or not. If a statement or representation becomes a term of the contract, the effect of its becoming a term is to create an obligation; if the statement turns out to be untrue, that will result in a breach of contract.

The first issue to consider in this chapter, therefore, is whether and how pre-contractual statements may become terms of the contract. The basic principle is that it is a question of intention: did the maker of the statement intend it to be a term of the contract? But the test of intention is objective, i.e. whether a reasonable person would have taken the statement to be meant as a contractual term. That depends upon what exactly was said (or written) and upon the circumstances surrounding the transaction.

When representations become terms

If the representee (the person to whom the statement is made) has made it known that he attaches great importance to a certain fact, and the other party then states that that fact is true, it is likely that the statement will be treated as a contractual term. In *Bannerman v White* (1861), for example, an intending buyer of hops asked whether sulphur had been used in their treatment. He added that if it had, he would not even trouble to ask the price. It was held that the seller's (untrue) assurance that sulphur had not been used was a term of the contract.

A second point to note is that, if the person making the statement suggests that the other party should check it, the statement will not be treated as a term of the contract. In *Ecay v Godfrey* (1947) the seller of a boat stated that it was sound, but advised the buyer to have it surveyed. This showed that the seller did not intend that his statement should be taken as a term of the contract. On the other hand, if the person making the statement does so in a way which suggests that he has special knowledge, with the consequence that the other party is dissuaded from checking it, the statement will probably be held to be a contractual term. So, for example, in *Schawel v Reade* (1913, HL) the plaintiff was examining a horse with a view to buying it for stud purposes. The defendant said:

"You need not look for anything: the horse is perfectly sound. If there was anything the matter with the horse I would tell you."

The buyer in reliance on this statement bought the horse, which proved to be totally unfit for stud purposes. The seller's statement was held to be a contractual term.

If the maker of the statement has some special knowledge or skill compared with the other party, the statement may well be held to be a contractual term; if their degrees of knowledge are equal, or if the representee has the greater knowledge, the statement will probably be held to be a non-contractual representation. In *Oscar Chess Ltd v Williams* (1957, CA) the defendant traded in to the plaintiffs (car dealers) a Morris car which he honestly described as a 1948 model. He received an allowance for it of £290. It turned out to be a 1939 model, worth £175. The statement that the car was a 1948 model was held not to be a term of the contract. The seller was a private individual, who had taken his information from the registration book, which only later turned out to be forged. The buyers were car dealers and so were in at least as good a position as the seller to know the true age of the car.

In *Dick Bentley Productions Ltd v Harold Smith (Motors) Ltd* (1965, CA) the defendant, who was a dealer, sold a Bentley, stating that it had only done 20,000 miles since a replacement engine had been fitted. In fact it had done nearly 100,000 miles since then. The Court of Appeal held that the defendant's statement was a term of the contract and that the plaintiffs were entitled to damages.

LIVERPOOL JOHN MOORES UNIVERSITY
LEARNING & INFORMATION SERVICES

In the *Dick Bentley* case Lord Denning suggested that an inducing statement should be presumed to be a term of the contract, but that the presumption can be rebutted if the representor has not acted negligently or fraudulently. It would be going too far to suggest, however, that the courts usually use this as a basis for deciding this kind of issue.

The parol evidence rule

The parol evidence rule is to the effect that extrinsic evidence, particularly oral evidence, cannot be admitted to add to, vary or contradict a deed or other written instrument. An example of the working of the rule is to be found in *Henderson v Arthur* (1907, CA). A covenant in a lease provided for payment of rent in advance. The lessee was not permitted to give evidence of a previous oral agreement that payment should be made by a bill of exchange maturing in three months' time.

The rule excludes extrinsic evidence of the contents of a contract, but not extrinsic evidence relating to its validity. Evidence of matters outside the writing can be given to show some invalidating cause, such as misrepresentation, mistake, incapacity or absence of consideration.

If the parol evidence rule was applied over a broad front it would lead to injustice in many cases, but over the years it has been made subject to many exceptions so that its scope is quite limited. The main exceptions are considered below.

Rectification

In litigation concerning a contract two issues are often raised, construction and rectification. The plaintiff argues on the construction point that the meaning of the contract is "X". He further argues, in case the court decides against him on construction, that "X" was the subject of a previous express agreement between the parties before the contract was reduced to writing and that, if the contract as written does not mean "X", its wording should be rectified to bring it into line with "X". On the construction point the parol evidence rule applies, shutting out extrinsic evidence. On the rectification point the parol evidence rule does not apply; indeed the point depends entirely on extrinsic evidence of a pre-contract agreement between the parties. See *Joscelyne v Nissen* (1970, CA) and *Prenn v Simmonds* (1971, HL).

It is important to bear in mind that rectification is an equitable remedy, which is available only at the discretion of the court. The rules governing the granting of equitable remedies thus come into play here; so, for example, rectification will not be granted in favour of a plaintiff who is guilty of excessive delay in seeking the remedy, since "delay defeats Equity".

Non-operation

The parol evidence rule does not prevent extrinsic evidence being given to prove that the contract does not yet operate or has ceased to operate. In *Pym v Campbell* (1856) the parties entered into a written agreement for the sale of an invention. When the plaintiff sued for a breach of this agreement the defendants were permitted to give evidence of an oral agreement that the written agreement was not to operate until a third party had approved the invention and that the third party never had approved it.

Incompleteness

The most important limitation on the parol evidence rule is that it does not apply where the court finds that the written agreement is not the whole agreement. Thus, where one party is reasonably entitled to assume that the writing does contain all the terms of the contract, the other party will not be allowed to give evidence that it does not.

Two contrasting cases illustrate the point. In *Malpas v L. & S.W. Railway Co* (1866) Malpas orally contracted with the defendants to carry his cattle from Guildford to King's Cross. He signed (without noticing its contents) a consignment note by which the cattle were "to be sent to Nine Elms Station" (a station between Guildford and King's Cross). The cattle were delayed at Nine Elms and suffered injury. The plaintiff was allowed to give evidence that the full contract was for conveyance to King's Cross via Nine Elms. In *Hutton v Watling* (1948, CA) there was a document headed "To sale of business". The document set out a number of terms, and contained a receipt for the price of the goodwill. The purchaser sued to enforce one of the written terms; the vendor argued that the document was only a memorandum and tried to give evidence that there was an antecedent oral agreement different in its terms. This evidence was held inadmissible. Lord Greene M.R. said:

"If the other party to the alleged contract, interpreting it as a reasonably intelligent person would do in the light of the relevant circumstances, takes it to be of a contractual nature, that concludes the matter and it is not possible to call oral evidence that it was a mere memorandum".

In *J. Evans & Son (Portsmouth) Ltd v Andrea Merzario Ltd* (1976) Roskill L.J. said that where there is a contract which is partly oral, partly in writing and partly by conduct, "the court is entitled to look at and should look at all the evidence from start to finish in order to see what the bargain was that was struck between the parties".

Collateral contracts

One way of avoiding the problems posed by rules such as the parol evidence rule is to resort to the device commonly called a collateral contract. By means of this device the courts hold that a statement which is not a term of the main contract is nevertheless not a "mere" representation, because it is a term of another contract, standing side by side with the main contract. A good example of this is *De Lassalle v Guildford* (1901, CA). The facts were that the defendant was negotiating to let his house to the plaintiff. The plaintiff refused to hand over the counterpart of the lease until he was assured that the drains were in order. The defendant gave such an assurance, and the plaintiff then delivered the counterpart. The drains were not in order. The plaintiff sued for damages and succeeded in the Court of Appeal, on the grounds that there had been a breach, not of the tenancy contract (the lease did not refer to the condition of the drains) but of the collateral (drains) contract.

A similar conclusion was reached in *City & Westminster Properties (1934) Ltd v Mudd* (1959). Here, a tenant was presented with a lease which contained a covenant to use the premises for business purposes only. He had in fact been living at the premises for some time. When he queried the covenant he was given an oral assurance that he would be allowed to continue living at the premises. So he signed the lease. The lessors then brought an action for forfeiture of the lease for breach of covenant. It was held that the tenant could defend the action by relying on the oral assurance as giving rise to a collateral contract.

In such cases the collateral contract doctrine not only bypasses the "mere" representation argument; it also bypasses the parol evidence rule. It is able to bypass the parol evidence rule because although the collateral contract may add to the total obligations of the promisor it does not add to the main contract. It is not open to the courts to find a collateral contract unless all the necessary elements of a valid contract are present: agreement, consideration and an intention to be legally bound. In the case of consideration the consideration must be separate from the consideration in the main contract. In *De Lassalle v Guildford* it could not be said that the rent in the main contract was the consideration for the promise relating to the drains in the collateral contract. The consideration for the drains promise was the (implied) promise to enter into the main contract. It can be paraphrased thus: "If you will promise that the drains are in order I will execute the lease".

In *De Lassalle's* case the main contract and the collateral contract had the same parties. But it is also possible for the collateral contract to be between A and B although the main contract is between A and C, as happened in *Shanklin Pier Ltd v Detel Products Ltd* (1951). The plaintiff owners of the pier, B, had engaged a firm, C, to paint the pier. B had the right to specify the materials to be used. The defendants, A, induced B to specify a particular paint (manufactured by A) by assuring B that it would last seven or 10 years. So C bought the paint from A. In fact it lasted about three months. B sued A and won. B was suing on the collateral (A–B) contract. The consideration given by B was that they caused C to enter into the A–C contract (the contract for purchase of the paint, the main contract).

A recent example of the use of the collateral contract is to be found in *Barry v Heathcote Ball & Co (Commercial Auctions) Ltd* (2001), in the context of an auction. In that case, auctioneers advertised that they would sell by auction without reserve two new engine-analyser machines, for each of which the manufacturers' list price was £14,521. The claimant made the only bid of £200 for each of the machines but the auctioneers purported to withdraw the machines from the sale. The Court of Appeal upheld the trial judge's decision in favour of the claimant. They said that the promise to hold the auction without reserve was an offer of a collateral contract which was accepted by the claimant making his bid.

THE NATURE OF CONTRACTUAL TERMS

A contract may be made by words or conduct or partly by words and partly by conduct. The words may be written or spoken or partly written and partly spoken. The words, whether written or spoken, which the parties use in formulating their agreement are the express terms of the contract. But those express terms do not always constitute the whole contract; there may be other terms which fall to be implied into it. Implied terms will be examined at the end of this chapter.

Where the contract is wholly in spoken words, the main task of the judge is to decide exactly what words were used. Where the contract is wholly in writing other problems may arise. The terms of a contract may be contained in more than one document. If the one document expressly refers to another, then that other document, so far as the reference extends, is incorporated into the contract. Thus, in a contract for the sale of land, there may be a clause stating: "The sale is subject to clause [X] of the National Conditions of Sale." Although it is not essential that the conditions should be provided to the other party, it is sensible to give the other party a copy of the conditions, to prevent disputes arising. *BCT Software Solutions Ltd v Arnold Laver & Co Ltd* (2002) is an example of the problems that can arise. In this case, BCT were providing Laver both with software and a software service. For various reasons Laver purported to terminate the software service by giving notice. BCT argued that they were entitled to recover the software because the software licence was part of a single package which went with the service contract. This was a reasonable construction of standard terms which BCT had recently adopted. Previously, they had had separate contracts for the supply of software and the provision of services. Under that system the software, once provided, was treated as licensed for ever. Under the new system, the provision of the software was tied to the service contract so that, in principle, the software licence was terminable. The change was clearly of great importance but BCT had not drawn it to the attention of Laver and, further, it was not clear that all BCT's staff understood the effect of the changes. The judge examined the history of the contractual negotiations between the parties with care and concluded that the parties' express agreement about the terms on which they would contract prevailed over and was inconsistent with the standard conditions.

If one contractual document does not expressly refer to another, it may yet be held by the courts that that other document forms part of the contract. Thus in *Edwards v Aberayron Mutual Ship Insurance Society Ltd* (1876) it was held that a policy of insurance could be read together with the rules of the mutual insurance society that had issued it, although the policy did not expressly refer to the rules.

The question whether a particular term has been incorporated into a contract is important in the context of exclusion clauses. In such cases, one of the issues may be whether a term not contained in a particular signed agreement has nevertheless been incorporated into the contract so as to bind the parties. This matter is considered in Chapter 5.

EXPRESS TERMS

The classification of express terms

As has been seen, the main primary obligations of the contract are created by the express terms of the contract. But the parties rarely set out all the obligations they intend to create. This may be because at the time they made the contract it did not occur to them to cater for a particular event which later happened; it may be because they did not think about the matter because it was obvious. Whatever the reason for failing to include an express term in the contract, many obligations are left to be dealt with later as the need arises. This is done by means of implied terms, which are considered later in this chapter, at p.73.

In a contract it is unlikely that all the express terms will be of equal importance. The courts recognise this inequality, and since the end of the nineteenth century there has grown up a terminology to distinguish two degrees of importance. The more important terms are referred to as "conditions"; the less important as "warranties". Breach of condition gives the victim the right to treat the contract as repudiated, as it would be unjust to force him to accept something which differed in an important way from that which he contracted for. The victim is not bound to treat the contract as repudiated; he may instead affirm the contract. In either event he may claim damages. Breach of warranty, on the other hand, does not entitle the victim to treat the contract as repudiated, but only to claim damages. That is just, because a minor breach can be

67

adequately remedied by a money payment. Looked at from the point of view of the party at fault, if his breach is a breach of condition he cannot enforce the contract if the other party has elected to treat it as repudiated; if his breach is only a breach of warranty he can enforce the contract, though he must pay damages for his breach. A third type of term is an "innominate" or "intermediate" term, which may be classified as a more or less important term depending upon the effects of the breach. These are considered after the nature of conditions has been examined.

In this context, it should be noted that the phrase "fundamental terms" is sometimes used. It is probably wise to avoid use of this phrase because it is by no means settled what it means and it tends to mean different things to different judges. A similar but distinct phrase found in the cases is "fundamental breach". This phrase, too, has not had a uniform meaning attached to it. In *Photo Productions Ltd v Securicor Transport Ltd* (1980, HL), however, Lord Diplock said that this phrase (if it is to be used at all) should, in the interests of clarity, be used to mean a breach which has the effect of depriving the innocent party of substantially the whole benefit that it was intended that he should get under the contract. In other words, "fundamental breach" is the equivalent, for breach of an intermediate term, of "breach of condition".

Conditions and innominate terms

It is important to identify what is meant by the word "condition" in the present context. It may sometimes mean an external fact upon which the existence or continuance of the contract depends, rather than a term of a contract. Thus in *Pym v Campbell* (1856) a contract for the sale of an invention was conditional on the approval of the invention by a third party.

A condition in the present context of contractual obligations may thus be described as a major or main obligation in the contract. A breach of the obligation will entitle the innocent party to treat the contract as repudiated and himself as discharged from further performance of any obligations under the contract. The problem lies in identifying whether a particular term is to be treated as a condition. Although the court will tend to follow the parties' own classification of a term as a condition, it will not do so if that will lead to an unreasonable result. In *L. Schuler A.G. v Wickman Machine Tools Sales Ltd* (1973) the contract said: "It shall be a

68

condition of this agreement ...". The clause provided for weekly visits over four-and-a-half-years to six named firms. The House of Lords said that a single failure to make one of the visits would not entitle the other party to end the contract. Lord Reid said:

> "Use of the word 'condition' is an indication—even a strong indication—of such an intention but it is by no means conclusive. The fact that a particular construction leads to a very unreasonable result must be a relevant consideration. The more unreasonable the result the more unlikely it is that the parties can have intended it ...."

Diplock L.J.'s suggestion (in the *Hong Kong Fir Shipping* case, below) that a term should be treated as a condition "where every breach ... must give rise to an event which will deprive the party not in default of substantially the whole of the benefit which it was intended that he should obtain from the contract" has been rejected in later cases. Nevertheless, it helps to indicate the nature of the terms which are to be regarded as conditions. They are the principal obligations of the contract.

The traditional approach to the classification of contractual terms was challenged in *Hong Kong Fir Shipping Co Ltd v Kawasaki Kisen Kaisha Ltd* (1962, CA). The facts were that the plaintiffs chartered a ship to the defendants for a period of 24 months. A clause in the contract stated that the ship was "in every way fitted for ordinary cargo service", whereas in fact it was unseaworthy, because the engine machinery was old. As a result, 20 weeks of the charter were lost. The defendants claimed to treat the contract as at an end. The plaintiffs sued for wrongful repudiation. They argued that their breach did not entitle the defendants to put an end to the contract, only to claim damages. The plaintiffs won. Diplock L.J. (as he then was) said:

> "There are, however, many contractual undertakings of a more complex character which cannot be categorised as being 'conditions' or 'warranties' ... Of such undertakings all that can be predicated is that some breaches will, and others will not, give rise to an event which will deprive the party not in default of substantially the whole benefit which it was intended that he should obtain from the contract; and the legal consequences of the breach of such an undertaking, unless provided for expressly

in the contract, depend upon the nature of the event to which the breach gives rise and do not follow automatically from a prior classification of the undertaking as a 'condition' or 'warranty'."

These types of terms have come to be called "innominate" or "intermediate".

The decision of the Court of Appeal in *Cehave N.V. v Bremer Handels GmbH*; *The Hansa Nord* (1976, CA) is an example of the usefulness of classifying a term in this way, so as to avoid the serious consequences involved in classifying it as a condition. The case involved a contract for the sale of 12,000 tons of citrus pulp pellets, to be used as an ingredient in cattle food. There were two main issues in the case: the one relevant here was whether a clause in the contract of sale that the pellets were to be shipped "in good condition" was a condition, a warranty or an intermediate term. It was held that the clause was an intermediate term, that its breach did not deprive the buyers of substantially the whole intended benefit under the contract, and that the buyers were not entitled to reject the whole cargo (i.e. treat the contract as at an end) but were only entitled to claim damages.

The disadvantage of the *Hong Kong Fir Shipping* approach is that it leaves the parties in a state of uncertainty. On the other hand, the advantage of using innominate terms is that it gives the court an element of flexibility and enables it to achieve what it considers to be a fair result in a particular case.

It is clear from later cases that the courts have been concerned to limit the effect of the *Hong Kong Fir Shipping* decision, particularly where a particular type of clause common in commercial contracts has been accepted as having the effect of a condition. In such cases, the courts have preferred the desirability of commercial certainty to the flexibility given by the innominate term approach. An example of this is time clauses. These have been consistently interpreted as conditions and the courts have regarded it as desirable that that interpretation should be maintained. This approach may be seen in *The Mihalis Angelos* (1971, CA), which involved a clause stating that the vehicle was "expected ready to load" on July 1, 1965 at Haiphong. They held that the expected readiness to load clause was not innominate, but was a condition. Any breach of the clause therefore entitled the charterers to treat the contract as repudiated irrespective of the consequences of the breach. In *Bunge Corporation v Tradax Export S.A.* (1981) Megaw L.J. said that time clauses should usually be treated as conditions, an approach which was approved by the House of Lords in *Cie Compagnie Commerciale Sucres et Denrées v C. Czarnikow Ltd* (1990). This approach to time clauses was later followed by the Privy Council in *Union Eagle Ltd v Golden Achievement Ltd* (1997). A contract for the sale of land provided that completion of the contract was to take place before a stipulated time and that time was of the essence of the contract. The purchaser was 10 minutes late in tendering the documents for completion. The Privy Council held that the seller was entitled to rescind the contract once the time for completion of the contract had passed and emphasised the need for certainty.

The effect of the various decisions considered above may be summarised by means of a series of questions which help in determining whether, when a breach occurs, the innocent party is entitled to treat the contract as at an end. The first question is whether the contract expressly provides that breach of a particular term will entitle the innocent party to put an end to the contract. If the answer is "Yes", then that concludes the matter: see, for example, *Lombard North Central Plc v Butterworth* (1987, CA). If the answer is "No", then the second question is whether the contract impliedly provides for such a result. If the term is described in the contract as a "condition", that points towards the answer "Yes". But it is not conclusive, as may be seen from the House of Lords case *L. Schuler A.G. v Wickman Machine Tool Sales Ltd* (1974, HL), considered above. If the term is described as a "warranty", that is not conclusive of the answer "No". If the answer is "Yes", that concludes the matter. If the answer is "No", then a third question arises. Although the contract does not expressly or impliedly create a right to treat the contract as terminated, does some rule of law create that right? The answer may be "Yes" because of: (a) a statute; or (b) a judicial decision. An example of (a) is the group of implied terms laid down by ss.12(1), 13, 14 and 15 of the Sale of Goods Act 1979. (Notice, however, that *The Hansa Nord* expressly holds that an express term in a contract of sale of goods may be neither a condition nor a warranty but an innominate term.) An example of (b) is the decision in *The Mihalis Angelos*, which said that the "expected readiness to load" clause in a charter party is a condition entitling the innocent party to treat the contract as terminated. (See also *Cie Compagnie Commerciale Sucres et Denrées v C. Czarnikow Ltd* (1990, HL) and *Union Eagle Ltd v Golden Achievement Ltd* (1997, PC).) If the answer to question three is

"Yes", that concludes the matter. If the answer is "No" (i.e. neither 3(a) nor 3(b) applies) then a final, fourth, question arises: has the innocent party been deprived substantially of what it was intended that he should get under the contract? If the answer is "Yes", then he is entitled to treat the contract as terminated. If the answer is "No", then he can only claim damages. One might call question (4) "the Hong Kong Fir question". An example of the answer "No" is the decision of the Court of Appeal in *The Hansa Nord*, above.

Effect of a breach of condition

Breach of condition gives the innocent party the right to treat the contract as repudiated, as it would be unjust to force him to accept something which differed in an important way from that which he contracted for. The innocent party is not bound to treat the contract as repudiated; he may instead affirm the contract. In either event he may claim damages.

There has been a considerable confusion of terminology in discussing the effect of a breach of condition and it is best to describe it with the phraseology used above. Use of the terms "rescind" and "rescission" should be confined to the context of misrepresentation. A useful phrase to have in mind, therefore, is "repudiatory breach", which covers every kind of breach that entitles the innocent party to treat the contract as terminated by reason of its having been repudiated by the defaulting party.

This discussion of conditions and warranties has spoken of the innocent party ending the contract or terminating the contract or treating the contract as at an end or as terminated. This is because they are phrases which were used in numerous cases before the *Photo Productions* case, above. But in the *Photo Productions* case the House of Lords emphasised that the phrases are shorthand expressions and are not strictly accurate because it is not really the contract itself which is ended; what is ended is the obligation of the innocent party to perform any further his contractual duties.

A further point to note is that the repudiation by the party at fault gives the innocent party the choice: he may choose or "elect" to affirm the contract or he may choose to treat the contract as at an end. Whatever decision he reaches, that decision is irrevocable. In addition, in either case, he still has the right to claim damages. If he affirms the contract, both parties must then continue to perform their obligations under the contract. This means that a later failure of performance by the innocent party may itself become a breach:

72

see, for example, *Motor Oil Hellas (Corinth) Refineries S.A. v Shipping Corporation of India* (1990). A question which may arise is whether the innocent party in fact elected to accept the repudiation or not. In *Vitol S.A. v Norelf Ltd* (1996) Lord Steyn said that it was a question of fact whether the election to treat the contract as repudiated had been communicated to the party in breach, depending upon "the particular contractual relationship and the particular circumstances of the case".

The effects of breach are discussed more fully in Chapter 18.

IMPLIED TERMS

The express terms do not always make up the whole contract, although they usually contain the main obligations of the contract. But the parties may not express all the main obligations or may not provide for every contingency. In that case, there may be other terms which fall to be implied into the contract. For example, if A contracts to sell a pair of jeans to B there will be an express term relating to the price of the jeans. A and B do not discuss the quality of the jeans. Even so, if when B put the jeans on they proved to have defective stitching so that they were falling apart, he would expect to have a remedy against A. Putting it into technical language, it is possible to say that it is reasonable to expect that a person selling jeans will sell jeans which are capable of being worn. In other words, there is an implied term that the seller will sell jeans of suitable quality. In addition, in the example given, the term implied would be a term derived from statute, the Sale of Goods Act 1979.

It should also be noted that a term will not be implied in relation to a particular matter if there is an express term governing the same matter. But if there is scope in the express term for the way it is applied, the courts may be prepared to imply a term governing the manner of its application: see *Johnstone v Bloomsbury Health Authority* (1991) and *Equitable Life Assurance Society v Hyman* (2000), considered more fully below.

Terms implied by the courts

The basic principle of implied terms is that a term will be implied where it is necessary in order to bring the contract into line with the intention of the parties. The intention of the parties, in relation to implied terms, is sought, as in other contexts, from an objective rather than a subjective standpoint. What is being sought is the presumed intention of the parties, and the presumption must be made from a study of the whole circumstances of the transaction. An unexpressed term, then, is implied by the court to give effect to the presumed intention of the parties in the particular transaction which is before the court.

When an implied term has become well settled by a series of judicial decisions in similar circumstances it tends to harden, as it were, into a substantive rule of law. For example, in a contract of employment many matters which were originally implied terms, and are still called so, have become duties imposed by law. Thus, the employer has a duty to provide safe plant and machinery, a safe system of work, and reasonably competent fellow-employees. In recent years, implied terms have played an important part in the development of the law governing the employment relationship. An example is the implication of a term in an employee's contract that the employer will not conduct himself in a manner calculated or likely to destroy or seriously damage the relationship of confidence and trust between employer and employee: see *Courtaulds Northern Textiles Ltd v Andrew* (1979). In some areas of law this hardening process has gone a stage further: implied terms have been written into a statute, as is the case, for example, with the Sale of Goods Act 1979, originally the Sale of Goods Act 1893.

A useful starting point in considering implied terms is the case of *The Moorcock* (1889, CA). The defendants were wharfingers who had contracted to allow the plaintiff to discharge his ship at their jetty. Both parties realised that the ship would ground at low water. When the tide ebbed the ship settled on a ridge of hard ground beneath the mud and suffered damage. Although there was no express term that the berth would be safe, the plaintiff won his case. It was held by the Court of Appeal that there must be implied into the contract an undertaking by the wharfingers that the river bottom was, so far as reasonable care could make it, in such a condition as not to endanger the ship. Bowen L.J. said:

"[T]he law is raising an implication from the presumed intention of the parties, with the object of giving to the transaction such efficacy as both parties must have intended that at all events it should have. In business transactions such as this, what the law desires to effect by the implication is to give such business efficacy to the transaction as must have been intended at all events by both parties who are businessmen."

Although this process of implication is a convenient way of repairing oversights or omissions, there is the risk of overworking it. Judges have regularly warned against treating Bowen L.J.'s words as a principle of law. A recent example of this view is to be found in *Equitable Life Assurance Society v Hyman* (2000), in which the House of Lords considered the implication of a term based on an intention imputed to the parties from their actual circumstances. Lord Steyn called this an "individualised term" and said:

"Such a term may be imputed to the parties: it is not critically dependent on proof of an actual intention of the parties.... The legal test for the implication of such a term is a standard of strict necessity."

He went on to point out that a term may never be implied in conflict with the express terms of the text. This case is considered in more detail below.

For the courts to imply a term it is not enough that the term should be reasonable; it must be both obvious and necessary: see *Liverpool City Council v Irwin* (1977, HL). There Lord Cross said:

"What the court is being in effect asked to do is to rectify a particular—often a very detailed—contract by inserting in it a term which the parties have not expressed. Here it is not enough for the court to say that the suggested term is a reasonable one the presence of which would make the contract a better or fairer one; it must be able to say that the insertion of the term is necessary."

This approach was confirmed by the House of Lords in the later case of *Hughes v Greenwich London Borough Council* (1993).

In *Shirlaw v Southern Foundries* (1926) Ltd (1939, CA) Mac-Kinnon L.J. said:

"Prima facie that which in any contract is left to be implied and need not be expressed is something so obvious that it goes without saying; so that, if, while the parties were making their bargain, an officious bystander were to suggest some express provision for it in their agreement, they would testily suppress him with a common 'Oh, of course!' "

It follows from this test that a term will not be implied if one of the parties is ignorant of the matter to be implied. In *Sethia (1944) Ltd v Partabmull Rameshwar* (1950, CA, and affirmed by HL) the buyers of Indian jute sued the sellers for non-delivery. The sellers had been unable to deliver because they failed to obtain a quota for export to Genoa. The sellers argued that a term should be implied that the contract was "subject to quota". The Court of Appeal refused to imply the term. The buyers knew of the quota system, but they did not know that the sellers had no quota for Italy. Similarly, in *Walford v Miles* (1992), the House of Lords refused to imply a term into a lock-out agreement that the vendor would not negotiate with anyone except the other party for an unspecified period, on the grounds that such a term would be uncertain.

Nevertheless, the process of implying terms is an important instrument in regulating the relationship between the parties to a contract. Three examples from recent cases show this. In *Johnstone v Bloomsbury Health Authority* (1991) the Court of Appeal said that the exercise of an express term in a contract may be cut down by an implied term obliging the party relying on it to act reasonably. This last case arose in the context of hospital doctors' hours of work, under a clause in their contracts which stipulated a standard working week of 40 hours and an additional requirement to be available on call up to an average of 48 hours a week over a specified period. The second example is *Scally v Southern Health and Social Services Board* (1991) in which the House of Lords said that in cases where a contract (in this case, a contract of employment) gives a valuable benefit, the court may imply a term obliging the other party to it to take reasonable steps to bring to the attention of that person a term in the contract, so that he may enjoy its benefit. This decision may be contrasted with the later decision in *University of Nottingham v Eyett (No.1)* (1999), in which the court held that the trusts and confidence term did not require the employer to volunteer advice, in circumstances where the employee had all the relevant rules in his possession. The facts were that the employee asked his employers to inform him of his pension position if he retired on July 31, 1994. They gave him correct information but did not point out that he would have received a higher pension had he served another month and retired on August 31, 1994. In *Scally's* case, Lord Bridge talked in terms of the term being a "necessary incident of a definable category of" contractual relationship. This formulation was approved by Lord Woolf in *Spring v Guardian Assurance Plc* (1994). He referred to "normal practice" in contracts of the particular kind and to the fact that it would be reasonable to expect the party to enter into the contract on the basis of the suggested implied term. See also *Crossley v Faithful & Gould Holdings Ltd* (2004).

The third example is the House of Lords decision in *Equitable Life Assurance Society v Hyman* (2000), which involved the interpretation of an article of the Society's articles of association and the question whether a restriction could be implied into the article. The article (art. 65) provided that the directors "shall apportion the amount of [the] declared surplus by way of bonus among the holders of the participating policies on such principles, and by such methods, as they from time to time may determine." Some of the policies offered by the Society contained a condition for conversion of the capital sum payable on maturity to an annuity at a guaranteed annual rate ("GAR"). When the Society found itself liable to pay out annuities at a GAR which was well above market rate, they tried to get round this problem by paying a smaller final bonus to those who had opted for the GAR and arguing that art.65 permitted them to do so. The House of Lords held that they had acted in breach of art.65. Lord Steyn said:

"The supposition of the parties must be presumed to have been that the directors would not exercise their discretion in conflict with contractual rights. These are the circumstances in which the directors of the Society resolved upon a differential policy which was designed to deprive the relevant guarantees of any substantial value. In my judgement an implication [of a term] precluding the use of the directors' discretion in this way is strictly necessary. The implication is essential to give effect to the reasonable expectations of the parties ..."

Terms may also be implied on the basis of custom. An example of a custom being imported into a contract as an implied term may be seen in *Hutton v Warren* (1836). A tenant who had been given notice to quit a farm was allowed to give evidence of a local custom entitling him to a fair allowance for seeds and labour. The court held that the lease made between the parties must be read as including the custom.

Terms implied by statute

Some implied terms develop from being terms implied by the courts to being terms implied by statute. Thus, many of the implied terms set out in the Sale of Goods Act 1893 had been habitually implied by the courts in the years before 1893, and so the statute was simply declaring the existing common law. One of the more important terms implied by the Sale of Goods Act 1979, as amended by the Sale and Supply of Goods Act 1994, is an implied term that the goods are of "satisfactory" quality. The original wording talked in terms of "merchantable quality". The new implied term as to satisfactory quality is further defined in ss.14(2A), (2B) and (2C), which state:

"(2A) For the purposes of this Act, goods are of satisfactory quality if they meet the standards that a reasonable person would regard as satisfactory, taking account of any description of the goods, the price (if relevant) and all the other relevant circumstances.

(2B) For the purposes of this Act, the quality of goods includes their state and condition and the following (among others) are in appropriate cases aspects of the quality of goods—

(a) fitness for all the purposes for which goods of the kind in question are commonly supplied,
(b) appearance and finish,
(c) freedom from minor defects,
(d) safety, and
(e) durability.

(2C) The term implied by subsection (2) above does not extend to any matter making the goods unsatisfactory—

(a) which is specifically drawn to the buyer's attention before the contract is made,
(b) where the buyer examines the goods before the contract is made, which that examination ought to reveal, or
(c) in the case of a contract for sale by sample, which would have been apparent on a reasonable examination of the sample."

Whether this revised wording will make any difference remains to be seen.

Under s.14(3) of the Act there is a further implied term that the goods will be fit for the purpose for which they are bought, where the buyer makes known to the seller a particular purpose for buying the goods in question. It should be noted that both these terms implied by s.14 are stated by s.14(6) of the Act to be conditions.

Just as statutory implied terms commonly (though not always) derive from earlier common law implied terms, so in their turn statutory implied terms are sometimes adopted, by analogy, in the courts. For example, in *Samuels v Davis* (1943, CA) the plaintiff dentist contracted to make a set of dentures. The defendant refused to pay for them on the ground that they were so unsatisfactory that they could not be used. There was argument whether the contract was a contract for sale of goods or a contract for work and materials. The Court of Appeal held that the question was irrelevant. If it was a contract for the sale of goods, the Sale of Goods Act 1893 imported a term that they should be reasonably fit for their purpose; if it was a contract for work and materials, the court would imply a term to the same effect.

Terms of reasonable fitness have been implied into all manner of contracts, including contracts of hire and contracts for repair. In the Sale of Goods Act the implied term of reasonable fitness is absolute, in the sense that the seller is liable for breach even if he has not been at all negligent. When the courts have applied a similar term to contracts other than for sale of goods they have usually implied the term in this absolute form. The contractor is said to be under "strict liability". In other contracts, where the implied term has grown up independently of the Sale of Goods Act, the undertaking is usually in a qualified form; thus, for example, a carrier of passengers is not absolutely liable, he has only "negligence liability".

The Supply of Goods and Services Act 1982, as amended by the Sale and Supply of Goods Act 1994, greatly extended the field of statutory implied terms. The Act introduced statutory implied terms for: (1) contracts for the supply of goods, being (a) contracts for the transfer of property in goods (other than contracts, such as contracts of sale of goods and contracts of hire-purchase, already covered by statutes) and (b) contracts for the hire of goods; and (2) contracts for the supply of services. (Group (1)(a) includes contracts for work and materials.) It is noteworthy that in contracts for the supply of goods (both (1)(a) and (1)(b), above) the implied terms regarding quality and fitness impose strict liability, whereas in contracts for the supply of services ((2), above) the implied terms regarding quality and fitness impose only negligence liability. An example of this last implied term is to be found in *Wilson v Best Travel Ltd* (1993), a case in which a tourist suffered serious injuries whilst staying in a hotel on a holiday booked through the defendant tour operators. The court said that the duty of care owed by a tour operator to its customers under the Act was a duty to exercise reasonable care to exclude from the accommodation offered any hotel whose characteristics were such that guests could not spend a holiday there in reasonable safety. The obligations of suppliers of package holidays have been increased by the United Kingdom Package Travel, Package Holidays and Package Tours Regulations 1992 (SI 1992/3288), introduced in response to Council Directive 90/314 ([1990] O.J. L158/9). The purpose of the Directive is to harmonise the law relating to package holidays and the contracts governing them in all the Member States. This is an example of the increasing tendency to regulate particular types of contracts by the statutory imposition of terms.

Apart from the classification of terms implied by s.14 of the Sale of Goods Act 1979 (as amended) as conditions, it is not possible to classify implied terms until the time of litigation, since, by their very nature, they were not known to, or contemplated by, the parties until then. When the court decides to imply a term, it is then open to it to indicate whether the particular term is a condition or warranty. They will probably do this after looking at the consequences of the breach which has been held to have occurred.

EXEMPTION CLAUSES

AN EXEMPTION clause is a term in a contract which tries to exempt one of the parties from liability in certain events. The principles involved also apply to limitation clauses, which are clauses which seek to limit (rather than wholly exclude) a party's liability, and clauses which provide that complaints must be made within a certain period of time.

An exemption clause may be a perfectly legitimate device in contracts between parties of equal bargaining power. But where the parties are unequal, such a clause may cause injustice. This is particularly so in what are called "standard form contracts". They usually arise where there is a monopoly or near-monopoly, or where there is a strong trade association. Fields in which standard exemption clauses operate include travel by air, carriage of goods and insurance. In these and other fields, the contracts are sometimes called "contracts of adhesion".

A party wishing to rely on an exemption clause must show that it was a term of the contract, and that, properly construed, it covers the loss or damage which has occurred. Even if he can show both these things, the clause may still fail for one or more of several possible reasons. These matters will be examined in turn: term of the contract; construction; and possible causes of failure.

It should be remembered that in most (but not all) contracts, exemption clauses may fail because of the effect of the Unfair Contract Terms Act 1977 or the Unfair Terms in Consumer Contracts Regulations 1999: see below, at p.94.

TERM OF THE CONTRACT

An exemption clause may become a term of the contract by signature or by notice.

Signature

If a person signs a contractual document he is bound by its terms, including any exemption clause it may contain, even if he does not read the document. In *L'Estrange v Graucob* (1934) the plaintiff, who was a cafe proprietress, bought a cigarette vending machine. She signed, without reading, a "sales agreement" which contained a number of clauses "in regrettably small print but quite legible". The machine did not work properly. The defendants were held to be protected by a clause which excluded their liability. Nevertheless, like many older cases on exemption clauses it should be remembered that, if the facts were to recur today, the result might be affected by subsequent legislation, such as the Unfair Contract Terms Act 1977.

Notice

If the contractual document is not signed, the question of notice arises. The exemption clause may be printed on a document which is handed to one party by the other or is posted up in the shop or booking hall or other place where the contract is made. In such a case the clause will only be incorporated into the contract, so as to become a term of it, if: (a) the party affected knows of the clause, or (b) reasonable steps are taken to bring it to his notice.

It is worth pointing out at this stage that there is no special magic relating to exemption clauses in this respect. An express clause of any kind will only be effective if it is incorporated into the contract. All the points considered below as to how it may become incorporated apply to any kind of clause: Was the clause contained in a signed contract? If not, was it contained in a document which was clearly meant to have contractual force? Was reasonably sufficient notice of it given? Was it given in time?

What kind of document?

The exemption clause will only be effective if it is contained in a document which is part of the contract. If the person concerned knew that the document was intended to form part of the contract, he is bound; if he did not know, then the test is whether a reasonable person would have taken the document to be a contractual document, as distinct from (for example) a mere receipt. In *Chapelton v Barry UDC* (1940, CA) the plaintiff hired a deck chair at the seaside, and he was handed a ticket for which he paid 2d. On the back of the ticket it was stated that the Council was not liable in the event of "any accident or damage arising from the hire of the chair". When he sat on the chair, it collapsed and he was injured. The exemption was held not to protect the Council; the ticket was a mere receipt. On the other hand, a prominently displayed notice is capable of being a contractual document.

What degree of notice?

There is a large number of decided cases on this topic, often referred to as "the ticket cases". The guiding principle, however, can be deduced from one case, *Parker v South Eastern Railway* (1877, CA). The plaintiff left a bag in a railway cloakroom and paid for a ticket. On the front of the ticket were a number, a date, the opening times of the office, and the words "see back". On the back of the ticket was a clause (amongst others) stating: "The company will not be responsible for any package exceeding the value of £10." The plaintiff, later that day, presented his ticket, but the bag could not be found. He claimed the value of the bag, which exceeded £10. The company pleaded the exemption clause. The jury was asked two questions: (1) Did the plaintiff read the clause? and (2) Was he under any obligation to read it? The jury answered "No" to both questions. The Court of Appeal ordered a new trial; the jury had been asked the wrong question; the correct second question (assuming the plaintiff had not read the clause) was: Did the railway company do what was reasonably sufficient to give the plaintiff notice of the clause? This case was applied by the Court of Appeal in *Interfoto Picture Library Ltd v Stiletto Visual Programmes Ltd* (1988), where in fact an exclusion clause was not involved. The court made it clear that, where a term in a contract is particularly onerous or unusual and would not generally be known to the other party, the person wishing to enforce the term must show that it was fairly and reasonably brought to the other party's attention. It is clear that the restrictive approach to incorporation taken in *Parker*'s case, above, is still followed.

Most of the cases turn on such matters as: what was said and done when the contract was entered into, what was on the front of the ticket, what was on the back of the ticket, whether the ticket was folded, whether the clause was obliterated by a date stamp, and whether the clause was buried in a mass of advertisements. But sometimes the decisive point lies in earlier dealings between the parties. In *Kendall v Lillico* (1969, HL) the sellers sold some goods to the buyers under an oral contract and the next day sent them a "sold note" containing an exemption clause. As this "sold note" came after the contract had been made, it was too late to be of any effect. (On this, see below.) But there had been a consistent course of dealing between the parties over the previous three years, involving some 100 similar contracts, during which the sellers had, after each oral contract, sent the buyers a "sold note" containing the same clause. The House of Lords held that, before the instant contract, reasonable notice of the exemption clause had been given. The same result may be reached even where there have been no previous dealings between the parties, provided that the parties are in the same line of business and know that similar clauses are in common use in the business: see *British Crane Hire Corporation Ltd v Ipswich Plant Hire Ltd* (1975, CA).

When was the notice given?

An exemption clause becomes a term of the contract only if notice of it is given before, or at the time of, contracting. In *Olley v Marlborough Court Ltd* (1949, CA) a guest booked in at the reception desk of an hotel and paid for a week's stay. She then went up to the bedroom. On its wall was a notice stating that the hotel would not be liable for articles lost or stolen unless handed in for safe custody. She left her furs in the bedroom, closed the self-locking door and hung the key on a board in the reception office. The furs were stolen. The exemption clause did not help the defendants, because the contract was made at the reception desk and the plaintiff did not see, and could not have seen, the exemption clause until later. That subsequent notice could not affect her rights; it was simply not part of the contract.

In relation to exemption clauses, it may be very important to determine when the contract was made. The cases show that where a ticket (for example, a railway ticket) is bought at a booking-office, the request of the passenger is thought of as an invitation to treat, the clerk's handing out of the ticket as an offer, and the passenger's paying the fare as an acceptance. In *Thornton v Shoe Lane Parking* (1971, CA) the Court of Appeal had to deal with a case where the ticket was dispensed by an unattended machine. Lord Denning said that in such a case the offer lay in the sign "Parking" on the outside of the garage, and the acceptance lay in the customer's placing his car on the spot that caused the machine to operate. Conditions printed on the ticket which was then given out to the customer by the machine came too late.

CONSTRUCTION OF EXEMPTION CLAUSES

To construe means to interpret; construction means interpretation. This is a task which faces a court when dealing with any written contractual term. It is not possible here to go into all the rules of construction. Two rules are of particular importance in construing exemption clauses: (1) the contra proferentem rule and (2) the main purpose rule. At one time some judges tended to construe exemption clauses in isolation. In *Photo Productions Ltd v Securicor Transport Ltd* (1980, HL) that idea was exploded; what has to be construed is the whole contract including any exemption clause. In other words, like any language in any document, it has to be considered in its context.

Contra proferentem rule

This rule is to the effect that any ambiguity, or other doubt, in an exemption clause must be resolved against the person who is seeking to rely on it; that is, against the person who is proffering it. In *Baldry v Marshall* (1925, CA) the plaintiff asked the defendants, who were motor dealers, for a car "suitable for touring purposes." The defendants suggested that a Bugatti car would be appropriate.

After delivery it was found to be remarkably unsuitable for touring purposes, and the plaintiff sued to get his money back. The written contract included a guarantee for 12 months against mechanical defects, but expressly excluded "any other guarantee or warranty, statutory or otherwise". The Court of Appeal held that the stipulation for suitability for touring purposes was a condition, not a warranty, and that therefore the exemption clause did not apply.

In *Andrews v Singer* (1934, CA) the plaintiffs contracted to buy some "new Singer cars" from the defendants. By a clause in the written contract "all conditions, warranties and liabilities, implied by statute, common law or otherwise" were excluded. One of the cars, when delivered, turned out to be a used car. The plaintiffs sued for damages and won. The Court of Appeal held that though the term "new Singer car" was a condition, it was not an implied, but an express, condition, and therefore the exemption clause did not apply to it, since it was expressed only to protect the sellers from liability for breach of implied conditions.

In *L'Estrange v Graucob* (above, p.82), however, the seller defeated even the ingenuity of the Court of Appeal. The clause there in issue stated that "any express or implied condition, statement or warranty, statutory or otherwise, is hereby excluded". That comprehensive clause successfully protected the defendant seller. The contra proferentem rule could not help the buyer, although the validity of such a draconian clause would now be affected by the Unfair Contract Terms Act 1977.

Liability for negligence

A very important aspect of the contra proferentem rule is that very clear words must be used before a party will be held to be exempt from liability for negligence.

We saw at the end of Chapter 4, that, by an implied term, a contractor is sometimes held to have a strict liability and is sometimes held to have only negligence liability. If there is any doubt whether the words of an exemption clause exclude liability for negligence, they will be held to do so only if that is the only liability that the party has. In *Alderslade v Hendon Laundry* (1945, CA) the defendants contracted to launder the plaintiff's handkerchiefs. The contract limited their liability for lost or damaged articles to 20 times the laundering charge. (This is a good example of a limitation clause, as distinct from a complete exemption clause.) The handkerchiefs were lost through the defendants' negligence. The Court of Appeal held that the limitation clause must apply, because if it did not apply to negligence liability it would "lack subject-matter"; there was no other liability it could apply to, since the launderers did not have strict liability. On the other hand, a contractor may be under a strict liability, as in *White v John Warwick & Co Ltd* (1953, CA) where the plaintiff hired a tradesman's cycle from the defendants. The written agreement stated that "nothing in this agreement shall render the owners liable for any personal injuries". While the plaintiff was riding the cycle, the saddle tilted forward and he was injured. The Court of Appeal held that the clause did not protect the owners. They were under strict liability as well as negligence liability. The somewhat vague wording of the clause was sufficient to exclude their strict liability but not their negligence liability.

But it must be remembered that this is only a rule of construction. If the words are clear enough, an exemption clause can exclude negligence liability as well as strict liability. On the other hand, if the words used are very unclear, they will not protect the contractor against negligence liability even where negligence is the only possible ground of liability. See *Hollier v Rambler Motors* (1972, CA).

In this field there is a kind of borderland between contract and tort. The negligence liability in a contract overlaps with negligence as a tort. A party to a contract cannot defeat an exemption clause by threatening to sue in tort. If an exemption clause does protect a defendant from liability for contractual negligence, it equally protects him from liability for tortious negligence.

Where the Unfair Contract Terms Act 1977 applies, that Act lays additional restrictions on a party's ability to protect itself from liability for negligence whether contractual or tortious: see p.94, below.

Main purpose rule

In *Glynn v Margetson* (1893, HL) Lord Halsbury said:

> "Looking at the whole of the instrument, and seeing what one must regard ... as its main purpose, one must reject words, indeed whole provisions, if they are inconsistent with what one assumes to be the main purpose of the contract."

In that case, oranges were to be carried by ship from Malaga to Liverpool. The bill of lading contained a clause permitting the ship to call at almost any port in Europe or Africa. The ship went east from Malaga, then back again, and only then to Liverpool. When it docked, the oranges were found to have deteriorated because of the delay. The carrier was held liable in spite of the permissive clause. The wide words of the clause must be cut down so as not to defeat the main object and intent of the contract, the carriage of oranges from Malaga to Liverpool. The clause only justified the carrier in calling at ports on the route between those places.

The "main purpose rule" then, is that in construing an exemption clause there is a presumption that it was not intended to defeat the main purpose of the contract. The rule was endorsed by the House of Lords in *Suisse Atlantique Société d'Armement Maritime S.A v N.V. Rotterdamsche Kolen Centrale* (1967, HL). There is no doubt that the main purpose rule is a powerful instrument for limiting the effect of exemption clauses. Section 3 of the Unfair Contract Terms Act 1977 (where it applies) gives statutory support to the "main purpose rule".

Fundamental breach

In the years before 1967 there grew up what appeared to be a substantive rule of law that if a party committed a fundamental breach of his contract he was not entitled to rely on any exemption clause in the contract. In that year the *Suisse Atlantique* case (1967, HL) was decided by the House of Lords. Their Lordships "decided" (though, strictly, what they said on this point was obiter) that there is no rule of law that an exemption clause can never apply where there has been a fundamental breach; it is simply a question of construction whether an exemption clause applies in the events that have happened.

In *Photo Productions Ltd v Securicor Transport Ltd* (1980, HL) the House of Lords reaffirmed the law as stated in *Suisse Atlantique*. In the *Photo Productions* case the plaintiffs were a company which owned a factory. They entered into a contract with the defendants, a security company, whereby the defendants were to provide a visiting patrol at night and at weekends. One Sunday night the duty patrol, one Musgrove, lit a small fire inside the factory; the fire got out of control, and the factory and its stock, together worth £615,000, were completely destroyed. The plaintiffs sued the defendants. The defendants relied on an exemption clause in the contract which provided:

"Under no circumstances shall [Securicor] be responsible for any injurious act or default by any employee of [Securicor] unless such act or default could have been foreseen and avoided by the exercise of due diligence on the part of [Securicor] as his employer ...".

The plaintiffs did not allege that Securicor were negligent in employing Musgrove. The House of Lords held that although Securicor were in breach of their obligation to operate their service with due and proper regard to the safety and security of Photo Production's premises, all that the court had to do was to construe and apply the exemption clause; it was clear and unambiguous and it protected Securicor from liability. There was no question of Securicor being disqualified, because of their breach, from relying on the clause.

The *Photo Productions* case confirms that the question is simply one of construction: does the exemption clause cover the events which happened? On the whole, we can say that the more serious the breach (or the consequences of the breach), the less likely is the court to interpret the exemption clause as applying to the breach. But it remains possible for a party to a contract to exclude liability for breach of a fundamental term or a breach which has serious consequences—provided that he uses clear words to cover the events which occur.

The contract in the *Photo Productions* case was made before the coming into force of the Unfair Contract Terms Act 1977 and so the Act did not apply, but it is interesting to note that the decision of the House of Lords is entirely in line with s.9(1) of the Act: see below.

POSSIBLE CAUSES OF FAILURE OF AN EXEMPTION CLAUSE

Even where an exemption clause is undoubtedly a term of the contract, and even where, on its true construction, it covers the loss or damage which has occurred, it may yet fail. Five possible causes of failure will be discussed here.

1. Misrepresentation

In *L'Estrange v Graucob* (above, p.82) Scrutton L.J. said:

"When a document containing contractual terms is signed, then in the absence of fraud, or ... misrepresentation, the party signing it is bound, and it is wholly immaterial whether he has read the document or not."

In *Curtis v Chemical Cleaning and Dyeing Co* (1951, CA) the plaintiff took to the defendants' shop a white satin wedding dress to have it cleaned. The dress was trimmed with beads and sequins. The shop assistant gave her a form to sign. The plaintiff asked what it was all about. The assistant replied that it exempted the company from the risk of damage to the beads and sequins. The plaintiff then signed the form, which in fact contained a clause stating that the company was not to be liable for any damage, however caused. When the dress was returned it was found to be stained. The plaintiff sued for damages and the defendants sought to rely on the clause. Following the observation of Scrutton L.J. in *L'Estrange v Graucob*, the Court of Appeal held that the defendants could not rely on the clause, because the assistant had misrepresented its effect. There was no suggestion of fraud. Of course, if there were fraud, then the clause would certainly fail.

2. Overriding oral undertaking

Evans (J.) & Son (Portsmouth) Ltd v Andrea Merzario Ltd (1976, CA) illustrates this point. The plaintiffs were importers of machines from Italy. The defendants were forwarding contractors. The course of dealing between the parties was on the standard conditions of the forwarding trade. Until 1967 the defendants had arranged for transportation of the plaintiff's goods in crates under deck, because the machines were liable to rust if carried on deck. In 1967 the defendants proposed to change over to transportation in containers. The defendants gave the plaintiffs an oral assurance that machines subsequently transported in containers would be shipped under deck. On the faith of that oral assurance, the plaintiffs agreed to the change-over to container transport, and gave the defendants an order for the carriage of a machine in a container. Because of an error on the part of the defendants, the container was shipped at Rotterdam on deck. The container fell off the deck and was lost overboard. The printed standard conditions of the forwarding trade which were incorporated into the contract gave the defendants complete freedom in respect of the means and procedure to be followed in the transportation of the goods, and contained exemption and limitation clauses. The plaintiffs sued for breach of contract and the defendants relied on the printed conditions. The Court of Appeal held unanimously that the oral undertaking overrode such of the clauses of the printed conditions as were repugnant to it. The majority of the Court reached this decision on the ground that the oral undertaking constituted a term of the main contract. Lord Denning, though reaching the same decision, did so, on the ground that the oral undertaking formed part of a collateral contract: see below.

3. Collateral contract

The collateral contract device (see pp.64, et seq.) may, on occasion, neutralise an exemption clause. In *Webster v Higgin* (1948, CA) the plaintiff was a garage proprietor. His agent said to the defendant: "If you buy the Hillman 10 we will guarantee that it is in good condition." The defendant then entered into a hire-purchase contract with the plaintiff, and the contract contained an exemption clause. When the car was delivered it was not in a very good state; it was, in Lord Greene's words "nothing but a mass of second-hand and dilapidated ironmongery". Not unnaturally, the defendant did not pay the instalments. The plaintiff sued for the return of the car and for the instalments due. The Court of Appeal held that the exemption clause in the main (hire-purchase) contract did not affect the "guarantee" in the previous (collateral) contract. The effect of the judgment was that the defendant could return the car and get back his deposit money.

In *Webster v Higgin* the main contract and the collateral contract were both between the same parties, but the same principle can work where this is not so. In *Andrews v Hopkinson* (1957) the plaintiff wanted a second-hand car. The defendant car dealer recommended one, using these words: "It's a good little bus. I would stake my life on it." The plaintiff agreed to take it on hire-purchase. The normal arrangements were made: the dealer sold the car to a finance company and the finance company let it on hire-purchase terms to the customer, the plaintiff signed a delivery note stating that he was "satisfied as to its condition". A week later the car suddenly swerved into a lorry; the car was wrecked and the plaintiff was seriously injured. It was established that the car had a long-standing fault in the steering. The terms of the delivery note might well have prevented the plaintiff from suing the finance company, but he sued the dealer for breach of the collateral contract, the "good little bus" contract, and obtained damages.

The collateral contract device does not, strictly speaking, cause the exemption clause to fail. The exemption clause does not itself fail, but it fails to prevent the plaintiff from getting a remedy. A response to this has been the adoption of so-called "entire agreement clauses" in commercial contracts of the kind found in *Watford Electronics Ltd v Sanderson CFL Ltd* (2001, CA). Here the clause stated:

> "The parties agree that these terms and conditions ... represent the entire agreement between the parties relating to the sale and purchase of the equipment and that no statement or representations made by either party have been relied upon by the other in agreeing to enter the Contract".

Such a clause would likely be sufficient to exclude liability in respect of a collateral contact. A much more difficult matter is whether the second half of the clause would also exclude liability for misrepresentation (see p.126 below). In the case itself Chadwick L.J. rejected the argument that an acknowledgement of non-reliance amounts in reality to an exclusion clause to which s.3 of the Misrepresentation Act 1967 could apply. The cases are not, however, entirely clear and it remains to be seen on what side of the line between substance and form the courts will draw the line.

4. Third parties

A "third party" is a person who is not a party to a contract. Chapter 12 deals with the doctrine of privity of contract at greater length. Stated briefly, the doctrine is that a person who is not a party to a contract cannot benefit from the contract or suffer from it. This applies as much to an exemption clause as to any other kind of clause. The leading authority on the application of the doctrine to exemption clauses is *Scruttons Ltd v Midland Silicones Ltd* (1962, HL). A drum of chemicals belonging to Midland Silicones was shipped from the United States to England. The contract of carriage limited the liability of the carrier to US $500 per packet. (So it was a limitation clause, not an exemption clause, but the principles are the same.) The drum was damaged to the extent of £593, through the negligence of a company of stevedores (Scruttons), whom the carriers had employed to unload the ship. It was held by the House of Lords that the stevedores could not rely on the limitation clause in the contract of carriage, because they were not parties to that contract. It was also said that the stevedores could not rely on a similar limitation clause contained in the contract between the stevedores and the carrier. It should be noted that there were two contracts. The case decides that C cannot take the benefit of an exemption clause contained in a contract between A and B; and it assumes that C cannot impose on A the burden of an exemption clause contained in a contract between C and B.

An important point to grasp is that an employee is a third party in this context, so that, even if his employer has a perfectly good exemption clause, the employee cannot benefit from it. In *Cosgrove v Horsfall* (1945, CA) a person was travelling on a bus under a free pass which contained a term that neither the London Passenger Transport Board nor its servants would be liable to him for injury, however caused. The passenger was injured through the negligence of the bus driver. The passenger could not, or at any rate did not, sue the LPTB, because of the exemption clause, but he successfully sued the driver. The driver was not a party to the licence or contract, and so could not rely on its exemption clause. This was so, even though the clause had expressly mentioned the Board's "servants".

A way round *Scruttons Ltd v Midland Silicones Ltd*, which was found to be commercially inconvenient, has been opened up by a decision of the Privy Council on appeal from New Zealand, *New Zealand Shipping Co Ltd v A.M. Satterthwaite & Co Ltd*; *The Eurymedon* (1975, PC). In that case the Privy Council, by a majority of three to two, held that the benefit of an exemption clause in a contract of carriage can be claimed by a stevedore provided that four conditions are satisfied: (1) the contract of carriage makes it clear that the stevedore is intended to be protected; (2) the contract of carriage makes it clear that the carrier is contracting not only on his own behalf but also as agent for the stevedore; (3) the carrier has authority from the stevedore so to contract; and (4) there is some consideration moving from the stevedore. In the instant case the consideration was held to be the performance of the unloading services by the stevedore. It did not matter that the stevedore was already under a contractual obligation to the carrier to perform unloading services. The case of *Scotson v Pegg* (see p.40, above) was expressly approved.

5. Legislation

Before the Unfair Contract Terms Act 1977, the legislature intervened in a modest way to control exemption clauses in some specific fields. That Act, however, was a massive intervention over a very wide field.

Examples of previous statutory intervention include s.149 of the Road Traffic Act 1988 (as it now is), which deals with an agreement or undertaking between the user of a motor vehicle and a passenger seeking to restrict any liability of the user towards the passenger; s.29 of the Public Passenger Vehicles Act 1981, which renders void any provision in a contract that seeks to exclude or limit liability for death or personal injury of a passenger in a public service vehicle. Section 3 of the Misrepresentation Act 1967 stated that a provision in an agreement that sought to exclude or restrict liability for misrepresentation was to have effect only to the extent that a court thought fair and reasonable. (Misrepresentation will be looked at in Chapter 7). Where it applies, the Contracts (Rights of Third Parties) Act 1999 may also allow third parties to be protected by exemption clauses made in their favour.

Unfair Contract Terms Act 1977

Despite its title, the Unfair Contract Terms Act 1977 deals only with unfair exemption clauses, not all unfair contract terms.

In order to understand the Act it is first necessary to study two definitions, "business liability" and "deals as consumer". This is because most of the provisions in the Act apply only to business liability and because a consumer has a specially favoured status under the Act. "Business liability" is liability arising from things done by a person in the course of a business or from the occupation of business premises: see s.1(3). A person "deals as consumer" (see s.12) if he does not make (or hold himself out as making) the contract in the course of a business and the other party does make the contract in the course of a business. If the contract is for the supply of goods, there is an additional point, that the goods must be of a type ordinarily supplied for private use or consumption. One effect of this definition is that where a non-business person contracts with another non-business person (e.g. in selling a second-hand car) neither party "deals as consumer".

The main provisions of the Act are as follows:

94

(1) Liability (that is, business liability) for death or personal injury resulting from negligence cannot be excluded or restricted by any contract term or notice: s.2(1).

(2) In the case of other loss or damage a person cannot so exclude or restrict his (business) liability for negligence except in so far as the term or notice satisfies the requirement of reasonableness: s.2(2). The requirement of reasonableness "is that the term shall have been a fair and reasonable one to be included having regard to the circumstances which were, or ought reasonably to have been, known to or in the contemplation of the parties when the contract was made": see s.11(1). Guidelines for the application of the reasonableness test are laid down in s.11(4) and (so far as concerns the supply of goods) in Sch.2.

An example of the application of these provisions is the case of *Phillips Products Ltd v Hyland and Hamstead Plant Hire Co Ltd* (1987, CA), where the second defendants, Hamstead Hire, hired an excavator plus driver (the first defendant) to the plaintiffs. Condition 8 of the contract of hire provided that the driver was to be regarded as the employee of the hirers; they were to be responsible for all claims arising in connection with the operation of the excavator by the driver. An accident occurred as a result of the driver's negligence; the plaintiff's factory suffered considerable damage. So they sued the driver and the hire company, which relied on condition 8. The plaintiff argued that the condition did not cover the driver's negligence; alternatively, if it did, it was caught by s.2(2) of the Act and failed to satisfy the requirement of reasonableness. The hire company argued that the condition did not exclude or restrict liability; rather, it transferred liability to the hirers. The Court of Appeal rejected this argument and held the defendants liable. They said that the court must look at the substance and effect of the term rather than its form. Here, the effect of condition 8 was to negative a common law duty in tort which would otherwise have fallen on the hire company. This meant that the condition had the effect of excluding liability and so fell within s.2(2).

This case may be contrasted with a case decided later in the same year, *Thompson v T. Lohan (Plant Hire) Ltd and J.W. Hurdiss Ltd* (1987, CA), which was decided by a different division of the Court of Appeal. The facts were similar to those of the preceding case; the condition in question was a new version of condition 8, but the variations are not significant for the purposes of the decision. The accident in this case occurred as a result of the driver's negligence, which caused the death of a fellow-employee, the plaintiff. The first defendants were the driver's general employers; the second defendants were the hirers. The plaintiff's widow sued the first defendants successfully; they then claimed that they should be indemnified by the second defendants (in other words, they wanted the second defendants to meet their liability to the plaintiff). The second defendants argued that condition 8 was contrary to s.2(1) of the Act. The Court of Appeal said that it was not. They said that s.2(1) was intended to prevent the restriction or exclusion of liability in relation to the victim of negligence and was not concerned with arrangements made by a wrongdoer with others for sharing or transferring the burden of compensating the victim. Condition 8 was therefore effective to transfer the liability for the driver's negligence to the second defendants.

The important distinction between the two cases is that in the *Phillips Products* case there was an attempt to exclude liability towards the victim; whereas in *Thompson*'s case there was no such attempt.

(3)   When one party deals as consumer or on the other party's written standard terms of business, that other party cannot:

    (a)   when himself in breach of contract, exclude or restrict his (business) liability in respect of the breach, or

    (b)   claim to be entitled to render a contractual performance substantially different from that which was reasonably expected of him; or

    (c)   claim to be entitled to render no performance at all, except (in all these cases) subject to the requirement of reasonableness: see s.3. This section applies to strict liability as well as liability for negligence.

Whilst much of the impact of the Act is felt in the consumer field, it is important to note that commercial parties too can be affected. This is illustrated by the leading judgment of the House of Lords in *George Mitchell (Chesterhall) Ltd v Finney Lock Seeds Ltd* (1983), which also serves as a good example of how a court now approaches exclusion clauses. The defendant had sold seed to the plaintiffs which turned out to be both unmerchantable (or unsatisfactory as s.14 of the amended Sale of Goods Act 1979 now states) and not of the agreed variety. The seed merchant relied on an exemption clause which purported to, "exclude all liability for any loss or damage arising from the use of any seeds ... supplied by us and for any consequential damage whatsoever." The House of Lords, in adopting what was essentially Lord Denning's approach in the Court of Appeal, decided that although a limitation clause was to be construed contra proferentem and had to be clearly expressed, recent legislation, by which was particularly meant the Unfair Contract Terms Act 1977, "had removed from judges the temptation to resort to the device of ascribing to the words appearing in exemption clauses a tortured meaning so as to avoid giving effect" to them, (per Lord Diplock). On this basis the clause, which had undoubtedly been incorporated into the agreement between the parties, was therefore enforceable at common law. This was not, however, the end of the story. Because the contract had been conducted on the basis of the seller's standard terms, the Act applied and the seller's term failed the statutory test of reasonableness. An important factor in favour of the finding of unreasonableness was said to be that, in the past, the seller had negotiated a settlement of farmers' claims rather than seeking strictly to rely on this clause. This suggested, it was said, that they themselves did not regard the term as reasonable. Quite whether this is an altogether convincing argument must be open to doubt. It may often be commercially expedient to settle disputes without relying on the parties' strict legal rights in order to preserve the goodwill of customers, and it rather appears that the seller was penalised for its generous attitude in the past. There seems more to be said for the reasoning that the supply of defective seed was negligent and that it was a risk against which the seller could easily have insured with a marginal impact on the price of the seeds.

The restriction placed upon performing the contract in a "substantially different form" (s.3(2)(b)) is particularly wide. It does not require that there be a conventional breach of contract, only that, in the court's view, the different mode of performance was reasonable. For example, suppose a contract states that accommodation "will be provided" in the Ritz Hotel (and therefore arguably a special or unique experience) "or, if accommodation in the Ritz Hotel is unavailable, in another hotel of comparable quality." Such a clause might fall foul of s.3(2)(a) of the Act. But, even if it is only meant to provide for an alternative mode of performance of the contract, it could still be caught by s.3(2)(b). If a plaintiff could reasonably be expected to be put up only in the Ritz Hotel the clause would be ineffective unless a defendant can show that it satisfies the Act's test of resonableness.

(4) In contracts for the sale and hire-purchase of goods, implied terms as to title cannot be excluded at all; implied terms as to conformity of goods with description or sample or as to their quality or fitness for a particular purpose cannot be excluded as against a person dealing as consumer and, as against non-consumers, can only be excluded subject to the requirement of reasonableness (s.6). This section is not confined to business liability.

(5) For other contracts under which possession or ownership of goods passes (e.g. hire) there are similar (but not identical) rules in s.7.

(6) Where the requirement of reasonableness applies, a term which satisfied the requirement remains effective even though the contract has been terminated by breach or by a party electing to treat it as repudiated: s.9(1).

This section makes absolutely clear that the doctrine of fundamental breach (above p.88) is abolished.

(7) Where on a breach the contract is nevertheless affirmed by a party entitled to treat it as repudiated, this does not of itself exclude the requirement of reasonableness: s.9(2).

The Act does not set up a generalised prohibition of exemption clauses or a generalised requirement of reasonableness. There are many contracts to which it does not apply or does not fully apply, such as contracts of insurance and contracts relating to the transfer of land. Thus, in *Electricity Supply Nominees Ltd v IAF Group Plc* (1993), the dispute was between a landlord and a tenant and concerned the terms of a covenant in a lease. The judge held that the lease was outside the provisions of the Act: see also s.1(2) and Sch.1.

The Act leaves some uncertainty as to what clauses are caught as being exemption clauses. This is a difficult problem. Compare two contracts. Contract A provides: "I undertake to deliver the goods by November 30. If delivery is delayed by strikes I shall not be liable." Contract B provides: "I undertake (subject to strikes) to deliver the goods by November 30." In Contract A there is clearly an exemption clause—that is to say, a clause restricting the contractor's liability. In Contract B the same result is achieved by restricting the contractor's duty. Is that restriction controlled by the Act? Section 13 deals with the matter. It seems from that section that the restriction of duty in Contract B is subjected to many of the provisions of the Act but not to (the very important) s.3 (see point (3), above). See *Smith v Eric S. Bush* (a firm); *Harris v Wyre Forest District Council* (1989, HL) and *Stewart Gill Ltd v Horatio Myer & Co Ltd* (1992), where s.13 is considered.

A recent example of the problems of deciding whether a particular clause is an exemption clause or not, is *St Albans City and District Council v International Computers Ltd* (1994). The defendants, a computer company, had a contract with standard terms and conditions, one of which limited their liability for loss to £100,000. The company supplied software containing an error to the Council; as a consequence, the Council set its community charge too low. It suffered a loss of more than £1 million. The company tried to rely on the limitation of liability clause, but the judge said that this was an exclusion clause which was affected by s.3 of the Act, since the Council had dealt on the company's standard terms of business. He went on to hold that the term was not fair and reasonable. A particular factor he considered was that the company was able to insure itself against this type of loss, whereas if the loss fell on the Council it would ultimately be borne by the local population. He said that it was not unreasonable that the person who made the profit should also carry the risk. The practical consequences counted in the Council's favour. The Court of Appeal, in affirming the decision, also made the important point that an appellate court should treat a trial judge's finding of reasonableness with the "utmost respect".

As was mentioned earlier, the short title of the Act is misleading. The Act does not only apply to contract terms generally nor only to contractual liability; it applies also to non-contractual notices and to tortious liability. The Act does not affect at all the principles upon which a court is to decide whether a particular exemption clause is or is not a term of the contract. The Act does affect very considerably the construction of exemption clauses—if it applies. A court dealing with the matter will have to decide whether the Act knocks out a particular clause entirely or makes it subject to the test of reasonableness or leaves it untouched. The Act adopts the contra proferentem rule in regard to the requirement of reasonableness: s.11(5) declares: "It is for those claiming that a contract term or notice satisfies the requirement of reasonableness to show that it does." The main purpose rule is given statutory support by s.3(2)(b). Where it applies, s.9(1) of the Act (see point (6), above) reaches the same result as the House of Lords reached (without the aid of the Act) in the *Photo Productions* case (see p.88, above), that breach (whether fundamental or not) does not put an end to an otherwise valid exemption clause; it simply remains to be construed. Section 9(2) of the Act (see point (7), above) is presumably designed to knock out any possibility of a kind of converse argument, namely an argument that where a party who is entitled to treat a contract as repudiated chooses instead to affirm the contract, the other party is freed from an otherwise applicable requirement of reasonableness. In that case, it remains a question of construction as to whether the requirement of reasonableness is or is not fulfilled.

Unfair Terms in Consumer Contracts Regulations 1999

These regulations are the United Kingdom's response to the European Directive 93/13. They are certainly the most significant European Union measure to impact upon the domestic law of contract. It is perhaps only because their existence is not widely known by the consuming public that their existence has not had a more dramatic effect, no doubt aided by the fact that they are secreted within a statutory instrument rather than in an Act of Parliament. They also reflect the growing tendency of the law of contract to diverge into two distinct areas; what one might call commercial and consumer contract law.

There is an obvious overlap with the Unfair Contract Terms Act 1977, although the Regulations are in some ways wider and in others more narrowly drawn that the 1977 Act. They are wider in that they apply a test of "good faith" to contract terms, a concept relatively novel to English contract law, and potentially they may strike at a wide range of terms, not simply exemption clauses. They also apply to areas such as insurance which falls outside the ambit of the 1977 Act. They are narrower in that they do not say some terms will have no legal effect at all as stated, for example, in ss.2 or 7 of the 1977 Act. There is no attempt to codify or rationalise the law relating to exemption clauses. The Regulations merely paste on another layer of legislative provisions to what existed already.

The crucial distinction between the Regulations and the Act is that the Regulations apply only to consumer transactions and that they include clauses which confer rights on a party. They are not limited to exclusion clauses and apply to many, although not all, the likely important terms in a consumer contract.

The term "consumer" is defined in a way that is similar to the 1977 Act. The sort of agreement targeted by the Regulations is the typical consumer standard form contract where the terms are not individually negotiated. Where the Regulations apply, s.8 states that an "unfair term ... shall not be binding on the consumer." This means that such a term may still be binding on the supplier of goods or services. Section 5 defines an unfair term as one which, "has not been individually negotiated [and] ... causes a significant imbalance in the parties' rights and obligations ... to the detriment of the consumer." This is clearly a broad test but s.6(2)(b) makes clear that this does not apply to the price of goods. It was thought to be impracticable for the courts to become enmeshed in this kind of dispute. Further detailed guidance is given in Sch.2 of the Regulations which sets out a list of terms which may be regarded as unfair. For example para.1(i) refers to terms which, "irrevocably bind the consumer to terms with which he had no real opportunity of becoming acquainted before the conclusion of the contract." This might be effective in the common situation where, for example, a consumer contracts for goods or services over the telephone paying with a credit card.

Section 7 states that contracts must be in, "plain, intelligible language." The sanction for failure to do so is that any ambiguity will be resolved in favour of the consumer, a statutory version of the contra proferentem rule. This in itself is a provision which should cause all those relying on standard form business contracts to look closely to see if their terms are indeed likely to be held valid.

The first reported case on the Regulations is the decision of the House of Lords in *Director General of Fair Trading v First National Bank Plc* (2002) which concerned a common clause relating to interest found in loan agreements. The effect of such a clause is that interest can continue to accrue on a loan even after a court judgment. The practical effect is that a consumer can be faced with a large claim for interest even after paying off the judgment. The House of Lords nevertheless decided that such a term was not unfair. One had to look at the contract as a whole, there had to be open dealing, and this required that terms should be expressed clearly, fully and legibly, which here they were. This suggests that, as in *Interfoto Picture Library Ltd v Stiletto Visual Programmes* (1989) (above p.84), the more onerous a term the more likely it is to be regarded as unfair if it is not sufficiently drawn to the consumer's attention.

The monetary amounts in cases involving the Regulations are such that cases are unlikely to appear in the law reports. Anyone wishing to assess the effect of the Regulations needs to consult the bulletins issued by the Director General of Fair Trading. A characteristic example of an occasion where the Regulations led to a change in business practice related to a standard form for the hire of video tapes. One company's agreement contained a clause which stated the supplier of the video tape was not liable for damage caused to a player by a defective tape but that the consumer was liable for damaging the tape. The effect was to create a clear imbalance in the rights of the parties adverse to the consumer. The result was that the company amended the clause to remove the imbalance.

PART THREE

DEFECTS IN THE AGREEMENT

ABSENCE OF REQUIRED FORMALITY

IN GENERAL, contracts can be made quite informally and writing is not usually necessary; a spoken word will do. But a few contracts require certain formalities. These are considered here.

DEEDS

A seal is no longer necessary for the valid execution of an instrument as a deed, as was seen in Chapter 2. The rule was abolished by s.1(1)(b) of the Law of Property (Miscellaneous Provisions) Act 1989. For a discussion of the relevant provisions, see p.50.

CONTRACTS WHICH MUST BE IN WRITING

There are a few contracts which are required by statute to be in writing. Amongst these are share transfers, bills of exchange, promissory notes and certain consumer credit agreements, including regulated hire-purchase agreements. The most important contracts in this category are contracts relating to land.

Contracts relating to land are now governed by s.2 of the Law of Property (Miscellaneous Provisions) Act 1989. Section 2(1) stipulates that a contract for the sale (or other disposition) of an interest in land may only be made in writing; all the terms which the parties have expressly agreed must be incorporated in one document, or, where contracts are exchanged, in each document. It is possible for the terms of the agreement to be incorporated in the document by reference to some other document: see s.2(2). Further, the document incorporating the terms must be signed by or on behalf of each party to the contract: s.2(3). Where contracts are exchanged, the same document need not bear the signatures of both parties, who may sign separately.

The provisions of s.2(2) were considered in *Record v Bell* (1991), a case which involved a letter of variation containing additional terms. The judge said that the letter could only be incorporated into the contract if the contract referred to or identified it. It could not be done by the letter referring to the contract. In this case, the letter of variation was attached to one of the contracts but not the other. The judge suggested that, had it been attached to both, s.2 would have been satisfied. He went on to hold, however, that there was a collateral contract. This was on the basis that the letter of variation was an offer of a warranty by the vendor's solicitor to the purchaser's solicitor as to the state of the title to induce him to exchange and that the offer was accepted by the exchange of contracts. In *Firstpost Homes Ltd v Johnson* (1995) the document in question referred to an attached plan. The purchaser signed the plan, but not the principal document. The Court of Appeal found that the requirements of s.2 had not been complied with.

In *Tootal Clothing Ltd v Guinea Properties Ltd* (1992) the landlord agreed, during negotiations for a lease of premises, to contribute to the cost of shop-fitting works. The lease did not mention that the landlord would contribute to the shop-fitting works. However, a second agreement was entered into on the same day as the lease agreement. This stated that it was supplemental to the lease agreement and that the landlord would contribute to the cost of the shop-fitting. The agreement was duly signed by both parties. When the work had been completed, the tenant asked for payment of the landlord's contribution, but the landlord refused on the grounds that s.2 barred recovery. The Court of Appeal held that s.2 only applies to executory land contracts and that, once the land contract had been executed by completion, the section had no further relevance to the enforceability of the supplemental agreement. Scott L.J. said that there was nothing to prevent the enforceability of such an agreement if parties chose to hive off part of the terms of their agreement into a separate contract distinct from the written land contract. This decision appears to be contrary to the intention, as expressed in s.2(1), that the terms of a land contract should be incorporated in that contract. See also *Grossman v Hooper* (2001) and *Dolphin Quays Developments Ltd v Mills* (2006).

The grant of an option to purchase land falls within the scope of s.2; the exercise of the option, however, does not and so does not need to be signed by both parties: see *Spiro v Glencrown Properties Ltd* (1991). The Act does not apply to lock-out agreements: see *Pitt v PHH Asset Management Ltd* (1993); see also p.27, above. In *McCausland v Duncan Lawrie Ltd* (1996), the Court of Appeal held that a variation of a contract for the sale or other disposition of land must satisfy the requirements of s.2, in the same way as the original contract. On the other hand, s.2 does not apply to an agreement by a party to a contract to waive a term inserted for his benefit, as such an agreement does not vary the contract: see *Glen Courtney v Corp Ltd* (2006).

Certain types of contract are excluded by s.2(5) (as amended) from the operation of s.2 and need not be in writing: (1) contracts to grant a lease for a term of less than three years; (2) contracts made in the course of a public auction; and (3) contracts regulated under the Financial Services and Markets Act 2000 (Other than regulated mortgage contracts).

Section 2(6) defines "interest in land" as meaning "any estate, interest or charge in or over land or in or over the proceeds of sale of land". This is a wide definition which embraces contracts to create an interest in land (e.g. a right of way), options and commercial contracts which affect land.

Non-compliance with the requirements of s.2 of the 1989 Act will mean that the contract will be completely invalid; in effect there will be no contract. This gives rise to the question whether there are any means of protection against someone who relies upon the defect in the formal requirements to claim to be released from the agreement. It may be possible to rely upon rectification, which is provided for expressly by s.2(4), so that the contract could be amended to include matters which had been agreed between the parties but omitted from the written contract. It may be possible also to rely upon the device of the collateral contract. So, in *Tootal Clothing Ltd v Guinea Properties Management Ltd* (1992), above, the agreement by the landlord to contribute to the cost of the shop-fitting to be carried out by the tenant was held to be "supplemental" so that it did not need to be in writing. The final possibility is the doctrine of proprietary estoppel, which applies where one party has been encouraged by another to believe that he will acquire an interest in property and he has acted to his detriment in reliance on that belief. This possibility has been considered in a number of recent cases. In *United Bank of Kuwait v Sahib* (1996), for example, Sahib purported to give security for a loan by depositing a land certificate relating to the property in question. The Court of Appeal said that the deposit of the land certificate was ineffective because the terms of s.2 had not been met. Peter Gibson L.J. was prepared to accept that an estoppel would operate between Sahib and the party with whom the land certificate had been deposited. The problem was that it did not bind an assignee from Sahib who knew nothing about the facts which brought the estoppel into operation. In *McAusland v Duncan Lawrie Ltd* (1996) the parties agreed to vary the date for completion of a contract for the sale of land, but the agreement did not satisfy s.2. After the agreement the parties went ahead on the basis of the new date, but neither challenged the validity of the variation. The issue arose as an interlocutory matter (a motion to strike out the statement of claim). The Court of Appeal said that the doctrine of estoppel might be available but left the question whether it could be established on the basis of the evidence until trial of the action. In *Cobbe v Yeoman's Row Management Ltd* (2006) the Court of Appeal held that s.2 did not preclude the application of proprietary estoppel.

The other possible exception to s.2 arises from the *Tootal Clothing* case, above. The Court of Appeal there said that the section only applies to executory contracts, not executed contracts. This interpretation of the section appears to be contrary to what was intended.

Finally, it may be that incomplete compliance with s.2 will make an agreement enforceable in equity. But this will only be possible if what has happened will persuade a court that the situation should be treated as giving rise to an implied, resulting or constructive trust. The creation and operation of such trusts is expressly preserved by s.2(5) of the Act. This is not the place to consider the complex rules relating to such trusts, which should be pursued in a book on trusts.

CONTRACTS WHICH MUST BE EVIDENCED IN WRITING

There is a distinction between a requirement that a contract must be in writing and a requirement that a contract must be evidenced in writing. The first requirement can only be met by the making of a complete contract in writing; the second requirement can be met by something much less formal, as will be discussed below.

Contracts of guarantee

The Statute of Frauds 1677 required six classes of contracts to be evidenced in writing. Two have survived; the rest were repealed by the Law Reform (Enforcement of Contracts) Act 1954. The two remaining classes are contracts of guarantee and contracts relating to land. This latter class is now further affected by the Law of Property (Miscellaneous Provisions) Act 1989 and is considered above, p.105.

A contract of guarantee is described by the Statute of Frauds as a "promise to answer for the debt, default or miscarriages of another person"; hence, it applies to the liabilities of that other person. Such a promise is a guarantee. A typical example is the guarantee of a bank overdraft, a loan from a bank to a customer. If A's father (B) undertakes to A's bank (C) that he, B, will hold himself responsible if A does not pay off his overdraft when requested, B is guaranteeing A's overdraft. There are three parties, A, B and C: the primary debtor is A; B will be liable only if A does not pay; C is the creditor. It should be noted that B makes his promise to C, the creditor. If B makes his promise to A, the debtor, that is not a guarantee within the Statute of Frauds. Also notice the form of B's promise; he promises that A will pay. If A does not pay, B becomes liable. If B promises C to pay off A's overdraft on request, that is not a guarantee but an indemnity, and is not within the Statute. That is because such a promise is not a promise to answer for the debt of another; it is a promise to pay a debt which the promisor is adopting as his own. A recent example is to be found in *Action-strength Ltd (t/a Vital Resources) v International Glass Engineering IN.GL.EN SpA* (2002). The case involved a building contract and three parties: the main contractor (B), a subcontractor (A, the claimant), and the employer (C). Because B continually paid late, A threatened to pull his labour off site. A alleged that C then promised that if A kept the workforce on site, he (C) would see that A was paid anything which was due, if necessary by deducting the money from money due from C to B. A sued C relying on the alleged agreement. The House of Lords agreed with C's argument that, if A's claim was true, the contract involved was a contract of guarantee which was required to be in writing and rejected the argument that estoppel could be invoked to avoid the operation of s.4.

A guarantee is caught by the Statute only if it stands alone. Thus, if a guarantee is given as part of a larger transaction, the Statute does not apply. An example is to be found in a *del credere* agency. If an agent is employed to sell goods on behalf of a principal and promises, for an extra commission, that if any particular buyer should fail to pay for goods, he (the agent) will make up the loss to the principal, he becomes a *del credere* agent. It is true that he enters into a contract of guarantee with his principal, but it has been held that, because that contract is only a part of the larger contract of agency, it is not within the Statute. See, for example, *Couturier v Hastie* (1856).

Another aspect of the same principle is that, where an owner of property gives a guarantee in order to protect that property, the Statute does not apply. Thus in *Fitzgerald v Dressler* (1859) C sold goods to A; A resold them to B at a higher price. C held a lien on the goods (that is, he was entitled to keep them until he was paid by A). B wanted possession of the goods, so he made an (oral) promise to C that, in return for C handing over the goods, he (B) would pay A's debt if A did not pay. It was held that the Statute did not apply, and that B was bound by his promise though it was not evidenced in writing.

The vast majority of guarantees are given in respect of contractual liabilities, but it has been held that the word "miscarriages" in the Statute is apt to include tortious liabilities. In *Kirkham v Marter* (1819) A rode the plaintiff's horse without permission and killed it. The plaintiff threatened to sue A in tort. B, A's father, promised the plaintiff to pay him the agreed value of the horse if the plaintiff would drop his action. It was held that B's promise, which was oral, was not enforceable because of the Statute.

It is not necessary that the agreement should itself be in writing; it is sufficient if there is a signed note or memorandum in writing, containing all the material terms. In the case of a note or memorandum of the agreement, the intention or capacity of the person signing the memorandum is irrelevant: see *Elpis Maritime Co Ltd v Marti Chartering Co Inc.; The Maria D* (1991, HL).

CHAPTER SEVEN

MISREPRESENTATION

IN THE negotiations leading up to a contract many statements may
be made. Some of those statements will be incorporated into the
final contract, thus becoming contractual terms. Other statements,
though not incorporated into the main contract, may be held to
constitute a collateral contract. Still other statements may not be
incorporated into any contract at all. If a statement becomes a term
in a main contract or in a collateral contract and then turns out to
be untrue, its untruth amounts to a breach of contract. The party
who suffers by the untruth has a right of action for breach of
contract. His exact rights will depend on how important the statement was (a "condition" or a "warranty" in traditional language)
or how serious are the effects of the breach.

Some statements do not become terms of any contract at all—
main or collateral. Such statements have sometimes been called
"mere representations", but are better called non-contractual

111

representations. If such a statement turns out to be untrue, its untruth is not a breach of contract, but the innocent party does have some remedies, as will be seen.

A non-contractual representation which is untrue is a misrepresentation. There are three kinds of misrepresentation: fraudulent, negligent and innocent misrepresentations. The remedies for misrepresentation vary, depending on the state of mind of the representor. That is not the case with contractual misstatements; there the remedy is not affected at all by the innocence or otherwise of the defendant. A misrepresentation is an untrue statement made by one party to the other, which induces him to enter into the contract.

This chapter will look first at the nature of the statement involved and then at the nature of the inducement. After that, fraudulent, negligent and innocent misrepresentations, and their effects, will be examined.

If one party has been induced to enter into a contract by some factual statement which turns out to be untrue, (in other words a misrepresentation) the injured party may have a remedy despite the fact that the inaccurate statement never actually became a term of the agreement. It is this situation which has given rise to the cluster of overlapping legal principles brought together under the heading of "Misrepresentation."

The justice of allowing someone who has been misled into entering a contract the opportunity of escaping from it is more obvious that the legal devices which try to achieve this aim. It is unfortunate that the Misrepresentation Act 1967, far from clarifying or codifying the various legal remedies at that date, appears to have added another layer of complexity on the uncertain foundation of the previous common law. Nevertheless, there are clearly two issue which require attention, namely: (1) What sort of statement or conduct will amount to a misrepresentation? and (2) What redress does a plaintiff have in these circumstances? The rather complex range of remedies available is a reflection of the fact that a misrepresentation can range from outrageously fraudulent to the entirely innocent and therefore more than one solution may be appropriate.

The meaning of misrepresentation

In the simplest type of case nobody could doubt the existence of a misrepresentation. Suppose that A wishes to sell his armchair to B.

A untruthfully tells B that it was a personal gift by the Queen to A, and B thereupon buys it. Assuming that this was not a term of the contract of sale (an assumption that is made of any mis-representation throughout this chapter) and that it was an induce-ment to B's purchase, then clearly this is a misrepresentation which gives rise to legal consequences. In some areas, however, the legal usage of the term "misrepresentation" is rather narrower than its use in every day speech, in others perhaps a little wider. A misrepresentation to be of legal effect must be of fact, not of opi-nion, intention or law; but in some cases silence itself will be regarded as a misrepresentation. These areas now require to be examined in more detail.

Statement of fact

A misstatement amounts to a misrepresentation only if it is a statement of fact.

Fact, not opinion

If the statement is a statement of opinion and not of fact, that is not a misrepresentation. In *Bisset v Wilkinson* (1927, PC), for example, Bisset was selling a holding in New Zealand to Wilkinson. The holding had not previously been used as a sheep farm, and Wilk-inson knew this. Bisset said that the land would support 2,000 sheep. This was held to be a statement of opinion and not of fact. But a statement of opinion may involve a statement of fact by implication. This point is well illustrated by *Smith v Land and House Property Corporation* (1885, CA). The vendor of a hotel described it as "let to Mr Frederick Fleck (a most desirable tenant)". The tenant was in fact in arrears with his rent. It was held that the statement was not a mere expression of opinion because the vendor was impliedly stating "that he knows facts which justify his opinion". See also *Esso Petroleum Ltd v Mardon* (1976, CA).

Fact, not intention

If the statement is a statement of intention and not of fact, that is not a misrepresentation. But a statement of intention may involve a statement of fact. In *Edgington v Fitzmaurice* (1885, CA) the directors of a company invited a loan from the public and stated that the money would be used to improve the company's buildings and to extend the business. The real intention of the directors was to use the money to pay off the company's existing debts. Their statement of intention was held to be also a statement of fact. Bowen L.J. said:

"There must be a misstatement of an existing fact: but the state of a man's mind is as much a fact as the state of his digestion".

The directors had made a misstatement of their present intention as to their future conduct. Similarly, in *Goff v Gauthier* (1991), the defendants exchanged contracts when they were told by the plaintiff's solicitor that the sale would be called off if they did not do so and a contract for sale would be sent to another purchaser. There was in fact no such purchaser. This was held to amount to a misstatement of fact as to the vendor's intention.

Fact, not law

If the statement is a statement of law and not of fact it is not a misrepresentation. That is an easy thing to say but extremely hard to apply. At first sight one would think that the statement "John and Mary are married" is a statement of fact. But it may be that John has been married before and that there is some doubt as to whether his previous marriage has been legally terminated. In view of that doubt, the statement that John and Mary are married begins to look like a statement of law. Probably, a bald assertion that they are married, without mention of the doubt, is a statement of fact.

Anomalously, a statement as to private rights, such as that there are no restrictive covenants affecting a piece of land, although sounding like a statement of law, is treated as equivalent to a statement of fact.

Silence as misrepresentation

The general rule is that mere silence is not misrepresentation. For example, in *Fletcher v Krell* (1873) a woman applied for a post of governess without revealing, at a time when such things were felt to be important, that she was a divorcee. It was held that that did not amount to misrepresentation.

114

There are situations, however, where a failure to speak does amount to misrepresentation.

Change of circumstances

In *With v O'Flanagan* (1936, CA) the defendant wanted to sell his medical practice. Negotiations for the sale to the plaintiff began in January. The defendant said that the practice was worth £2,000 a year, which at that time it was. The defendant then fell ill, and by May 1, when the contract of sale was signed, the practice had become virtually worthless. It was held that the defendant's silence in the face of this development was a misrepresentation.

A more recent application of the same basic principles is to be found in *Spice Girls Ltd v Aprilia World Service BV* (2002, CA). In this case the defendant had entered into negotiations with the Spice Girls whereby the former would sponsor a concert tour in return for the latter promoting the defendant's scooters. Before the contract was signed one of the group gave notice to the others of her intention to leave, but no mention of this was made to the defendant. The Court of appeal held that a false impression had therefore been given which the claimants should have corrected. This therefore amounted to a misrepresentation.

The truth but not the whole truth

In *Nottingham Patent Brick and Tile Co v Butler* (1886, CA) the purchaser of some land asked the vendor's solicitor whether the land was subject to restrictive covenants. The solicitor replied that he was not aware of any. He did not go on to explain why he was not aware of any; namely, that he had not bothered to read the relevant documents. It was held that the solicitor's statement, though literally true, amounted to a misrepresentation. In *Dimmock v Hallett* (1886–67) a vendor of property stated that the farms on his land were let, but failed to reveal that the tenants had given notice of their intention to leave. This failure to disclose so distorted the positive information given that the court similarly held there had been a misrepresentation.

Contracts of the utmost good faith (uberrimae fidei)

There are some contracts, called contracts uberrimae fidei, in which there is a duty to disclose material facts. The reason for the rule is that they are contracts in which one party is in a particularly strong position, compared with the other party, to know the facts.

An example of such a contract is an insurance contract. The duty of disclosure laid upon the insured is very heavy. He must disclose "all material facts"; that is, every circumstance "which would influence the judgment of a prudent insurer in fixing the premium, or determining whether he will take the risk" (Marine Insurance Act 1906, s.18(2)). In *Woolcott v Sun Alliance and London Insurance Ltd* (1978) a failure to disclose criminal convictions was held to be material to a contract of fire insurance, since they could affect the moral hazard which the insurers had to assess. A clear example of the rule, which incidentally makes the point that the loss does not have to be a result of the non-disclosure, is the case of *Seaman v Fonereau* (1743). The assured here concealed the fact that the ship involved was in a position of danger when last sighted. In fact, it escaped from that difficulty but was subsequently captured by the Spaniards. It was held that the failure to disclose was sufficient to render the contract voidable.

Some fiduciary relationships

A duty of disclosure may arise from the relationship of the parties. There are some relationships which require more than mere disclosure, where there is a fiduciary duty to make full disclosure of all material facts. This arises in the case of contracts between principal and agent, between partners and indeed prospective partners (see *Conlon v Sims* (2006, CA)), and between a solicitor and a client. A similar duty to disclose certain information exists, by virtue of legislation, between the promoters of a company and the public. The duty in this class of contract arises from the relationship of the parties, whereas in contracts uberrimae fidei the duty arises from the nature of the contract.

THE NATURE OF THE INDUCEMENT

A misstatement is a misrepresentation only if it induces the person to whom it is made to enter into a contract. It cannot be said to induce him if he does not rely on the misstatement. Thus, if a misstatement is made to a person, and that person then makes his own investigations to test the truth of the statement, he cannot claim relief on the ground of misrepresentation. Obviously he cannot if he discovers the truth, but the point is that he still cannot claim even if he does not discover the truth. In *Attwood v Small*

(1838, HL) a vendor offered to sell a mine and made exaggerated statements as to its capacity. The buyers appointed expert agents to investigate the mine. The agents reported (wrongly) that the statements were true. The contract of sale was then completed. It was then held that the buyers' subsequent action must fail because they had not relied on the vendor's statements, but on their own independent investigations.

On the other hand, if a person is given an opportunity to test the accuracy of a statement but does not take that opportunity, he is not shut out from relief. In *Redgrave v Hurd* (1881, CA) a man was induced to buy a solicitor's practice by a misstatement of its value. He was given an opportunity to examine the accounts. If he had examined the accounts he would have discovered the truth. He did not examine them. The misstatement was held to be an operative misrepresentation. Both in contract and in criminal deception it is no defence that the victim could have found out the truth had he gone to even a little more trouble.

Although the representation must be an inducement to enter the contract, it need not be the only one. In *Edgington v Fitzmaurice* (1885, CA, above) the plaintiff was induced to take debentures in a company, partly by a misstatement in the prospectus as to how the money was going to be used, and partly by his own incorrect belief that the debenture holders would have a charge on the company's property. He admitted that he would not have lent the money but for his own incorrect belief, but it was held that he was nevertheless entitled to claim the misstatement as an operative misrepresentation.

TYPES OF MISREPRESENTATION AND THEIR EFFECTS

There are three kinds of misrepresentation, depending upon whether the maker of the statement is fraudulent, negligent or innocent.

Fraudulent misrepresentation

In *Derry v Peek* (1889, HL) it was decided by the House of Lords that a false statement is fraudulent at common law only if it is made (1) knowingly, (2) without belief in its truth, or (3) recklessly, careless as to whether it be true or false. More simply, this amounts to saying that a fraudulent statement is one that the maker does not honestly believe to be true. It must, therefore, be more than just foolish, inaccurate or unreasonable.

A fraudulent misrepresentation makes a contract voidable. The party who has been misled may "avoid" the contract. He may also sue for damages. He is not suing for breach of contract; he is suing in tort. Fraud is a tort, in which context it is called "deceit". The case of *Doyle v Olby* (1969, CA) shows very clearly that for fraudulent misrepresentation the damages must be calculated on tort principles and not on contract principles. (See also e.g. *East v Maurer* (1991)).

In addition to suing for damages, the injured party may, as indicated, avoid the contract. He need not do so. He may content himself with an action for damages. But he has a choice, to affirm or avoid the contract. If he decides to avoid the contract he need not go to court; all he needs to do is to give notice, by words or conduct, that he refuses to be bound by it. The effect of that notice, if it is justifiable, is that the contract is cancelled. Of course, the most appropriate person to whom to give this notice is the other party to the contract. But it may happen that the other party, being a fraud, disappears. That happened in *Car and Universal Finance Co Ltd v Caldwell* (1965, CA). A man was induced by fraud to sell his car to a rogue called Norris. Norris's cheque "bounced" and Norris disappeared. The former owner at once notified the police and the Automobile Association and asked them to find the car. It was held that he had done all he could in the circumstances and that his actions had successfully avoided the contract. The importance is this: if a third party in good faith and for value obtains the property that has passed under a voidable contract before the contract is avoided he gets a good title; if he gets the property after it has been avoided he does not (except where s.9 of the Factors Act 1889 or s.25(1) of the Sale of Goods Act 1979 applies).

The party misled by a fraudulent misrepresentation may, instead of, or as well as, merely notifying his "avoidance", apply to the court for a formal order of "rescission". He will want to do this if the other party refuses to hand back what the misled party has paid or transferred under the contract. The word "rescission" (and its verb "to rescind") can mean the order of a court cancelling a contract, and it can also mean the party's act of cancellation without going to court or before going to court. Rescission is available, not only for fraud, but also for negligent and innocent misrepresentation, and will be discussed more fully after these types of misrepresentation have been considered. But there is one feature that applies only in fraud. In general, rescission, whether in court or out of court, involves each party in handing back what it got under the contract; a process which is called restitution. But where a person has been induced by fraud to enter into a contract, he need only hand back what he got under the contract if he himself sues for rescission. If he is taken to court by the other party he can plead fraud as a defence and still refuse to return what he got under the contract. For example, an insurer, where the contract of insurance has been induced by fraud, can deny liability under the policy and keep the premiums.

It is implicit in what has just been said that fraud is a defence to an action brought by the defrauder.

Negligent misrepresentation

At one time the law made no distinction between negligent misrepresentation and wholly innocent misrepresentation. If a misrepresentation was not fraudulent it was treated as innocent; damages were not obtainable for innocent misrepresentation. The only remedy was the equitable remedy of rescission. But two developments (one at common law and one by statute) have altered all this, and now there is a distinction between negligent and wholly innocent misrepresentation and there is a remedy in damages for negligent misrepresentation.

Negligence at common law

In *Hedley Byrne & Co Ltd v Heller & Partners Ltd* (1964) the House of Lords stated, obiter, that the duty of care, which is the foundation of the tort of negligence, can extend to careless statements where a "special relationship" exists between the parties. For some time it was unclear how, if at all, the principle of *Hedley Byrne* applied to a misstatement leading up to a contract. It is now clear from *Esso Petroleum Co Ltd v Mardon* (1976, CA) that a "special relationship" may exist between the parties in a pre-contractual negotiation if one party has some relevant special knowledge, expertise or skill, and that, if a contract is induced by a careless misstatement made by the expert, the resulting contractual relationship between them does not prevent the non-expert from suing the expert in the tort of negligence. (See also *Banque Financière de la Cité S.A. v Westgate Insurance Co Ltd* (1989, CA).) But there must be a "relationship of proximity" between the parties giving rise to a duty of care. Thus a person may make a statement which is put into general circulation and may reasonably be relied upon by strangers for a variety of different purposes; but he will not be liable to a person who relied upon the statement unless it is shown that he knew that the statement would be communicated to the person relying upon it (either as an individual or as a member of an identifiable class) specifically in connection with a particular transaction or a transaction of a particular kind and that that person would be very likely to rely on it for the purpose of deciding whether to enter into that transaction. This principle was set out by the House of Lords in *Caparo Industries Plc v Dickman* (1990). They held that an auditor of a public company's accounts owes no duty of care to a member of the public at large who relies on the accounts to buy shares in the company; nor does the auditor owe a duty of care to an individual shareholder in the company who wishes to buy more shares in the company: the auditor's statutory duty to prepare accounts is owed to the body of shareholders at large to enable them as a body to exercise informed control of the company. (See also *Al Saudi Banque v Clarke Pixley (a firm)* (1989), *Al-Nakib Investments (Jersey) Ltd v Longcroft* (1990) and *Morgan Crucible Plc v Hill Samuel Bank Ltd* (1991).)

Liability under the principle of *Hedley Byrne* flows from the law of tort, even though the context in which it arises may be contractual negotiations. Accordingly, as this is, like deceit, a separate tort, the restrictions that the statement must be fact (not law, opinion or future intention) do not apply. For this reason a tortious claim may sometimes give a plaintiff an advantage which a purely contractual misrepresentation does not.

Negligence under the Misrepresentation Act 1967

The Misrepresentation Act 1967 distinguishes between negligent and wholly innocent misrepresentation, and gives a remedy in damages for the former. Section 2(1) of the Act provides:

"Where a person has entered into a contract after a misrepresentation has been made to him by another party thereto and as a result thereof he has suffered loss, then, if the person making the misrepresentation would be liable to damages in respect thereof had the misrepresentation been made fraudulently, that person shall be so liable notwithstanding that the misrepresentation was not made fraudulently, unless he proves that he had reasonable ground to believe and did believe up to the time the contract was made that the facts represented were true."

There have not been very many reported cases on the Misrepresentation Act, but *Howard Marine and Dredging Co Ltd v A. Ogden and Sons (Excavations) Ltd* (1978, CA) is worthy of study. The facts (about the payload of some hired barges) are interesting, and the case shows differences of judicial opinion concerning "reasonable ground to believe" in s.2(1), and also concerning reasonableness in s.3 (exemption clauses). It is clear, however, that the burden on the person making the representation is heavy and not easy to discharge. As Lord Bridge stated: "the statute imposes an absolute obligation not to state facts which the representor cannot prove he had reasonable ground to believe".

It is convenient to refer to the misrepresentation dealt with in s.2(1) as "negligent misrepresentation". But it must be noticed that it bears very little relation to the tort of negligence. The word "negligence" is not used in the subsection, nor is the classic phrase "duty of care". Significantly, the burden of proof is on the defendant, whereas in tort it is on the plaintiff.

It is not clear whether the subsection can apply to non-disclosure, particularly of the kind that arose in *With v O'Flanagan* (1936, CA, above). The difficulty is this: can it be said of the plaintiff in a *With v O'Flanagan* situation that "a misrepresentation has been made to him"? The decision of the Court of Appeal in *Banque Financière de la Cité v Westgate Insurance Co Ltd* (1989) suggests that the answer to this question is "No".

In summary, the present state of the law is that a person induced to enter into a contract by negligent misrepresentation may sue for damages, either under the principle of *Hedley Byrne* or under s.2(1) of the Misrepresentation Act. The latter course is much the easier, because it places the burden of proof concerning carelessness on the defendant. It has also been held that damages under the Act are to be assessed on the more generous basis of the tort of deceit (*Royscot Trust Ltd v Rogerson* (1991). But where the misrepresentor is not a party to the contract, s.2(1) is not available and the misrepresentee can only sue under the common law principle of *Hedley Byrne*. He would have to show a "special relationship" between himself and the misrepresentor, and he would have to prove negligence.

In addition to, or instead of, suing for damages the misled party may rescind the contract either in court or out of court. This remedy will be discussed further after wholly innocent misrepresentation has been considered. Negligent misrepresentation can be used as a defence.

Wholly innocent misrepresentation

If the misrepresentor has been neither fraudulent nor negligent, his misrepresentation is wholly innocent. In such a case the misled party has no right to damages; the only remedy is rescission, in or out of court. Notice that I have said that the misled party has no right to damages. That is true, but the court has a discretion, where the misled party would be entitled to rescind the contract, to award damages instead of rescission. That is laid down by s.2(2) of the Misrepresentation Act 1967. Section 2(2) is absolutely different from s.2(1). Section 2(1) deals only with negligent misrepresentation, and gives the misled party a right to damages in addition to his right of rescission. Section 2(2) deals with both negligent and wholly innocent misrepresentation and it gives the court a discretion to award damages instead of rescission. But notice the overlap: the court has a discretion, even where there is negligent misrepresentation, to say to the misled party: "No, we won't give you rescission, but we will give you damages." So this situation may arise: a misled party sues in respect of negligent misrepresentation for damages and rescission. The court may award him damages under s.2(1), and then, under s.2(2), refuse rescission, awarding damages instead. Section 2(3) deals with this situation by providing that in such a case the damages under s.2(2) should be taken into account in assessing the damages under s.2(1).

Thus the position in wholly innocent misrepresentation is that the misled party starts off with a right to rescission and no right to damages. The court, however, may decide to award him damages instead of rescission. The court may do this "if of opinion that it would be equitable to do so, having regard to the nature of the misrepresentation and the loss that would be caused by it if the contract were upheld, as well as to the loss that rescission would cause to the other party" (s.2(2)). A judge will probably be inclined to award damages and not rescission where the point of fact which has been misrepresented is of only slight importance. An example of this is *Sindall v Cambridgeshire CC* (1994). The court expressed the view that damages, not rescission, would have been appropriate where the loss flowing from the misrepresentation was £18,000 in the context of a loss to the defendant of some £6 million if the contract had been rescinded.

Wholly innocent misrepresentation can be used as a defence to an action by the other party.

All three kinds of misrepresentation give the misled party a right to rescind. But rescission does not happen automatically when a misrepresentation is made. Misrepresentation makes a contract voidable. This means that the innocent party must take steps to rescind it.

Restitution and indemnity

Where a court orders rescission it will also order mutual restitution—"a giving back and taking back on both sides". The principle is to put the parties back into their former positions as though the contract had never been made. In some cases that can only be done by ordering a money payment. But such a money payment is not damages. The principle is quite different: with damages, the aim of the court is to put the parties into the positions they would have been in had the contract been performed; with restitution, the aim is to put the parties into the positions they would have been in had the contract never been made. A money payment in connection with rescission is called, to distinguish it from damages, an indemnity.

In *Whittington v Seale-Hayne* (1900) the plaintiffs, who were poultry breeders, were induced to take a lease of certain premises by the defendant's innocent misrepresentation that the premises were in a thoroughly sanitary condition. The premises turned out to be unsanitary: the water supply was poisoned. The manager of the poultry farm became seriously ill and most of the poultry died. To add to the plaintiffs' troubles, the local council declared the premises unfit for habitation and required the drains to be put in order, which expense, by a term of the lease, fell upon the plaintiffs. The defendant submitted to rescission, and agreed to pay £20 in respect of rent, rates and repairs. The plaintiffs claimed for loss of profits and also loss of stock, removal expenses and medical expenses. The court rejected not only the claim for loss of profits (which would clearly have amounted to damages), but these other expenses claims as well. It was said that indemnity can only be claimed in respect of obligations which inevitably arise under the contract. The plaintiffs had to pay rent and rates and had to repair the drains, but they did not have to stock up the farm and carry on business. If this case is rightly decided, an indemnity does not even put the plaintiff fully into his pre-contract position. Those expenses which he did not inevitably incur have, so to speak, gone down the drain. If the facts of this case were to recur today, a claim could perhaps be made on the basis of either a collateral warranty or negligent misrepresentation. The principle of an indemnity might still, nevertheless, be relevant where a representor has discharged the burden of proof under s.2(1) of the Misrepresentation Act 1967 and a court does not order damages in lieu of rescission under s.2(2).

Loss of the right to rescind

Although a party misled by misrepresentation starts off with a right of rescission, that right may be lost. There are now three circumstances which may lead to the loss of the right of rescission. There used to be five, but the Misrepresentation Act 1967 removed two. Thus it used to be the law, possibly, but not certainly, that where a statement began life as a misrepresentation (thus giving a right of rescission) and then became embodied in a contract as a warranty (as distinct from a condition), the right of rescission was lost. That rule was abolished by s.1(a) of the Act. Again it used to be the law, at any rate in some kinds of contract, that where a contract had been performed (for example, where a contract for sale of land had been executed), the pre-existing right of rescission was lost (except in fraud). That rule was abolished by s.1(b) of the Act.

Affirmation of the contract

If the party who has been misled by a misrepresentation affirms the contract, he cannot afterwards claim rescission. Affirmation occurs when the party misled either declares his intention to proceed with the contract or does some act from which such an intention may be inferred. Lapse of time is not in itself affirmation, but it is some evidence of affirmation. In *Leaf v International Galleries* (1950, CA) the plaintiff was induced to buy a picture by a non-fraudulent representation that it was a Constable. Five years later when he wished to sell it he discovered that it was painted by someone else. There was no suggestion of fraud and the plaintiff applied for rescission of the contract as soon as he discovered the truth. Nevertheless, the Court of Appeal refused to grant the remedy and stated that:

> "it behooves the purchaser either to verify or, as the case may be, to disprove the representation within a reasonable time, or else stand or fall by it."

No doubt the position would have been quite different if the misrepresentation had been fraudulent. In that case it seems likely that time would only have started to run once the fraud had been discovered.

Restitution impossible

The misled party will lose the right of rescission if something happens, in which the misled party has participated, which makes it impossible to restore the parties to their former position. For example, the purchaser of a mine cannot get rescission after he has worked out the mine. But rescission is still available if substantial restoration is possible, even though precise restoration is not. Thus deterioration in the condition or value of property is not a bar to rescission. The court can accompany its order for rescission with financial adjustments between the parties.

Third-party rights

If a third party acquires a right under the contract in good faith and for value the misled party loses the right of rescission. So, for example, A sells goods to B on credit, being induced to do so by B's misrepresentation as to his creditworthiness. B sells the goods to C, who takes them and pays for them and has no knowledge of B's misrepresentation. A, having never been paid by B, now seeks rescission of the contract of sale between himself and B, coupled with restoration of the goods. A will fail in his action. This links up with the point made on p.118, that if a third party in good faith and for value obtains property that had previously passed from A to B under a voidable contract before that contract is avoided, he obtains a good title.

MISREPRESENTATION AND BREACH

An untrue statement may begin life as a non-contractual representation and then later be incorporated into a contract as a term. This may give the innocent party two causes of action; one for misrepresentation and one for breach of contract.

Sometimes, however, an action for misrepresentation might be more beneficial than a claim for breach of contract. In *Naughton v O'Callaghan* (1990) the plaintiffs bought a horse whose pedigree had been hopelessly misdescribed and which subsequently turned out to be a poor racer worth much less than the 26,000 guineas paid for it. The problem was that, even if accurately described, it might still have been worth a similar amount at the time of sale. There was therefore an argument that the plaintiffs had suffered no loss of bargain as a result of the breach. This was avoided by bringing the claim under the heading of misrepresentation. The plaintiffs had bought and kept the horse because of the misrepresentation concerning its pedigree. Had they known the truth at the time of sale they could have sold the horse immediately with almost no loss. Because they had kept it instead, by which time it had become much less valuable, they had suffered the loss of the difference between its value at the time of sale and at the date of judgment. This was recoverable as damages which flowed directly from the misrepresentation.

Exempting liability

The remedies available to a plaintiff would clearly be of no use if it was possible to insert into a contract a term excluding all liability for misrepresentation. Section 3 of the 1967 Act, as amended, states that if a contract contains a term which would exclude or restrict any liability or remedy for misrepresentation:

> "That term shall be of no effect except in so far as it satisfies the requirement of reasonableness as stated in s.11(1) of the Unfair Contract Terms Act 1977; and it is for those claiming that the term satisfied that requirement to show that it does".

It is noteworthy that the onus rests firmly on the person relying upon it to show that it was reasonable and that, unlike the 1977 Act which excludes certain types of contract (e.g. insurance) from its ambit, s.3 of the 1967 Act has general application.

An example of the application of s.3 occurred in *Walker v Boyle* (1982). The vendor of a house made an innocent but incorrect statement that there were no disputes regarding the boundaries of the property. This was an incorrect misrepresentation which on the face of it gave a right to rescission of the contract. The contract had, however, been concluded using the National Conditions of Sale which contained a cl.17(1) stating, "no error, mis-statement or omission in any preliminary answer concerning the property ... shall annul the sale." The vendor therefore relied on this term as excluding his liability. The court granted rescission. One of the grounds for the judgment was that cl.17(1) was an unreasonable exclusion clause. Not only does the case illustrate the operation of s.3 of the 1967 Act but it is also of interest in that the occurrence of the offending term in a common-form clause in a long used standard form contract did not prevent its demise in the circumstances of the case. As Dillion J. commented:

"I do not think it can be said that its precarious survival until 1977 entitles it to the automatic accolade of fairness and reasonableness."

The extent to which including an appropriately drafted "entire contract agreement" can exclude liability for misrepresentation, or is caught by s.3, is not entirely clear (see above p.92) Where the parties are commercial parties of relatively equal bargaining power there may not be much cause for concern since the term may well be found to be reasonable anyway. Where this is not so, it would seem somewhat unsatisfactory if by such a simple drafting mechanism a defendant could evade the protection offered by s.3 of the 1967 Act.

CHAPTER EIGHT

DURESS AND UNDUE INFLUENCE

WHERE A person is driven into a contract by duress or by undue
influence the contract is voidable and may be set aside by a court.

DURESS

Duress traditionally means actual violence or threats of violence to
the person; it is a common law doctrine. A threat to the goods of a
person is not duress. There are very few instances of duress in the
law reports in modern times. However, in 1976 a case of duress
came on appeal to the Privy Council from Australia: *Barton v
Armstrong* (1976, PC). Armstrong held the largest shareholding in a
company called Landmark and Barton held the next largest. Hos-
tility developed between the two, and in the end Barton executed a
deed on behalf of the company buying out Armstrong on terms
very favourable to Armstrong and disastrous to the company and
to Barton. During the period leading up to the execution of the
deed Armstrong made many threats to Barton. The Privy Council,
by a majority, held that the deeds were executed by Barton under
duress and should be declared void so far as they concerned him.
The majority held that duress was like fraud in that the threats need
not be the only factor inducing the contract so long as it was a
factor.

In *Pao On v Lau Yiu Long* (1980, PC) the Privy Council accepted in principle that the traditional doctrine of duress (personal violence) could, given strong facts, be extended to provide a remedy in the event of "economic duress" (commercial pressure). In that case, the plaintiffs agreed to sell a building which was under construction to the defendants; in exchange they were to receive 60 per cent of the shares in the defendants' company for a year at a price of $1 per share. They would then sell them back to the defendants at $2.50 per share. There was a possibility of the share price going up, which would result in a windfall profit to the defendants, so the plaintiffs threatened to breach the contract unless the arrangements were cancelled and replaced by an indemnity contract. This would provide protection for the plaintiffs but without the chance of a windfall profit. The defendants agreed to these demands. The plaintiffs later sued on the indemnity contract. Lord Scarman accepted that, in principle, economic duress may be a factor making contracts voidable. He said that the essence of the rule is that "there must be a coercion of will such that there was not true consent ... it must be shown that the contract entered into was not a voluntary act". But he said that it is important to distinguish between mere commercial pressure, which is an everyday fact of life in the business world, and duress. It is a question of fact in each case. It should be noted that in that case the Privy Council accepted that duress makes a contract voidable, rather than void from the beginning.

In *Universe Tankships Inc. of Monrovia v International Transport Workers Federation; The Universe Sentinel* (1983, HL), which involved pressure applied by a trade union by "blacking" the plaintiff's ship in port and refusing to release it until they made certain payments, both Lord Diplock and Lord Scarman agreed that to establish duress there must first be established coercion or compulsion of the will and, secondly, that that coercion or compulsion must be brought about by pressure which the law regards as illegitimate.

The principle has been applied subsequently to an agreement between two commercial organisations: see *Atlas Express Ltd v Kafco (Importers and Distributors) Ltd* (1989). In *CTN Cash and Carry Ltd v Gallaher Ltd* (1994), however, the Court of Appeal emphasised that it would be difficult, though not impossible, to maintain such a claim in the context of arm's-length commercial dealings between two trading companies, especially where the party making the threat bona fide believes that its demand is valid. For recent discussions of duress, reference may be made to *Nurdin & Peacock Plc v DB Ramsden & Co Ltd* (1999) and *Alf Vaughan & Co Ltd (in administrative receivership) v Royscot Trust Plc* (1999). The last case contains a useful survey of the law of duress. See also *Drew v Daniel* (2005) and *Halpern v Halpern* (2007).

UNDUE INFLUENCE

Courts of equity regarded the common law doctrine of duress as narrow, and, under the general doctrine of equitable fraud, they developed a much wider jurisdiction over contracts made under pressure. There thus grew up the doctrine of undue influence, designed to give relief where, in circumstances not amounting to duress, a person enters into a disadvantageous transaction either of gift or of contract.

The cases can be divided into two categories: actual or express undue influence (Class 1) and presumed undue influence (Class 2). Class 2 comes into play where the person claiming undue influence establishes the existence of a relationship of trust and confidence between himself and the wrongdoer "of such a nature that it is fair to presume that the wrongdoer abused the relationship in procuring [him] to enter the impugned transaction". Class 2 is subdivided further. Class 2A consists of certain well-known relationships which the law will treat as relationships of trust and confidence; class 2B consists of other cases where the complainant establishes on the evidence that he was accustomed to place trust and confidence in the wrongdoer. This classification was approved by Lord Browne-Wilkinson in *Barclays Bank Plc v O'Brien* (1993) but was criticised by the House of Lords in *Royal Bank of Scotland Plc v Etridge* (No.2) (2001). In husband and wife cases, which have given rise to much of the recent case law, the courts may treat the case as falling within Class 1 or Class 2B, but not Class 2A.

Actual undue influence

In Class 1 cases, sometimes called "domination" cases, the person who complains that he was pressed into the contract must prove that actual pressure was applied. Thus a promise to pay money, for example, will be set aside if the promisor proves that he was pressed into the promise by a threat that if he did not promise he would be prosecuted, or his spouse or close relative would be prosecuted, for some criminal offence. The burden of proving the pressure lies upon the complainant. In *Williams v Bayley* (1866, HL), for example, a young man gave to his bank several promissory notes upon which he had forged the endorsements of his father, a colliery owner. There were meetings between son, father, bankers and solicitors. The bankers made it clear that, unless some arrangements were come to, the son would be prosecuted. Eventually the father agreed to mortgage his colliery to the bank, in return for the bank handing back the promissory notes. This agreement was set aside by the court on the ground that undue pressure had been exerted.

More recent examples of this class of undue influence are to be found in *Bank of Credit and Commerce International S.A. v Aboody* (1992) and *CIBC Mortgages Plc v Pitt* (1993, HL). In the first case, the judge found that the husband had exerted undue influence on the wife. There was evidence that the husband was a bully and that the wife was under pressure and had signed the relevant documents because she wanted peace. In the second, the wife was induced to agree to a second mortgage on the family home as security for a loan to finance share purchases. She did not want to go ahead but gave in after being put under pressure by her husband. See also *Drew v Daniel* (2005).

In such cases of actual undue influence, it is not necessary for the victim of the undue influence to prove in addition that he suffered manifest disadvantage, as is required in cases of presumed undue influence: see *National Westminster Bank Plc v Morgan* (1985, HL) and *CIBC Mortgages Plc v Pitt* (1993, HL). In the former, Lord Browne-Wilkinson said that actual undue influence is a "species of fraud" and "like any other victim of fraud, a person who has been induced by undue influence to carry out a transaction which he did not freely and knowingly enter into is entitled to have that transaction set aside as of right".

Presumed undue influence

Class 2 comes into play where the person claiming undue influence establishes the existence of a relationship of trust and confidence between himself and the wrongdoer "of such a nature that it is fair to presume that the wrongdoer abused the relationship in procuring [him] to enter the impugned transaction": see Lord Browne-Wilkinson in *Barclays Bank Plc v O'Brien* (1993, HL). In *Royal*

Bank of Scotland Plc v Etridge (No.2) (2001), the House of Lords reviewed this type of undue influence at considerable length. Lord Nicholls of Birkenhead said:

"The burden of proving an allegation of undue influence rests upon the person who claims to have been wronged ... . The evidence required to discharge the burden of proof depends upon the nature of the alleged undue influence, the personality of the parties, their relationship, the extent to which the transaction cannot readily be accounted for by the ordinary motives of ordinary persons in that relationship, and all the circumstances of the case ... . Proof that the complainant placed trust and confidence in the other party in relation to the management of the complainant's financial affairs, coupled with a transaction which calls for an explanation, will normally be sufficient ... to discharge the burden of proof. On proof of these two matters the stage is set for the court to infer that, in the absence of a satisfactory explanation, the transaction can only have been procured by undue influenced. In other words, proof of these two facts is prima facie evidence that the defendant abused the influence he acquired in the parties' relationship ... . So the evidential burden shifts to him. It is for him to produce evidence to counter the inference which otherwise should be drawn."

In these cases, therefore, the presumption arises from the relationship. The relationships involved are all relationships in which one person is in a position of some dominance over the other. The duty of the dominant person is to be faithful to the confidence that is reposed in him by the other. If it comes to litigation, it is his duty to prove that he has not taken unfair advantage of the other person. This duty is imposed by way of presumption. Where a transaction is challenged in the courts, it is for the dominant person, if he wishes to uphold the transaction, to prove that no undue influence was in fact used. If he cannot prove this absence of undue influence he fails, and the transaction will be set aside.

In cases in Class 2, there is the further requirement that the transaction was to the obvious and unfair disadvantage of the person subjected to the dominating influence: see *National Westminster Bank Plc v Morgan* (1985, HL). A "manifest disadvantage", as it has often been called, must be a disadvantage which is obvious as such to any independent and reasonable person who considered the transaction at the time with knowledge of all the relevant facts. It must amount to an "advantage taken of the person subjected to the influence which, failing proof to the contrary, [is] explicable only on the basis that undue influence ha[s] been exercised to procure it": see *National Westminster Bank Plc v Morgan*. In *CIBC Mortgages Ltd v Pitt* (1993, HL) Lord Browne-Wilkinson suggested that this may need to be reconsidered in the future. In *Royal Bank of Scotland Plc v Etridge (No.2)* (2001), Lord Nicholls of Birkenhead observed that the label "manifest disadvantage" had been causing difficulty and said that it should be discarded. He added that Lord Scarman's test (quoted above) should be adhered to instead. He also rejected the argument that this second requirement should be removed.

Class 2A: relationships giving rise to the presumption of undue influence

Certain relationships as a matter of law raise the presumption that undue influence has been exercised, for example doctor and patient, solicitor and client, parent and child, and trustee and beneficiary. The relationship between husband and wife does not fall into this category.

Class 2B: where a relationship of trust and confidence is proved to exist

If the relationship does not fall within Class 2A, the alleged victim of the undue influence may still prove the existence of a relationship under which he generally reposed trust and confidence in the wrongdoer; in that case, the existence of such a relationship raises the presumption of undue influence: see *Barclays Bank Plc v O'Brien* (1993, HL). The presumption does not apply as a matter of law between husband and wife, but there may be circumstances in which it does arise, e.g. where a wife assumes dominance over an ill husband or the evidence shows that the wife reposed trust and confidence in her husband in relation to their financial affairs. As Lord Browne-Wilkinson said in *Barclays Bank Plc v O'Brien*:

"In those cases ... where the wife relies in all financial matters on her husband and simply does what he suggests, a presumption of undue influence ... can be established solely from the proof of such trusts and confidence without proof of actual, undue influence".

In that case Lord Browne-Wilkinson also accepted that it is possible for a relationship of trust and confidence to arise where there is an emotional relationship between cohabitants, whether married or not. In *Massey v Midland Bank Ltd* (1995) Steyn L.J. took this a stage further and extended the category to include a couple who had a long-term emotional and sexual relationship and who had children but did not cohabit. In *Banco Exterior Internacional S.A. v Thomas* (1997, CA), the presumption was held to apply between close friends where one was in straitened circumstances and the other agreed to pay her a regular income if she would agree to guarantee his borrowing. A similar conclusion was reached in *Crédit Lyonnais Bank Nederland N.V. v Burch* (1997, CA), where a junior employee was prevailed upon by her employer to mortgage her flat as security for an increase in the company's overdraft. See also *Turkey v Awadh* (2005).

The list of relationships is not closed. In *Re Craig* (1971) Mr Craig was 84 when his wife died. He was then worth about £40,000. He employed a Mrs Middleton as secretary-companion until he died. During the six years of her employment he made gifts to Mrs Middleton amounting to about £30,000. The court set aside the gifts, holding that the circumstances raised a presumption of undue influence which Mrs Middleton had not succeeded in rebutting. See also *Goldsworthy v Brickell* (1987, CA), where the presumption was applied to a relationship of trust and confidence between an elderly farmer and his neighbour.

An interesting (and, in a sense, opposite) case is *Re Brocklehurst* (1978, CA). Sir Philip Lee Brocklehurst was the owner of an estate near Macclesfield. In 1972 his second wife left him and his old batman died. He was alone and lonely and in his eighties. He became friendly with a local garage proprietor called John Roberts. Sir Philip made his last will in 1974 and died eight months later. His executors then discovered that Sir Philip had, some six months before he died, severed the shooting rights from the estate by granting a 99-year lease of the shooting rights to Mr Roberts. This had the effect of reducing the value of the estate by some £90,000. A majority of the Court of Appeal (Lord Denning dissenting) held that there was no presumption of undue influence, mainly because, far from Mr Roberts being in a position of dominance, Sir Philip had tended to dominate Mr Roberts. The majority further held that, even if there was a presumption, Mr Roberts had rebutted it by proving that the gift of the shooting rights had been the spontaneous and independent act of Sir Philip.

Rebutting the presumption

The presumption of undue influence can be rebutted if the dominant person can show that the complainant was able to have "the free exercise of independent will". The usual way of doing this is to show that the complainant had independent advice. But the mere fact of independent advice will not necessarily save the transaction and, conversely, the mere absence of independent advice is not necessarily fatal to the transaction. In *Royal Bank of Scotland Plc v Etridge (No.2)* (2001, HL) Lord Nicholls Birkenhead said:

> "Proof that the complainant received advice from a third party before entering into the impugned transaction is one of the matters a court takes into account when weighing all the evidence .... . Proof of outside advice does not, of itself, necessarily show that the subsequent completion of the transaction was free from the exercise of undue influence. Whether it will be proper to infer that outside advice had an emancipating effect, so that the transaction was not brought about by the exercise of undue influence, is a question of fact to be decided having regard to all the evidence of the case."

Effect of undue influence on third parties

As between the original parties to the transaction, the effect of undue influence is to make the contract voidable not void, though in certain circumstances it may be lost: see below. Where the transaction is set aside by the court, it will be set aside completely: see *TSB v Camfield* (1995). Where it is not possible to restore the parties to their original positions, for example because the property has passed to a third party, the court may impose a "common-sense and ... fair remedy ... to achieve practical justice between the parties": see May J. in *Mahoney v Purnell* (1996).

The right to rescission may be lost where a third party has acquired rights over the property. If the third party has knowledge of the undue influence, it will take subject to the rights of the victim of the undue influence. This matter has become of increasing importance in recent years, as is shown by the number of cases involving transactions between husband and wife or between other cohabitants allegedly involving undue influence where the victim has tried to avoid a third party, usually a bank, acquiring an interest as a result of the allegedly tainted transaction. As Lord Browne-Wilkinson made clear in *Barclays Bank Plc v O'Brien* (1993, HL), the law should provide a solution which will enable a property to be available to creditors as security whilst at the same time providing proper protection to a party who risks dispossession.

In cases of this kind, the transaction is liable to be set aside as against the bank if the bank had actual, constructive or imputed notice that it was procured by improper means. The crucial question is likely to be whether the bank has constructive notice of the victim's rights; in other words, whether there were circumstances which put the bank on inquiry as to the existence of the victim's rights. In *Barclay's Bank Plc v O'Brien*, above, Lord Browne-Wilkinson said that a bank or other creditor would be put on inquiry when a wife offered to stand surety for her husband's debts by the combination of two factors: (a) that the transaction was on its face not to the financial advantage of the wife; and (b) there was a substantial risk in such transactions that, in procuring the wife to act as surety, the husband had committed "a legal or equitable wrong that entitles the wife to set aside the transaction." In the later case of *Royal Bank of Scotland Plc v Etridge* (No.2) (2001), Lord Nicholls of Birkenhead said that that meant, quite simply, "that a bank is put on inquiry whenever a wife offers to stand surety for her husband's debts." On this point, he rejected the views of the Court of Appeal, which had made the threshold higher. He pointed out that it is not essential that the bank is aware that the parties are cohabiting or that the particular surety places implicit trust and confidence in the principal debtor in relation to her financial affairs.

Once the bank or other creditor is put on inquiry, the next question concerns the steps it should take. In *Etridge (No.2)*, the House of Lords dealt with this issue in detail. They said that the bank need do no more than take reasonable steps to satisfy itself that the practical implications of the proposed transaction have been brought home to the wife, in a meaningful way, so that she enters into the transaction with her eyes open so far as its basic elements are concerned. Ordinarily, it will be reasonable for the bank to rely upon confirmation from a solicitor, acting for the wife, that he has advised her appropriately. Any deficiencies in the advice are a matter between the wife and the solicitor, and the bank is entitled to proceed in the belief that a solicitor advising the wife has done so properly. In their judgments, the members of the House of

Lords set out in detail the responsibilities of solicitors giving advice in such circumstances, but it is unnecessary to go into that aspect of the judgments here. They concluded by saying that if the bank or other creditor does not take reasonable steps to bring home to the individual guarantor the risks that he is running by standing as a surety, it will be deemed to have notice of any claim the guarantor may have that the transaction was procured by undue influence on the part of the debtor. See also *Yorkshire Bank Plc v Tinsley* (2004).

How the right to relief may be lost

A contract affected by undue influence is voidable. This means that the person alleging undue influence must bring an action for rescission to avoid it. The action will fail in the following circumstances: (1) if it can be shown that the claimant affirmed the transaction after the influence, or that the relationship giving rise to the presumption of influence had ceased; (2) if there has been "laches"; and (3) if third parties have acquired rights from the transaction, provided that they have acted in good faith, for value and without knowledge of the undue influence. For this third category of case, see the discussion above.

Laches is an equitable idea, meaning a person's prolonged neglect to assert his rights. An example is *Allcard v Skinner* (1887), in which undue influence was found to have been exerted, but the plaintiff was unable to recover the balance of the money paid as a result of the influence because she waited for six years before claiming; during that time the influence would have ceased to affect her and she could have taken independent advice.

Inequality of bargaining power?

In *Lloyds Bank Ltd v Bundy* (1975, CA), an elderly, ill farmer guaranteed the bank account of his son's ailing company and charged his farm (his only asset) to the bank. The Court of Appeal unanimously set aside the guarantee and the charge and dismissed the bank's action for possession of the farm. Lord Denning said that all the instances where the courts will intervene to set aside a transaction are based on a single principle, that of relief against inequality of bargaining power. The other two members of the court, however, reached their decision on the basis of undue influence by the bank.

In *National Westminster Bank Plc v Morgan* (1985, HL) the House of Lords held that Lord Denning's view was not correct and that the doctrine of undue influence is not based on the principle of relief against inequality of bargaining power but the prevention of the victimisation of one party by another. The House of Lords stressed that in exercising its equitable jurisdiction to grant relief against undue influence, a court must look at the facts of each case. The doctrine of undue influence therefore remains.

MISTAKE

AT FIRST sight it might seem obvious that if an agreement has been concluded on the basis of a mistake by one or both of the parties then the law will release them from their obligations. Such an approach, however, could never represent the law. Some mistakes are trivial, others fundamentally alter the basis of the contract. It would not be feasible or sensible to dissolve whole contracts merely because one party was labouring under a slight misapprehension as to some peripheral matter. Justice must not only embrace the interests of the immediate parties but also the requirements of certainty. If other parties have relied upon the existence of a contract, which on the face of it is perfectly valid, it may cause inconvenience and hardship to declare it invalid. For all these considerations the operation of the legal doctrine of "mistake" is a much more circumscribed notion than the use of the word in common speech would suggest. The result is that when things go wrong with a contract the doctrine of mistake is not likely to be the first thing a lawyer turns to. In order for it to be relevant, there must in general be something very seriously defective about the agreement or the subject-matter of the contract.

"Mistake" covers a wide range of situations and some have

doubted whether there really is a single doctrine of mistake at all. Many of the cases could be explained on the basis of a breakdown in the conjunction of offer and acceptance, albeit a breakdown of a serious kind. Some of the cases, however, would not readily lend themselves to this approach. If, for example, the parties reach perfect agreement on an entity which has ceased to exist then it is difficult to see how a failure of offer and acceptance is to blame for the resulting nullity.

There seem to be as many ways of describing types of mistake as there are judges or authors. Broadly speaking two threads can be followed through the web of terminology. One describes the situation where the parties agree between themselves but for some reason the contract is incapable of performance as they envisage it (i.e. Possibility Mistake). In a sense the contract is frustrated before it has even got off the ground. The second situation that may arise is where there is in fact no real consensus *ad idem* between the parties (i.e. Agreement Mistake).

Here, mistake is considered under three heads: "Agreement mistake", "Possibility mistake" and "Mistakes in documents".

AGREEMENT MISTAKE

If two (or more) persons agree in the same terms on the same subject-matter they are bound. A person will also generally be bound if his conduct would lead a reasonable person to suppose that he had agreed, even though he has not in his own mind agreed; but a court will depart from this usual objective view if it is satisfied that in reality there is no agreement. Agreement mistake, therefore, is a mistake as to the offer or the acceptance; mistake, that is, as to the agreement. This kind of mistake is sometimes called "mistake negativing consent", because it tends to arise either where it appears that the parties were at cross-purposes or where one party entered the agreement after being deceived by the other.

Agreement mistake may arise in one of three ways. There may, first, be mistake as to the person. A may intend to contract with B, only to find that the other party to the apparent agreement is C. Secondly, there may be mistake as to the subject-matter. A may intend to contract about a thing (X), whereas B intends to contract about another thing (Y). Thirdly, there may be mistake about terms. A may intend to buy a horse for £500, whereas B intends to sell it for £800. These three types of mistakes will now be examined in turn. It should be noted that where the court decides to uphold the mistake, the effect is that there is no contract; in other words, the contract will be void.

Mistake as to the person

This type of case usually involves fraudulent activity by a rogue who acquires property fraudulently and resells it to an innocent third party. For example, in *Cundy v Lindsay* (1878, HL) the plaintiffs, Messrs Lindsay, linen manufacturers, received an order for a large quantity of handkerchiefs from a rogue called Blenkarn, who gave his address as "37 Wood Street, Cheapside, London; entrance, second door in Little Love Lane". He signed his name to look like "Blenkiron & Co", a respectable firm, known by repu-tation to the plaintiffs and carrying on business at 123 Wood Street. The plaintiffs sent the goods on credit addressed to "Blenkiron & Co, 37 Wood Street". In that way Blenkarn got possession of the handkerchiefs. He did not pay for them and he sold 250 dozen of them to the defendants, Messrs Cundy. The plaintiffs sued the defendants in conversion. It was held by the House of Lords that there was no contract between the plaintiffs and Blenkarn, as the plaintiffs had no intention of dealing with him but with someone else. As there was no contract with Blenkarn he obtained no title to the goods and so could pass none to the defendants, who were liable in conversion. It makes no difference whether one thinks of the plaintiffs as offerors or as offerees. Either their offer was accepted by someone for whom it was not intended, or their acceptance was made to someone for whom it was not intended.

In *King's Norton Metal Co v Edridge, Merrett & Co Ltd* (1897, CA) the plaintiffs received by letter an order for wire from "Hallam & Co". On the notepaper was a picture of a large factory with numerous chimneys, and in one corner was a printed statement that "Hallam & Co" had depots and agencies at Belfast, Lille and Ghent. In fact "Hallam & Co" was simply an alias of a penniless rogue called Wallis. The plaintiffs, relying on the description of "Hallam & Co." contained in the letter, sent the goods on credit. Wallis thus got possession of them. He did not pay for them, and he sold them to the defendants. The plaintiffs sued for conversion. It was held by the Court of Appeal that the plaintiffs "had intended to contract with the writer of the letter". Thus there was a contract between the plaintiffs and Wallis, and thus Wallis was able to pass a good title to the defendants, who were not liable in conversion.

The distinction between *Cundy v Lindsay* and the *King's Norton* case is that in *Cundy v Lindsay* the plaintiffs made a mistake as to the identity of the person they were dealing with; they thought they were dealing with a different entity. In the *King's Norton* case the plaintiffs were not mistaken as to the identity of the person they were dealing with, only as to his attributes, particularly his creditworthiness. They did not think they were dealing with a different entity; there was no other entity.

There is a difference in effect. If there is no contract, as in *Cundy v Lindsay*, the innocent third party obtains no title and suffers the loss. If there is a contract, as in the *King's Norton* case, it is voidable for fraud, but provided the innocent third-party buyer obtains the goods before the contract has in fact been avoided, he is secure. Reference may be made back to Chapter 7, to the section on fraudulent misrepresentation, on the question of avoidance. (See also *Citibank NA v Brown Shipping & Co Ltd* (1991).)

The distinction between a mistake as to the person which prevents a contract coming into existence at all and a mistake as to the person which renders the contract voidable for fraud is a difficult distinction to make, and it is particularly difficult when the parties are not dealing by letter, but face to face. For example, in *Phillips v Brooks Ltd* (1919) a man whose real name was North went into the plaintiff's shop and asked to see pearls and rings. He selected pearls costing £2,550 and a ring costing £450. He took out a cheque book and said that he was Sir George Bullough. The jeweller (the plaintiff) had heard of Sir George Bullough as a wealthy man. North gave Sir George's address. The jeweller checked the address in a directory. He then allowed North to take away the ring in exchange for a cheque for £3,000. The cheque bounced. North pawned the ring with the defendant, a pawnbroker. The plaintiff jeweller sued the defendant pawnbroker, arguing that there was never any contract between himself and North, so that North had no title to the ring, and so the defendant had no title either. But the defendant won. The judge said that the plaintiff "had contracted to sell and deliver the ring to the person who came into his shop ... who obtained the sale and delivery by means of the false pretence that he was Sir George Bullough. His intention was to sell to the person present and identified by sight and hearing." The contract of sale was voidable for fraud, but it had not been avoided at the time when the defendant acquired his interest in the ring.

The more recent case of *Ingram v Little* (1961, CA) involved another rogue. The plaintiffs were three sisters, living in Surrey. They were joint owners of a car, and they advertised it for sale. The rogue, introducing himself as "Hutchinson", came to the house and negotiated for the purchase of the car. He eventually offered £717 for it. This price was agreed, and "Hutchinson" produced his cheque book. Elsie Ingram, who was conducting the negotiations, said she would not in any circumstances accept a cheque and the proposed deal was finished. The rogue then said that he was P.G.M. Hutchinson, with business interests in Guildford and living at Stanstead House, Caterham. Hilda Ingram, one of the sisters, went along the street to the local post office and checked in the telephone directory that there was such a person as P.G.M. Hutchinson living at that address. The sisters then let the rogue have the car in exchange for his cheque. The rogue was not P.G.M. Hutchinson, who had nothing whatsoever to do with the transaction. The cheque was dishonoured. The rogue sold the car to the defendant and disappeared. The plaintiffs sued the defendant in conversion. They won at first instance and the Court of Appeal, by a majority, affirmed this decision, on the ground that there was no contract between the plaintiffs and the rogue. The plaintiffs intended to deal with the Hutchinson of Stanstead House, and not with the separate entity, the so-called "Hutchinson" who was before their eyes. Thus they were mistaken, not merely as to his attributes (such as creditworthiness), but as to his identity.

In *Lewis v Averay* (1972, CA) the plaintiff advertised a car for sale. A man telephoned about it and subsequently called. He was a rogue, of course. Having said that he liked the car, the rogue introduced himself as "Richard Green", making the plaintiff believe that he was the well-known film actor of that name, who was, incidentally, known for his role as "Robin Hood". They agreed on a price of £450. The rogue wrote out a cheque for that amount, signing it "R.A. Green." The plaintiff was hesitant and asked for proof of identity. The rogue produced an admission pass to Pinewood Studios, bearing the name "Richard A. Green", and a photograph which was plainly that of the rogue. The plaintiff then let the rogue have the car and log book. A few days later the plaintiff was told by his bank that the cheque was worthless. Meanwhile the rogue had sold the car to the defendant, who bought it in good faith and without knowledge of the fraud. The plaintiff sued the defendant for conversion of the car. The Court of Appeal gave judgment for the defendant, holding that the rogue's fraud did not prevent there being a contract (albeit a voidable one) between him and the plaintiff. Consequently, as the contract had not been avoided in time, the rogue was able to pass a good title to the defendant.

The Court of Appeal made very plain their preference for *Phillips v Brooks* over *Ingram v Little*. Lord Denning said that he could see no valid distinction of fact between the two cases. He thought there was no substance in the idea (suggested by the majority of the Court of Appeal in *Ingram v Little*) that in *Phillips v Brooks* the contract of sale was concluded before the rogue made his misrepresentation, whereas in *Ingram v Little* the rogue made his misrepresentation before the contract was concluded. In Lord Denning's view the property in the goods did not pass in either case until the seller let the rogue have the goods. Lord Denning also said that the alleged distinction between a mistake as to identity and a mistake as to attributes was a distinction without a difference. The interest of *Lewis v Averay* goes beyond the bounds of contract law in that it is a very clear instance of the Court of Appeal refusing to follow a previous decision of its own, *Ingram v Little*. It might once have been possible to note the difficulty in reconciling these cases but at least conclude that the preferences of the Court of Appeal in *Lewis v Averay* represented the present law. The result was, therefore, that, at least where the parties are face-to-face, there is a presumption that the parties intend to deal with the person who is physically present. The recent decision of the House of Lords in *Shogun Finance Ltd v Hudson* (2004), whilst seeking to rationalise this area of law, makes clear that judicial opinion is still deeply divided on the issues raised by these cases. Here the rogue approached a motor dealer saying that he wished to acquire a car on hire-purchase. He produced the driving licence of a Mr Patel, who existed, but who knew nothing of the impersonation and whose licence had presumably been stolen. The finance company carried out the usual checks, albeit using the details of the real Mr Patel, and discovered nothing adverse in his credit record. The rogue then forged Mr Patel's signature on the contract between himself and the finance company and was allowed to take away the car having paid a 10 per cent deposit. The cheque bounced but in the meantime the rogue quickly sold on the car to Hudson. The finance company subsequently sued Hudson in conversion on the basis that, since the hire-purchase agreement was invalid, he could not take the benefit of s.27 of the Hire Purchase Act 1964 which protects the innocent purchaser from a claim when a hirer under a hire-purchase agreement sells a car to an innocent purchaser. In other words, the finance company claimed that the contract between themselves and the rogue was void for mistaken identity, and the House of Lords agreed.

The view of the majority appears to be that the situation was more like *Cundy v Lindsay*, a decision they clearly thought was correct, than the cases involving face-to-face transactions. In this case, the finance company had dealt with the rogue only by telephone and fax and the dealer was not regarded as having used their eyes and ears in dealing with him. The dissenting minority nevertheless cogently make the point, why should it make such a crucial difference that the parties are, or are not, in each other's presence? At the time *Cundy v Lindsay* was decided there was perhaps a clear distinction between presence and postal correspondence, but in a world of telephones, faxes, and even videophones the distinction is surely not as clear. This would suggest that the rule should be the same, and the minority's preference is that the contract should be voidable not void, which would protect innocent purchasers in the position of Mr Hudson. At present it seems that a completely innocent third party can end up incurring liability for someone else's voluntary acceptance of the inevitable risk of taking a cheque in payment.

For mistake as to the person to have any effect in law the mistake must be known to the other party. In *Upton RDC v Powell* (1942, CA) a farmer, whose barn was on fire, rang up the Upton police and asked for "the fire brigade". The police summoned the Upton fire brigade. It later turned out that though the farm was in the Upton police area, it was in the Pershore fire area. If the police had summoned the Pershore fire brigade it would have come to Farmer Powell's fire without charge. The Upton fire brigade was entitled to go to fires outside its own area and, if it did so, to charge for its services. The Upton fire brigade went to the fire, neither party knowing that there was any mistake. The court held that the Upton fire brigade was entitled, on an implied contract, to remuneration for its work. Similarly, if Blenkarn (see *Cundy v Lindsay*) had acted quite innocently—had had a genuine address in Wood Street and had ordered handkerchiefs over an unadorned signature "Blenkarn"—and really believed that the plaintiffs meant to contract with him, there would have been a contract.

For mistake as to the person to have any effect, it must also be a material mistake. That means that it must matter to the mistaken party. In *Mackie v European Assurance Society* (1869) the plaintiff instructed a man called Waddell to take out an insurance policy for him. Waddell had been agent for the X assurance society and the plaintiff thought that his policy would be effected with that society. In fact Waddell had just ceased to be agent for the X society and effected the policy with the defendant society. The defendant society argued that the contract of insurance was void because of this mistake. This argument was rejected by the court on the ground that it did not matter to the plaintiff which insurance society issued the policy; it was a matter of indifference to him. But on the other side of the line lies *Boulton v Jones* (1857). Jones had had dealings with a man called Brocklehurst and, at a time when Brocklehurst owed money to Jones, Jones sent to Brocklehurst a written order for 50 feet of leather hose. On that very day Brocklehurst had transferred his business to his foreman, Boulton. Boulton executed the order by sending the goods to Jones on credit. Jones accepted and used the goods in the belief that they had been sent by Brocklehurst. When, later, Jones was asked for payment he refused. His argument was that he had intended to contract with Brocklehurst, and that it mattered to him because of the set-off which he had against Brocklehurst and which he wished to utilise. The court held that Jones was not liable for the price of the goods.

Mistake as to the subject-matter

This kind of case arises where the parties are at cross-purposes. An example is *Scriven v Hindley* (1913). A man made a bid at an auction sale, thinking that he was bidding for hemp. In fact the bales in question contained tow. The bidder was sued for the price. The court held that there was no contract. "The parties were never *ad idem* as to the subject-matter of the proposed sale." A significant element in this case was that the description of the lots by the seller was arguably misleading. The objective approach would not therefore have yielded any firm conclusion, which therefore justified the finding that there was no contract.

Raffles v Wichelhaus (1864) may also be treated as a case of cross-purpose mistake. In that case, R agreed to sell, and W agreed to buy, a consignment of cotton which was to arrive "ex Peerless from Bombay". There happened to be two ships called Peerless sailing from Bombay, one in October and one in December. The seller tendered the cotton from the December Peerless. The buyer refused to accept it, on the ground that he had intended to buy cotton from the October Peerless. Judgment was given for the defendant. The court gave no reasons for its decision, but one would think that since there was an ambiguity and since, apparently, there were no circumstances which pointed to one meaning rather than the other, there was no contract, because the offer and acceptance did not match.

Mistake as to the terms of the contract

Mistake as to the terms of the contract is only rarely upheld. In *Wood v Scarth* (1858) the defendant offered in writing to let a public-house to the plaintiff for £63 a year. The plaintiff had a conversation about it with the defendant's clerk and then accepted the offer by letter. The defendant intended that a premium of £500 should be payable in addition to the rent, and he believed that his clerk had made this clear to the plaintiff. The plaintiff believed that the £63 a year was all that would be payable. It was held that the contract must stand; and the plaintiff was awarded damages for the defendant's refusal to grant the lease. Any reasonable observer would have seen a precise and unambiguous offer and acceptance which the defendant's mistake could not be seen to vitiate. It is interesting to note that the plaintiff, before bringing this action in a common law court, had sued for specific performance in an equity court. There he failed. Specific performance, along with other equitable remedies, is not given as of right but lies in the discretion of the court. A court may, instead of refusing specific performance outright, grant it on terms. This happened in *Bascomb v Beckwith* (1869). An estate was sold in lots on the terms that the purchaser of each lot should covenant not to build a public-house on it. The vendor kept one of the lots himself, and proposed to build a public-house on it. The plan of the lots did not make this clear. It was held that the vendor could have specific performance but only on terms that he covenanted not to build a public-house on the land retained by himself. A more recent example of the court holding a party to mistakenly agreed terms is *Centrovincial Estates Plc v Merchant Investors Assurance Company Ltd* (1983).

The refusal of specific performance, or the refusal of it except upon terms, does not amount to the court declaring there is no contract. But a court will, on occasion, make such a declaration. In *Hartog v Colin and Shields* (1939) the defendants intended to offer for sale to the plaintiffs some hare skins at a certain price "per piece". By a slip they offered to sell them at that price "per pound". The value of a piece was about one-third that of a pound. The prior negotiations had been conducted on the understanding that the skins would be sold at so much per piece as was apparently the custom in the trade. The plaintiffs sued for non-delivery of the skins. They failed. It was held that there was no contract. The plaintiffs must have known, from the previous negotiations, that "pound" was a slip for "piece". The judge stressed that the defendant had to establish that the plaintiff must have realised the mistake.

Thus the usual rule, as stated above, does not apply where the offeree knows (or, applying the objective approach, should be taken as knowing) that the offeror has made a mistake as to the terms of the offer. In that case, there is no genuine offer to accept.

Mistake as to quality is not operative

In *Smith v Hughes* (1871) the defendant was shown a sample of oats by the plaintiff, and bought them. The defendant thought they were old oats; new oats were no use to him. They were in fact new oats, and he refused to accept them. It was held that, if that was all his mistake, it was a mistake merely as to the quality of the oats and was without any legal effect, even if the other party knew of his mistake. But the court ordered a new trial so that another point could be investigated, whether there had been a mistake going further than quality, going indeed to the terms of the contract. The case is not a very clear authority on that point, which in any case is covered by *Hartog v Colin and Shields*, above. It is clear that mistake by one party as to the quality of the subject-matter, even if that mistake is known to the other party, does not affect the contract.

POSSIBILITY MISTAKE

This kind of mistake has nothing to do with a failure of the acceptance to correspond to the offer. In this situation there has been undoubted agreement, but the parties have made a common mistake about some underlying fact. To take the simplest example, suppose A has agreed with B for the sale of some article to B; unknown to both A and B the article does not exist. That particular mistake has the effect of rendering the contract void. The question here is what mistakes do have this effect and are "operative".

A party to a contract may make all manner of mistakes. In particular he may think that he is getting a good bargain and then later discover that the facts are not as he thought them to be, and that he has got a thoroughly bad bargain. Many such mistakes do not have any legal effect at all. Mistake in the legal sense is a very much narrower idea than it is in popular speech. Because mistake as a legal idea is so narrow, a lawyer acting for a client who has not obtained from a contract what he expected to does not think first of launching an action based on mistake. That is a last resort. He will consider, first, whether there has been a misrepresentation by the other party and, secondly, whether, having regard to the express and the implied terms of the contract, there has been a breach of contract. Only if there has been no misrepresentation (or if the right to rescission has been lost) and if there has been no breach of contract will the idea of suing for mistake be resorted to.

This kind of mistake is called possibility mistake because the parties have made a mistake as to the possibility of the contract's object being achieved. Thus, in the example given, the object of the contract was to transfer the ownership of an article from A to B in return for a sum of money. If the article does not exist, that object cannot be achieved. The impossibility here is antecedent impossibility or initial impossibility; because the impossibility already exists at the time the contract is made. There can also arise in a contract subsequent impossibility; that is, where the impossibility only arises after the contract has been made (but before it has been carried out). Thus, going back to the example, if the article perishes after A and B have made their contract for its sale (but before the sale has gone through), that is a case of subsequent impossibility. That kind of impossibility is called "frustration", and will be discussed in Chapter 17. The underlying idea is the same in both cases; whether the article perishes before the contract is made or after it is made, the object of the contract is frustrated. But it is better to confine the word "frustration" to mean subsequent impossibility. There is another similarity underlying both cases; antecedent impossibility and subsequent impossibility both excuse the parties. Since A is unable to deliver the article it looks as though this must be a breach of contract, but it is not. A is excused from his obligation to deliver

149

the article and, of course, B is excused from his obligation to pay the price. It is because impossibility excuses the parties that it is so important to determine the limits of the doctrine of impossibility. The rest of this section will consider antecedent, not subsequent, impossibility, but when reading Chapter 17, reference should be made back to this chapter. For a case where antecedent impossibility (common mistake) and frustration were pleaded in the alternative, see *Amalgamated Investment & Property Co Ltd v John Walker & Sons Ltd* (1977, CA).

Mistake as to existence

It is clear law that if, unknown to the parties, the subject-matter of the contract does not exist at the time that they make their agreement, the contract is void; in the older cases, this is called "*res extincta*". So, for example, in *Strickland v Turner* (1852) A bought from B an annuity on the life of X. Unknown to both A and B, X was already dead. It was held that as the annuity was not in existence at the time of the contract, the contract was void, and A was entitled to have his purchase money back. Similarly, in *Galloway v Galloway* (1914) a man and a woman entered into a separation deed, believing that they were husband and wife. This was not so, because the prior spouse of the husband turned out to be still alive. The separation deed was held to be void, because the "marriage" which was the basis of the deed did not exist.

A mistake as to existence does not always amount to an operative mistake, and consequently it does not always excuse the parties. This is because the contract may, by its terms, lay the responsibility for non-existence on one party or the other. If A agrees to sell something to B it may be clear from the terms of the contract that if that something does not exist then A is to be liable to B for failure to deliver it; alternatively, it may be clear that B is willing to take a risk, so that if it does not exist then B is to be liable to A for the price. It is only where the contract does not lay the responsibility on either party that non-existence excuses the parties. In an Australian case, *McRae v Commonwealth Disposals Commission* (1951), the Commission contracted to sell to the plaintiff a wrecked oil tanker described as lying on Jourmaund Reef, 100 miles north of Samarai. In fact there was no tanker lying anywhere near the latitude and longitude stated, and indeed there was no place known as Jourmaund Reef. In the High Court of Australia the plaintiff was awarded damages for breach of contract. The court held that the only proper construction of this particular contract was that it included a promise by the Commission that there was a tanker in the position specified.

Mistake as to ownership

In *Cooper v Phibbs* (1867) A agreed to let a fishery to B. Unknown to both parties, the fishery already belonged to B. The agreement was set aside by the House of Lords. The object of the contract— transfer of rights from A to B—was just as impossible of achievement as it would have been if the thing contracted about had been non-existent. Thus the principle applicable to a case of *res extincta* has been extended to the case of what is called "*res sua*" ("the thing was already his").

The mistake in *Cooper v Phibbs* w~ _____ \ of law, but rather of the ~~ _____ , *v Galloway*, th~ - ' ~f th~ ~~ral law ~~tement of law is never

~f quality

~ _____ ~h B for the sale of a thing from A to B, the c~ _____~ ~ to the construction point) is void for mistake if the thing~ ~ exist or if the thing already belongs to B. The questio~ ~w arises, can the contract be held void simply because A and B were mistaken about the quality of the thing? We have seen that a mistake as to quality cannot cause an operative agreement mistake. Here the question is whether it can cause an operative possibility mistake. Can it be said that a contract's object is impossible of achievement if the thing contracted about does not have some quality which the parties thought it had?

The answer to this question depends upon the correct interpretation of *Bell v Lever Brothers Ltd* (1932, HL). In 1923, the Lever Company, which had a controlling interest in the Niger Company, appointed Bell as chairman of the Niger Company at a salary of £8,000 a year. In 1926 the contract was renewed for another five years. Bell, by speculating in the company's business, committed breaches of duty which would have justified the Lever

Company in terminating his appointment. In 1929 the Niger Company amalgamated with another company and Bell became redundant. The Lever Company agreed to pay Bell, and did pay him, £30,000 as compensation for terminating his service contract. Later the Lever Company found out about Bell's breaches of duty. They brought an action claiming rescission of the compensation agreement and return of the £30,000. The jury found that Bell was not fraudulent; when he entered into the compensation agreement he had forgotten his breaches of duty. The trial judge held that the compensation agreement was void for mistake. The mistake was the belief of both parties that they were bargaining about a service contract which could only be terminated with compensation, whereas in fact it could have been terminated without compensation. The Court of Appeal affirmed this decision. The House of Lords allowed the appeal, holding that there was no operative mistake. The House so decided by a majority of three to two. Two Law Lords said that there was an operative mistake, as did the trial judge and the three Lords Justices in the Court of Appeal.

It is not at all clear from the speeches of the majority Law Lords what the true meaning of the decision is. The case is open to two interpretations: (1) that there is a doctrine of operative mistake as to quality, but that the mistake in the instant case was not great enough to bring the doctrine into play; and (2) that there is no such doctrine.

The true meaning of the decision in *Bell v Lever* is still open to argument, but in the 70 years which followed the decision in the case the courts seemed to adopt the second interpretation; that is, that there was no doctrine of operative mistake as to quality. In *Solle v Butcher* (1950, CA) the Court of Appeal held that a contract of letting was not void where the parties had both assumed, wrongly, that the premises were not subject to the Rent Restriction Acts. This was a fundamental mistake as to quality, yet the contract was held not to be void, in the light of *Bell v Lever*. *In Leaf v International Galleries* (1950, CA) the plaintiff bought from the defendants a picture which they both believed, mistakenly, to have been painted by Constable. The plaintiff sued for the return of the price. He based his claim on misrepresentation, so the issue of mistake did not have to be decided, but the Court of Appeal indicated that the contract was not void for mistake.

There are, however, a few cases which suggest that a contract can be rendered void by a mistake as to quality. In *Griffith v Brymer*

(1903) a contract was made at 11 am on June 24, 1902, for the hire of a room which overlooked the route of the coronation procession, due to be held on June 26. At 10 am on June 24, doctors decided to operate upon King Edward VII and, of course, this rendered the procession impossible. This decision was not known to the parties when the contract was made. The court held the contract void. This was a kind of mistake as to quality; the room which was the subject of the contract lacked a quality which it was thought to have. There was a similar mistake in *The Salvador* (1909). The defendant undertook to take a tug and two lighters in tow from Milford Haven to Rio de Janeiro for £570, of which £350 was to be paid in advance. This sum was paid, and the convoy started off. Four days later it put back into Milford Haven. Both parties believed, at the time the contract was made, that the tug was capable of towing the lighters to South America. The court held that there was no contract, as the supposed contract had been entered into "on the mistaken assumption that it could be performed". The plaintiff recovered back his £350. One view would be that these cases would not be followed today. As Lord Denning said in *Solle v Butcher*: "All previous decisions on this subject must now be read in the light of *Bell v Lever*."

But there are two cases decided since *Bell v Lever* in which a contract was held void for what was, in effect, a mistake of quality. In *Sheikh Bros Ltd v Ochsner* (1957, PC) a contract was made for the exploitation of sisal (a fibre used to make rope) growing on land belonging to A, which was to be cut and processed by B. It was a term of the contract that B should deliver to A an average minimum of 50 tons of sisal fibre a month. The profits were to be split between them. It turned out the land was not capable of producing 50 tons of sisal a month, so there was a mistake as to the quality of the land. The Privy Council, supposedly applying the principles laid down in *Bell v Lever*, held the contract to be void. The same result was reached most recently in *Associated Japanese Bank (International) Ltd v Crédit du Nord S.A.* (1988), in which a guarantee of an agreement relating to four non-existent machines was held to be void for common mistake. The rather inconclusive result of the cases appears to be that, whilst there is no doubt that any doctrine of common mistake at common law is extremely limited, it would be difficult on the strength of the authorities to deny its existence altogether. Steyn J. in particular, in the *Associated Japanese Bank* case, was unwilling to give what he regarded as an artificially restricted interpretation to the speeches in *Bell v Lever*.

The most recent authoritative review of this area of law is the Court of Appeal's important judgment in *Great Peace Shipping Ltd v Tsavliris Salvage (International) Ltd* (2002). Here the owners of a ship which had got into difficulties sought the services of another vessel which could, if necessary, rescue the crew. On the basis that the Great Peace was thought to be 12 hours away a contract was concluded for her to escort the stricken vessel. In fact, it subsequently became clear that the Great Peace was much further away than had been thought and would take some 39 hours to arrive. The defendant claimed that the contract was, as a result, void for mistake. Neither the trial court nor the Court of Appeal agreed. On the facts this does not seem surprising. If the ship had been three days away the point might have been more arguable. The particularly scholarly judgment of Lord Phillips M.R. acknowledges that the doctrine of *Bell v Lever Brothers* is extremely narrow, although cases of *res extincta*, such as *Associated Japanese Bank (International) Ltd v Crédit du Nord* (1988) and *res sua*, *Cooper v Phibbs* (1867) are regarded as entirely correct. If anything, however, the court narrows slightly Lord Atkin's statement in *Bell* that a contract might be void even if, "it may be possible to perform the letter of the contract." Lord Phillips states instead that, "for a contract to be void, the non-existence of the state of affairs must render performance of the contract impossible." This surely means that in cases where the parties make a mistake as to some quality or characteristic of the subject matter, it will be even more difficult now to claim that the contract is void for mistake.

The real importance of the decision is, however, that, at a stroke, the Court of Appeal has done away with a previous body of law which sought to give some relief from the strictures of the common law. In *Solle v Butcher* (1950, CA), Lord Denning formulated a principle of equitable mistake. This was said to apply where there had been a "fundamental" mistake, albeit one that might not be so fundamental as to justify regarding the contract as void at common law. The foundations of this doctrine were always regarded by most commentators as shaky, and in particular impossible to square with the decision of the House of Lords in *Bell v Lever Brothers*. It did, nevertheless, serve a certain pragmatic purpose in giving the courts the capacity to intervene where otherwise a claimant might be faced with the harsh consequences of going away completely empty handed. The result of a mistake being found to be operative in equity was that the agreement was said to be voidable, not void, so that it could be set aside, if necessary on terms, as in *Solle* itself. The decision in the *The Great Peace* makes clear that *Solle* was wrongly decided even though it was itself a decision of the Court of Appeal and had stood and been followed for over 50 years. Lord Phillips points out that the decision was indeed inconsistent with *Bell*'s case and that it was never clear what the distinction was between a fundamental mistake that was insufficient to render a contract void and one which did justify a contract being regarded as voidable.

A consequence of this case is that the precise ambit of the doctrine of mistake at common law is even more important than it was before. The all or nothingness of the law's response is not unlike the situation which can already arise in a case of mistaken identity such as *Shogun Finance v Hudson* (above, p.144). In both cases the litigation has given rise to dicta that some sort of legislative reform would help reduce the impact of the harsh, and sometimes arbitrary, consequences to the parties.

Although there is no mention of this in the judgments, and it concerns an unrelated area of law, the boldness of the Court of Appeal's decision raises the spectre that there may be other manifestations of a return to doctrinal orthodoxy. Another doctrine which was conjured by Lord Denning out of a dubious basis in the authorities, lacks authoritative consideration in the cases, is uncertain in its ambit but undoubtedly has some pragmatic attraction is the whole doctrine of promissory estoppel.

MISTAKES IN DOCUMENTS

Where a person signs a document, he is, as a general rule, bound by his signature. If he has not read the document he is still, in general, bound by it. Of course, he may be able to prove that he has been induced to sign it by fraud or other misrepresentation, or he may be able to prove the presence of a mistake, either an agreement mistake or a possibility mistake. If he can prove any of these things his possible remedies are as already discussed.

But there is one further remedy which may possibly be open to him. This is what is called the plea of "non est factum" ("this is not my deed"). This plea is peculiar to signed documents, and the law relating to it is quite separate from the general law of misrepresentation and mistake.

The plea of non est factum first made its appearance at the end of the sixteenth century. If a person who could not read had a deed "read over" to him, and the "reading" did not correctly state what was in the writing, he was not bound by the deed. The deed was not merely voidable for the fraud of the "reader", but was altogether void, with the consequence that if it came into the hands of even an innocent third party he could not acquire any rights under it. Later the plea was extended to written documents not under seal, and it was extended to persons who could have read, but did not read, the document.

At this stage in its development, the plea was very wide indeed, and the courts set about trying to bring it within more reasonable bounds. It became established law that the plea was not available to a signer who was mistaken merely as to the contents of the document, not as to its character or class. It was also established that the plea was not available to a signer who was negligent in signing.

The most important case on non est factum is the House of Lords decision in *Saunders v Anglia Building Society* (1971, HL). The plaintiff was Mrs Gallie, an old lady of 78, who owned a house held on long leasehold. She had a nephew called Wally Parkin. She had made a will leaving the house to Parkin, and she had handed over the deeds of the house to him. Parkin had a friend called Lee. Parkin and Lee together came to Mrs Gallie's house and asked her to sign a document. She got the impression that the point of the document was to enable Parkin and Lee to raise money jointly on the security of the house, and she had no objection to that. She thought that the document was an assignment of the leasehold by gift from herself to Parkin. She did not read the document because she had broken her spectacles. She signed it unread. In fact the document was an assignment from Mrs Gallie to Lee for £3,000. Lee did not pay Mrs Gallie the £3,000 or anything at all. Lee mortgaged the house to a building society and used the proceeds entirely for his own purposes, to the exclusion of Parkin. He defaulted on the mortgage payments, and the building society sought possession of the house. Mrs Gallie sued for a declaration that the assignment was void, on the basis of non est factum. Lee was the first defendant and the building society was the second defendant.

The trial judge gave judgment for Mrs Gallie. The Court of Appeal unanimously reversed his decision and the House of Lords unanimously affirmed the Court of Appeal. At first instance and in the Court of Appeal the case is called *Gallie v Lee*. In the House of

Lords it is called *Saunders v Anglia Building Society*. Mrs Gallie had died before the case reached the House of Lords, and Saunders was the name of her executrix. Lee ceased to be a party to the proceedings after the first instance decision.

The views of the House of Lords can be summarised as follows:

(1) The plea of non est factum can only succeed where the person who signed the document can show that there was a radical difference between what he signed and what he thought he was signing, and this test should replace the former distinction between the contents of a document and its character or class.

(2) The plea is not open to a signer who was careless in signing. The word "careless" is preferable to the word "negligent", because "negligent" has come to have a technical meaning (involving the breach of a duty of care) which is not appropriate in this context.

Mrs Gallie's executrix failed on the first point because, given Mrs Gallie's wish to enable Parkin and Lee to raise money on the security of the house, there was not a radical difference between what she signed and what she thought she was signing. Two of the Law Lords expressly approved the way Russell L.J. had put it in the Court of Appeal; namely, that Mrs Gallie was not mistaken as to the very "object of the exercise" as distinct from the details of the document or its parties.

In *United Dominions Trust Ltd v Western* (1976, CA) the Court of Appeal held that no valid distinction can be drawn between the carelessness of a person who signs a document without reading it and the carelessness of a person who signs a document in blank leaving the details to be filled in by a third party.

The most recent case involving a plea of non est factum confirms the narrow limits of the rule: see *Norwich and Peterborough Building Society v Steed (No.2)* (1993). A person who has been induced to sign a document which they have entirely misunderstood might well, if the facts permit, be better advised to seek a remedy in misrepresentation or undue influence.

CHAPTER TEN

ILLEGALITY

THIS CHAPTER is concerned with the situation where a contract, perfectly valid in other respects, comes into conflict with some legal rule and is thus tainted with illegality. The rule in question may be a rule laid down by a statute or it may be a rule of common law. Some contracts are prohibited by statute; some are prohibited by a rule of common law. Other contracts, though not absolutely prohibited, are denied their full validity by a statute or by a rule of common law. In the past, there have been attempts to classify illegal contracts by saying, for example, that some were illegal and void, some were merely void and others were unenforceable. Nowadays, it probably better reflects the attitude of the courts to say that the effect of illegality depends upon the nature and gravity of the illegality in question. In *Saunders v Edwards* (1987), Bingham L.J. said:

"Where issues of illegality are raised, the courts have (as it seems to me) to steer a middle course between two unacceptable positions. On the one hand it is unacceptable that any court of law should aid or lend its authority to a party seeking to pursue or enforce an object or agreement which the law prohibits. On the other hand, it is unacceptable that the court should, on the first indication of unlawfulness affecting any aspect of a transaction, draw up its skirts and refuse all assistance to the plaintiff, no matter how serious his loss or how disproportionate his loss to the unlawfulness of his conduct."

In this chapter the traditional categories are considered separately from contracts in restraint of trade, which are considered at the end of the chapter.

THE CATEGORIES OF ILLEGAL CONTRACTS

Wagering contracts

A bet upon some future event or upon some past or present fact is a wager if it has the following features: (1) there are two parties, or groups of parties, and no more; (2) each party stands to win or lose; and (3) neither party has any financial interest in the outcome other than the sum in issue. Because of point (1) a football pool is not a wager; because of point (2) a bet with "The Tote" is not a wager, since "The Tote" cannot lose: see *Tote Investors Ltd v Smoker* (1968, CA); because of point (3) a contract of insurance is not a wager, provided that the assured has a genuine "insurable interest".

Rights of the parties under a wagering contract
Section 18 of the Gaming Act 1845 provides as follows:

> "All contracts or agreements, whether by parole or in writing, by way of gaming or wagering, shall be null and void; and no suit shall be brought or maintained in any court of law or equity for recovering any sum of money or valuable thing alleged to be won upon any wager, or which shall have been deposited in the hands of any person to abide the event on which any wager shall have been made."

The section thus makes a wagering contract void. If the loser does not pay, the winner cannot sue. If the loser pays by cheque and then stops the cheque, the winner cannot sue on the cheque. If the loser does pay, he cannot sue to recover back his money.

The section also makes collateral contracts associated with gambling contracts unenforceable. In *Hill v William Hill (Park Lane) Ltd* (1949, HL), for example, the defendant owed some £3,600 to the plaintiffs for lost bets. The committee of Tattersalls ordered the defendant to pay his debt by stated instalments. The defendant did not pay. Then, in consideration that the plaintiffs would not enforce the order, the defendant made a fresh promise to

159

pay. He still did not pay. The plaintiffs sued him. The House of Lords held that the fresh promise was invalidated by s.18, as being the promise of a "sum of money alleged to be won upon a wager".

A third effect of the section is that it prevents the winner from suing the stakeholder if the stakeholder declines to pay over the money deposited with him by the loser. It does not prevent the winner or the loser suing the stakeholder to recover back his own stake.

Cases involving the Gaming Act 1845 are rare. An example is *City Index Ltd v Leslie* (1991), which involved wagers on stock market index movements. The case in fact turned on the construction of the relevant provisions of s.63 of the Financial Services Act 1986, which excludes from the ambit of s.18 of the 1845 Act activities listed in the Sch.1 to the 1986 Act. The Court of Appeal held that this type of bet fell within the 1986 Act and was therefore enforceable.

Rights on cheques and other securities

The winner of a wager cannot sue on the cheque if the loser pays by a cheque which then bounces. But can a third party, to whom such a cheque is negotiated, sue on it? It is necessary to distinguish here between gaming wagers and non-gaming wagers. Cheques given for money won on a game are deemed to be given for an "illegal consideration", by virtue of the Gaming Act 1835. The third-party holder of a cheque can sue on it if he can prove that he or some previous holder gave value for it and that he personally, when he took the cheque, had no notice of its origin. A cheque given on a non-gaming wager is given without consideration, since the wager itself is void, but it is not tainted with illegality. The third-party holder of such a cheque will succeed unless the defendant can prove that at no stage in its career has the cheque been transferred for value. It does not matter if the holder knew of its origin.

Contracts illegal by statute

A contract is illegal if it is prohibited by a statute. "Statute" for this purpose includes delegated or subordinate legislation, such as a statutory instrument. In some cases, the statute expressly prohibits the type of contract in question; in other cases, the statute is interpreted by the courts as having the effect of impliedly prohibiting a contract. The principle was stated by Devlin J. in *St John Shipping Corporation v Joseph Rank Ltd* (1957) as follows:

"The court will not enforce a contract which is expressly or impliedly prohibited by statute. If the contract is of this class it does not matter what the intent of the parties is; if the statute prohibits the contract, it is unenforceable whether the parties meant to break the law or not."

An example of express prohibition is to be found in the case of *Re Mahmoud and Ispahani* (1921, CA). A statutory order provided that no one should buy or sell linseed oil without a licence. The plaintiff had a licence to sell to other licensed dealers, and he was induced to sell to the defendant by the latter's fraudulent statement that he also had a licence. Subsequently, the defendant refused to take delivery and the plaintiff sued him for damages. Although the plaintiff was entirely innocent, he failed in his action. The order expressly prohibited any contract of sale if either party to it was unlicensed.

In *Mohamed v Alaga & Co (a firm)* (1998), the plaintiff entered into an agreement with a firm of solicitors. The terms of the agreement were that he would introduce Somali refugees to the firm, which would then apply for legal aid and represent the refugees on their asylum applications, and that he would help the firm in preparing and presenting the applications; in consideration for these services, the firm would pay him commission equivalent to one half of any fees received by them from the Legal Aid Board in respect of any Somali nationals who became clients of the firm and who sought and obtained legal aid. Lightman J. held that this agreement was expressly prohibited by the Solicitors' Practice Rules 1990, which were made under the Solicitors Act 1974 and amounted to subordinate legislation. He therefore held that the agreement was unenforceable; he also refused the plaintiff's claim for restitution.

Cope v Rowlands (1836) provides an example of an implied prohibition. A statute provided that any person who acted as broker in the City of London without a licence should forfeit the sum of £25 to the City. The plaintiff, who was unlicensed, did some work for the defendant in buying and selling stock. He failed in an action for his fee. Park B. said:

"The legislature had in view, as one object, the benefit and security of the public in those important transactions which are negotiated by brokers. The clause, therefore, which imposes a penalty, must be taken ... to imply a prohibition of all unadmitted persons to act as brokers, and consequently to prohibit by necessary inference all contracts which such persons make for compensation to themselves for so acting."

The courts will not lightly hold that a statute impliedly prohibits a contract. In *Archbolds (Freightage) Ltd v S. Spanglett Ltd* (1961, CA) the defendants agreed to carry for the plaintiffs 200 crates of whisky belonging to third parties from Leeds to London. The plaintiffs did not know that the defendants did not have the correct licence. The whisky was stolen on the way and the plaintiffs sued for damages. The defendants argued that the contract was prohibited under the Act. The Court of Appeal rejected this argument, and held that the Act did not prohibit the contract expressly, and did not even prohibit it by implication. The object of the statute was to promote the efficiency of transport services, and that object could be attained without invalidating every contract made by carriers in breach of its provisions; it could be attained by imposing penalties on such carriers.

Contracts contrary to public policy at common law

From at least the time of Elizabeth I, judges have regarded themselves as having jurisdiction to rule that certain contracts are injurious to society. There has thus grown up what is called the doctrine of "public policy", enabling judges to refuse relief to litigants claiming under contracts which are considered to be injurious to the public good. This is a vague and uncertain doctrine and was described by a judge in 1824 as being "a very unruly horse".

It is now settled that it is no longer open to the courts to invent a new head of public policy. The courts continue to act, however, on the heads of public policy established by earlier decisions. Thus the doctrine has now crystallised and the heads of public policy can be enumerated. There is scope for disagreement as to whether a particular point of public policy should be regarded as a separate head or should more properly come under some wider head.

A contract to commit a crime, tort or fraud

A contract which has as its object the commission of a crime, or of a tort, or of a fraud upon third parties, is illegal. A clear example is *Everet v Williams* (1725), where a contract between two high-waymen to rob a coach and then share the takings was held to be illegal, so that one highwayman could not sue the other for his share.

A more modern example is *Scott v Brown, Doering, McNab & Co* (1892, CA). Here, there was a contract to "rig the market"—that is, to enhance artificially the price of shares—by purchasing some of them at a fictitious premium. The plaintiff was unable to recover back money that he had paid to a firm of stockbrokers in pursuance of that contract.

A contract damaging to the country's safety

The most important example of this class of contract is a trading contract between a British subject and an alien enemy in time of war. If such a contract is made during war it is wholly illegal. If it is made in peacetime and then war comes, it can give rise to no further rights or obligations. But existing rights and obligations are only suspended; after hostilities cease they can be enforced.

A contract damaging to the country's foreign relations

A contract which tends to disturb the country's good relations with a friendly country is illegal. In *Regazzoni v K.C. Sethia (1944) Ltd* (1958, HL) the defendants agreed to sell to the plaintiffs jute twills, with the intention that they should be exported from India to Europe for resale in South Africa. Indian law prohibited the export of goods from India if they were destined for South Africa. The plaintiffs claimed damages for non-delivery of the goods. They failed. It was the common intent of both parties to violate the law of India and, since India was a friendly country, the contract was contrary to public policy in this country. See also *Lemenda Trading Co v African Middle East Petroleum Co Ltd* (1988).

A contract damaging to the administration of justice

The most important example of this class is a contract to stifle a prosecution; that is, to compromise a prosecution or to prevent a prosecution which has begun from taking its normal course. See *R. v Andrews* (1973).

Another example of a contract damaging to the administration of justice is a contract which involves maintenance or champerty. Maintenance in this context means stirring up litigation by giving aid to a plaintiff or defendant without just cause or excuse: see *Re*

Trepca Mines Ltd (application of Radomir Nicola Pachitch (Pasic)) (1962). Champerty is the maintenance of an action coupled with a bargain that the maintainer shall receive a share of whatever is recovered in the action: see *Ellis v Torrington* (1920). In *Re Trepca Mines Ltd*, Lord Denning M.R. said of champerty:

> "The reason why the common law condemns champerty is because of the abuses to which it gives rise. The common law fears that the champertous maintainer might be tempted, for his own personal gain, to inflame the damages, to suppress evidence, or even to suborn witnesses."

Both maintenance and champerty used to be criminal and tortious. The Criminal Law Act 1967 provides that neither shall any longer be criminal or tortious, but by s.14(2) it is provided that this abolition of liability "shall not affect any rule of ... law as to the cases in which a contract is to be treated as contrary to public policy or otherwise illegal". So the rule still stands that contracts involving maintenance or champerty are illegal. In *Giles v Thompson* (1993) the House of Lords refused to treat as champertous an agreement between a car-hire company and a potential plaintiff whose car needed repairs as a result of a motor accident by which the potential plaintiff received free car hire in return for agreeing that the company could bring an action for damages in the plaintiff's name. A similar conclusion was reached in the later decision in *Factortame Ltd v Secretary of State for the Environment, Transport and the Regions (No.2)* (2002), in which the Court of Appeal decided that contingency arrangements put into place to pay accountants for their professional services in relation to claims made by claimant companies which were in difficult financial circumstances were not champertous. Following Lord Denning's dictum, above, Lord Phillips M.R. said that the court must look at the facts of the particular case and consider whether those facts suggest that the agreement in question might tempt the allegedly champertous maintainer in the ways suggested by Lord Denning.

Changes in the way litigation is funded have caused the courts to re-examine agreements between lawyers and their clients relating to the payment of the lawyers' fees. Recently, the issue has arisen as to whether a contingency fee agreement or conditional fee agreement entered into by a solicitor or barrister is champertous. Whilst it is likely that at common law such arrangements would be champertous, this whole area has been overtaken by legislative developments. Their effect is that conditional fee agreements are permitted, provided that they satisfy the provisions of s.58 of the Courts and Legal Services Act 1990 (as amended by s.27(1) of the Access to Justice Act 1999, with effect from April 1, 2000). The view of the Court of Appeal is that s.58 embraces only agreements for the provision of litigation or advocacy services concluded by those with rights to conduct litigation or those with rights of audience: see *Factortame Ltd v Secretary of State for the Environment, Transport and the Regions (No.2)* (2002). The statutory provisions do not apply, therefore, to the provision of services by other categories of persons, such as accountants. Nor do they apply to an agreement involving payments by a solicitor for the introduction of clients, which are subject to r.7 of the Solicitors' Practice Rules 1990, made under s.31(1) of the Solicitors Act 1974: see *Mohamed v Alaga & Co (a firm)* (1999). See also *King v Telegraph Group Ltd* (2004).

Thus, for example, in *Bevan Ashford (a firm) v Geoff Yeandle (Contractors) Ltd (in liquidation)* (1998), questions arose relating to the validity of a conditional fee agreement entered into between a liquidator of a company and a firm of solicitors and a similar agreement entered into between the solicitors and a barrister who acted in arbitration on behalf of the liquidator. The agreement with the solicitors was that if the company won they would receive their disbursements and normal profit costs. The agreement with the barrister was that he would receive no fee for appearing for the company in the arbitration if it should fail but that he would receive an uplift of 50 per cent above the normal fee if it succeeded. Sir Richard Scott V.C. held that, if the conditional fee agreement relating to a particular cause of action was sanctioned for proceedings in court by s.58 of the Courts and Legal Services Act 1990 and by the Conditional Fee Agreements Order 1995 and the Conditional Fee Agreements Regulations 1995, the agreement was free from any public policy objection. Since the agreements in question complied with the Order and the Regulations, they were not champertous.

The courts have also considered agreements between liquidators and third parties who have agreed to fund litigation. In *Grovewood Holdings Plc v James Capel & Co Ltd* (1994) Lightman J. held to be champertous and an abuse of the process of the court an agreement by which a liquidator of a company engaged in litigation agreed with backers that, in return for funding to continue with litigation, they should receive a share of the recoveries of the action. The judge drew a distinction between selling a "bare" cause of action, which is permitted by the Insolvency Act 1986, and a sale of the fruits of litigation, which remains subject to the law of maintenance and champerty; so he ordered the action to be stayed. The Court of Appeal doubted this view in *Re Oasis Merchandising Services Ltd (in liquidation)* (1997). It held that a liquidator of an insolvent company had no power under the Insolvency Act 1986 to enter into a champertous agreement to assign to a third party the fruits of litigation in exchange for the third party financing the litigation.

Contracts to oust the jurisdiction of the courts

A contract which has the effect of taking away the right of one party, or both parties, to submit questions of law to the courts is contrary to public policy and is void. An example is *Baker v Jones* (1954), which involved an association formed to promote the sport of weightlifting. The association's rules, which constituted a contract between the members, provided that its council should be the sole interpreter of the rules and that the council's decision should in all cases be final. A member applied to the court for a declaration that the use of the association's funds for a particular purpose was against the rules. Lynskey J. held that the court had jurisdiction to entertain the action, and to consider whether the council's interpretation of the rules in a given case was correct in law. The rules, so far as they purported to oust the court's jurisdiction, were contrary to public policy and void.

An agreement between husband and wife for maintenance sometimes contains a term purporting to oust the jurisdiction of the courts. The wife, in return for an allowance, may promise not to apply to the court for maintenance. In *Hyman v Hyman* (1929, HL) the House of Lords held that such an agreement did not prevent the wife from applying to the court for maintenance. The effect of this decision has been overtaken by legislation.

It is possible, however, for parties to agree to submit a dispute to arbitration and arbitration clauses are enforceable.

A contract tending to promote corruption in public life

This is a fairly wide principle, but one example will suffice. In *Parkinson v College of Ambulance* (1925) the secretary of the defendant charity told the plaintiff that the charity was in a position to procure him a knighthood if he would make an adequate donation. After a certain amount of bargaining, the plaintiff paid £3,000 to the charity and undertook to do more when the knighthood was forthcoming. The plaintiff did not get a knighthood, and he sued for the return of his money. His action failed. See also *Lemenda Trading Co Ltd v African Middle East Petroleum Co Ltd* (1988).

A contract to defraud the revenue authorities

A contract to defraud the revenue authorities, whether national or local, is illegal. In *Miller v Karlinski* (1945, CA) the plaintiff was employed by the defendant. He was to receive a salary of £10 a week and repayment of his expenses. He was also entitled to include in his expense account the amount of income tax due in respect of his weekly salary. The plaintiff brought an action to recover 10 weeks' arrears of salary and £21 2s. 8d. for expenses. It emerged at the trial that about £17 of this latter sum represented his liability for income tax. It was held that the contract was illegal since it constituted a fraud on the revenue, and the plaintiff's action therefore failed. He was not only unable to recover the illegal "expenses"; he could not even recover his ordinary salary. By contrast, in *Hall v Woolston Hall Leisure Ltd* (2000), the Court of Appeal refused to accept that a contract was tainted by illegality where the employee did no more than at most acquiesce in the employer's illegal behaviour and had derived no rights from it. Unlike *Miller v Karlinski*, the illegality arose on a variation of the contract but the contract as varied did not incorporate a term that adopted the illegality.

Contracts damaging to the institution of marriage

A contract is void if it restrains a person from marrying at all, or if it requires someone to marry a particular person without a reciprocal obligation on that person. In *Lowe v Peers* (1768) a man made a contract under seal in these terms:

> "I do truly promise Mrs Catherine Lowe that I will not marry with any person besides herself: if I do, I agree to pay the said Catherine Lowe £1,000 within three months next after I shall marry anybody else."

The contract was held void.

A marriage brokage contract is a contract by which A undertakes for a fee to procure a marriage for B. Such contracts are illegal. Thus a contract between a client and a "marriage bureau" is void: see *Hermann v Charlesworth* (1905).

Contracts for future separation are illegal and void. Thus, a contract between husband and wife by which the husband promises his wife that he will make provision for her if she should ever live apart from him is void. On the other hand, a contract between husband and wife for immediate separation is valid and enforceable if it is in fact followed by immediate separation. If spouses have been separated and then come together again, the reconciliation agreement may make provision for the possibility of a renewed separation in the future.

A contract to promote sexual immorality

A contract tending to promote sexual immorality is illegal at common law. In *Upfill v Wright* (1911) a landlord let a flat to a woman whom he knew to be the mistress of a certain man. He also knew, or could be presumed to know, that the money for the rent would be given to her "as the price of her immorality". When the landlord sued for the rent, his action failed. In *Pearce v Brooks* (1866) the plaintiffs agreed to supply the defendant with a new miniature brougham. The defendant was a prostitute, and she intended to use the carriage, which was said to be "ornamental", in plying her trade, or plying for hire. The Court Exchequer Chamber was satisfied that the plaintiffs were aware of the defendant's intention. The plaintiffs' action for money due under the contract failed.

The effects of illegality

The general rule

The general rule is that neither party can sue on the contract which is thus unenforceable. This was reaffirmed by the House of Lords in *Tinsley v Milligan* (1993). For example, in *Keir v Leeman* (1846) the plaintiff, though he had performed his promise not to pursue a prosecution, could not sue on the counter-promise made by his friends to pay the debt owed to him. Leeman and his friend obtained what they promised to pay for and then got away without paying.

Sometimes, however, it is possible for a party to an illegal contract to succeed in a claim if the claim can be made without relying on the illegal contract. So, for example, in *Shelley v Paddock* (1980, CA) the plaintiff succeeded by suing for the tort of fraud; the fraud was not connected with the illegality. The facts were that a Miss Shelley wanted to buy a house in Spain. Mr and Mrs Paddock, who were resident in Spain, showed her a house near Alicante, telling her fraudulently that they were authorised agents of the owner to sell it. She agreed to buy the house, and paid a deposit of £80, and subsequently paid £9,320 into the Paddocks' bank account in England. These payments, without the consent of the Treasury, were illegal under the exchange control legislation, but Miss Shelley did not know that there was such a thing. (Exchange control, with minor exceptions, was abolished in 1979, but the facts of this case occurred in 1974.) Miss Shelley never got the house. In an action for fraud she recovered as damages a sum equal to the amount she had paid to the Paddocks, plus damages for mental and physical suffering, plus her expenses. A similar result was arrived at in *Saunders v Edwards* (1987, CA). See also *Hughes v Clewley (No.2)* (1996).

In this context, the device of the collateral contract (which was discussed in Chapter 4) is sometimes used. In *Strongman (1945) Ltd v Sincock* (1955, CA), for example, the plaintiff builders contracted to modernise some houses belonging to the defendant. It was illegal at the time to carry out the work without a licence from the Ministry of Works. Before the contract was made, the client (defendant) agreed to obtain the necessary licences. The plaintiffs did work to the value of over £6,000. The defendant paid about half this sum and tried to argue that, since licences had only in fact been obtained to the amount of £2,150, the contract had been illegally performed. The Court of Appeal held that the builders should succeed in their action for the unpaid balance. The builders could not succeed on the main contract, because they had taken part in the illegal performance of it. But since they were only technically (not morally) guilty, they could succeed on the collateral contract; the client's promise to obtain the licences in return for the implied promise of the builders to do the work on that understanding. More recently, the Court of Appeal has applied this line of reasoning to a claim by the guilty party. In *Euro-Diam Ltd v Bathurst* (1988, CA) the plaintiffs (diamond suppliers) sent diamonds to suppliers in West Germany (as it then was). The accompanying invoice understated the value of the goods with the intention of enabling the customers to avoid payment of German customs duty. Some of the diamonds were later stolen in Germany. The plaintiffs sued their insurers to recover the agreed value of the diamonds, but the insurers argued that the plaintiffs' claim was tainted with illegality, consisting of the avoidance of German customs duty. The judge found in the plaintiffs' favour; the Court of Appeal dismissed the insurers' appeal on the grounds that there was no direct, proximate connection between the plaintiffs' claim and the understated invoice. This was because: (a) the invoice was wholly unconnected with the plaintiffs' cause of action (which relied on the contract of insurance); (b) the invoice involved no deception on the insurers, since the value of the diamonds was agreed for the purposes of insurance and was thus unaffected by the value of the invoice; (c) the plaintiffs obtained no tangible benefit from the illegality; and (d) the fact that the invoice might prove an embarrassment to the plaintiffs in any other proceedings concerning the diamonds was not sufficient to enable the insurers to rely on illegality. A similar thought may be seen in *Tinsley v Milligan* (1993). The case involved a claim to a house which had been put into the name of only one of the parties to assist in a fraud on the Department of Social Security. The House of Lords said that a party to the illegality could enforce his property right provided that he could establish title without relying on his own illegality, even if it emerged that the title on which he relied was acquired in the course of carrying through an illegal transaction.

On the other hand, transactions related to the illegal contract between the parties are also illegal. Thus if A gives B security in respect of money due from A to B under an illegal contract, the security is illegal, and so unenforceable, in the same way as the original contract: see *Fisher v Bridges* (1854). But where a contract between A and B is illegal, a related contract between B and C will only be illegal if C knew of the illegality in the first contract. Thus, if B borrows money from C, to pay what he owes to A on an illegal contract, C will not be able to sue on the contract of loan if he knew that his loan was to be used to pay an illegal debt. On the other hand, if C did not know that his money was to be used in this way, he will be able to sue for money lent: see *Spector v Ageda* (1973).

Recovery of money or property

As has been seen, the general rule is that neither party can sue on the contract which is thus unenforceable. Consequently neither party can, in general, sue to recover back what it has paid or transferred under the contract. Thus, property or other rights transferred under an illegal contract become vested in the transferee: *Belvoir Finance Co Ltd v Stapleton* (1971, CA). There are exceptions, however.

Reliance on illegal contract unnecessary

A party can recover back money or property if he can establish his case without reliance on the illegal contract. In *Bowmakers Ltd v Barnet Instruments Ltd* (1945, CA) the defendants obtained some machine tools from the plaintiffs under illegal hire-purchase contracts. The defendants failed to make the payments. They also sold some of the goods, and refused to deliver the other goods to the plaintiffs on demand. The plaintiffs successfully claimed damages for the conversion of all the goods. A hirer under a hire-purchase contract has a "special property" in the goods, which he loses if he sells the goods. Thus the plaintiffs in suing in respect of the goods which had been sold were not relying on the contract of hire-purchase; they were simply asserting their rights in respect of goods owned by them. It is not entirely clear from the report how the court reached the same result in relation to the goods which the defendants kept in their own hands. The most likely explanation is that the hire-purchase contract contained a clause under which the contract terminated automatically on non-payment of hire, with the consequence that the hirer's "special property" ceased automatically. The House of Lords came to the same conclusion in *Tinsley v Milligan* (1993, HL), see above.

Plaintiff not equally guilty

A party can recover back money or property if he is not in *pari delicto* (not equally guilty). For example, some statutes have as their object the protection of a class or group of persons, so that, for instance, a tenant can recover back an illegal premium paid to a landlord. But in *Kiriri Cotton Co Ltd v Dewani* (1960, PC) the Privy Council were dealing with a foreign ordinance which, though it made the taking of a premium illegal, did not expressly say that the premium could be recovered back by the tenant. The Privy Council held that the tenant could recover back the premium by virtue of this common law principle.

A further example of this exception is to be found in *Marles v Trant* (1954, CA). The defendants sold some seed to the plaintiff. They believed it to be spring wheat and they sold it as spring wheat. In fact it was winter wheat. This contract was illegal as performed, because the defendants failed to comply with a statute which required an invoice to be delivered with the goods. The plaintiff, when he discovered that the wheat was winter wheat, sued the defendants for breach of contract. He won; the contract was illegal, but it was not illegal in itself, only in its performance, and he was innocent. The facts of *Marles v Trant* are similar to those of *Anderson Ltd v Daniel* (1924). The difference, however, is that in the latter case the sellers were suing on the contract, and they failed because they were not innocent; it was they who had contravened the statute. In *Marles v Trant* it was the buyer who was suing, and he succeeded, because he was innocent.

Withdrawal before performance of the illegal contract

A party can recover back what it has transferred to the other if it withdraws before the contract has been substantially performed. In *Taylor v Bowers* (1876, CA) the plaintiff was being pressed by his creditors. To prevent certain machinery from falling into his creditors' hands, he made a fictitious assignment of it to a man called Alcock. He then called two meetings of creditors in an attempt to reach a settlement, but no composition agreement in fact resulted. In the meantime Alcock had mortgaged the machinery to Bowers, who took it with notice of the fraudulent scheme. The plaintiff sued to recover back the machinery, and he won. The illegal purpose had not been carried out; no creditor had in fact been defrauded.

In *Tribe v Tribe* (1995, CA) a father agreed with his son to transfer some shares to him to avoid the risk of them being claimed by his creditors in the event of his bankruptcy. In the event, he was able to pay them without the need to resort to this scheme. He later claimed the shares back and argued that he had withdrawn before the illegal scheme was carried into effect. The Court of Appeal accepted this argument. It may be that their decision was coloured by their view of the son's behaviour, since he was aware of the reason behind the transfer and was trying to escape from the agreement.

Severance

Severance means the separating of the void part of the contract from the valid part. If severance is possible, it will enable an otherwise illegal contract to be enforceable by the parties once the void part has been removed. As will be seen, this rule is particularly applicable in the case of contracts in restraint of trade.

An example of severance is to be found in *Goldsoll v Goldman* (1915, CA). There, the defendant carried on business in London, selling imitation jewellery. He sold the business to the plaintiff and agreed that for a period of two years he would not deal in real or imitation jewellery in any part of the United Kingdom or in France, the United States, Russia or Spain, or within 25 miles of Pots-dammerstrasse, Berlin, or St Stefans Kirche, Vienna. The restraint over the whole United Kingdom was reasonable, as the business gained most of its customers from advertisements in national newspapers. The restraint relating to areas outside the United Kingdom was unreasonable. Also, whilst the prohibition against dealing in imitation jewellery was reasonable, the prohibition against dealing in real jewellery was not, since the business which the defendant had sold to the plaintiff was not concerned with real jewellery. The Court of Appeal held that the restraint clause could and should be severed in two ways: the references to places outside the United Kingdom were deleted, as also was the reference to real jewellery. That left a valid restraint against dealing in imitation jewellery in the United Kingdom.

In *Attwood v Lamont* (1920, CA) the plaintiffs had a general outfitters' business at Kidderminster. It was divided into several departments, each of which was supervised by one of their employees. The head of each department signed a contract promising that he would not, after leaving the plaintiffs' service, "be concerned in any of the following trades or businesses: that is to say, the trade or business of a tailor, dressmaker, general draper, milliner, hatter, haberdasher, gentlemen's, ladies' or children's outfitter" within 10 miles of Kidderminster. The plaintiffs were seeking to enforce this covenant against the former head of the tailoring department. They had to admit that the covenant was too wide in subject-matter to be enforced as it stood, but they argued that everything except the reference to tailoring should be cut out, thus leaving a valid covenant which they could enforce. This argument was rejected by the Court of Appeal. Severance would have altered the whole nature of the covenant. After severance the covenant would protect only that part of the business in which the defendant had worked, whereas the original covenant was "part of a scheme by which every head of a department was to be restrained from competition with the plaintiffs, even in the business of departments with which he had no connection". This was not a case of several distinct covenants: "there is in truth but one covenant for the protection of the respondent's entire business, and not several covenants for the protection of his several businesses. The respondent is, on the evidence, not carrying on several businesses but one business, and in my opinion this covenant must stand or fall in its unaltered form." It fell.

The main point of distinction between the two cases is that in *Goldsoll*'s case the deletions which the court made did not alter the whole nature of the covenant, but merely cut down its extent, whereas in *Attwood*'s case the deletions that were asked for, and refused, would have meant making, in effect, a new contract.

CONTRACTS IN RESTRAINT OF TRADE

General principles

The doctrine of restraint of trade is to the effect that a contract which comes within its ambit, and which restricts the liberty of a person to carry on his trade, business or profession in any manner he chooses, is contrary to public policy and void, unless it is justifiable as being reasonable.

The following general propositions of law may be stated:

(1) The doctrine of restraint of trade does not apply to every contract which, in any circumstances whatever, restricts a person's liberty to trade. It does not apply to restrictions which are part of the "accepted and normal currency of commercial or contractual or conveyancing relations". Thus an agreement by the lessee of a public-house that he will not sell beer on the premises except that brewed by his lessor is outside the doctrine of restraint of trade, as also is a negative covenant by which a lessee or purchaser of land agrees not to use the premises for trading purposes. The doctrine undoubtedly does apply to: (a) contracts under which an employee restricts his liberty to compete against his employer after he has left his present employment; and (b) contracts by which the vendor of a business restricts his liberty to compete against the purchaser. In other cases, the doctrine may or may not apply, depending upon the terms of the contract and the surrounding circumstances. "The classification must remain fluid and the categories can never be closed."

(2)   If a particular contract comes within the scope of the doctrine, and contains restrictions on a person's liberty to trade, it is prima facie void, and will only be saved if it is reasonable.

(3)   To pass the test of reasonableness the restraint must be reasonable as between the parties and reasonable in the public interest.

(4)   To be held reasonable, the restraint must protect, and protect only, some proprietary or other legitimate interest of the promisee; and consequently the restraint must not be excessive as regards its area, time of operation or the trades which it forbids.

(5)   In appropriate cases, it may be possible to sever a clause or part of a clause held to be unreasonable, but that will only be possible if the sense of the whole restraint is not destroyed by the severance.

Restraints in a contract of employment

A restraint imposed on an employee will not be held to be reasonable unless there is some proprietary interest of the employer which requires protection. Until recently, the only matters in which he would be held to have such an interest were his trade secrets (if any) and his business connection. Recently, the courts have accepted that an employer may also have an interest in retaining his workforce and preventing it from being poached, particularly by former employees: see *Hanover Insurance Brokers v Schapiro* (1994) and *Dawnay, Day & Co Ltd v de Braconnier d'Alphen* (1998).

A good example of a trade secrets case is *Forster & Sons Ltd v Suggett* (1918). The works manager of the plaintiff company was instructed in certain confidential methods concerning the correct mixture of gas and air in the furnaces for the manufacture of glass and glass bottles. He entered into a contract which contained a covenant that he would not, during the five years following the end of his employment, carry on in the United Kingdom, or be interested in, glass bottle manufacture or any other business connected with glass making as conducted by the plaintiff company. This restraint was held to be valid.

A good example of a case concerning business connection is *Fitch v Dewes* (1921, HL). A solicitor's managing clerk at Tamworth

175

entered into a covenant that after leaving his employer he would not, for the rest of his life, practise as a solicitor within seven miles of Tamworth Town Hall. This restraint was upheld.

In *Forster v Suggett* the area of the restraint was the whole of the United Kingdom, and in *Fitch v Dewes* the duration of the restraint was a lifetime. But it must be borne in mind that there are many cases where a restraint has been held void because it was too wide in area or too long in duration. It all depends on the circumstances, since they determine what is reasonable. Recent cases have tended to strike down restraints which prevent a former employee trading at all within a given area, and to uphold covenants which merely prevent him from soliciting the customers of his former employer.

If a restraint is imposed, not by a direct covenant but by some indirect means, the doctrine still applies, and the restraint will be void if it is not reasonable. In *Bull v Pitney-Bowes Ltd* (1967) the plaintiff was employed by the defendant company. It was a condition of his employment that he should become a member of a non-contributory pension scheme. Rule 16 of this scheme provided that a retired member should be liable to forfeit his pension rights if he engaged in any occupation which was in competition with the interests of the defendant company. After 26 years of service, the plaintiff voluntarily retired. He joined another company carrying on a business similar to that of the defendant company. He was warned that he might lose his pension if he did not leave his new employment. He sued for a declaration that rule 16 was in unreasonable restraint of trade and therefore void. Thesiger J. held that rule 16 was void. It was equivalent to a covenant in restraint of trade and was unreasonable. This is one of the comparatively rare cases where the court has stressed the public aspect of the unreasonableness, as distinct from the question of reasonableness between the parties. The judge held that it was contrary to public policy that the community should be deprived of the services of a man skilled in a particular trade.

In *Kores Manufacturing Co Ltd v Kolok Manufacturing Co Ltd* (1959, CA) two companies, manufacturing similar products, agreed that neither would employ any person who had been employed by the other during the last five years. The defendant company broke its promise. The Court of Appeal held that the plaintiff company's action must fail. The agreement was in restraint of trade and was unreasonable. More recently, the Court of Appeal has again considered such covenants, which are intended to prevent the poaching of employees: see *Hanover Insurance Brokers v Schapiro* (1994), in which the court refused to enforce such a covenant. It is clear that if it is to have any chance of enforcement it should be very narrowly drawn so as to be applicable to a small group or class of employees. See also *Dawnay, Day & Co Ltd v de Braconnier d'Alphen* (1998).

Restraints in a contract of sale of a business

The courts are more willing to uphold a restraint on the vendor of a business than one on an employee. The idea behind this is that buyers of a business would not be forthcoming if they could not have protection against competition by the vendor.

Such a restraint is valid, but only if it is connected with the proprietary interest which has been bought. In *British Reinforced Concrete Engineering Co Ltd v Schelff* (1921) the plaintiff company carried on a large business for the manufacture and sale of "BRC" road reinforcements. The defendant had a small business for the sale of "Loop" road reinforcements. The defendant sold his business to the plaintiff company and agreed not to compete with them in the manufacture or sale of road reinforcements. The covenant was held void. The interest which the plaintiff company had bought was the business of selling (not making) "Loop" reinforcements. It was therefore not justifiable to restrain the defendant from competing with the plaintiff company in road reinforcements in general. This case is a good example of unreasonableness residing in the excessive wideness of the forbidden trades: see proposition (4), above. But many more cases turn on unreasonableness of area or duration.

Restraints in other contracts

Proposition (1), above, said that in some cases there is no rigid rule of law that the doctrine of restraint of trade does apply, and no rigid rule of law that it does not. There are at least three fields in which the doctrine has been held to apply: in connection with trade associations; "*solus*" trading agreements; and agreements for exclusive services.

Trade associations

Sometimes a restraint is imposed by the rules of a trade association. One could call these "multilateral" restraints, as distinct from the unilateral restraints we have been considering. The principles are the same—the restrictions are prima facie void, and can only be enforced if they are reasonable.

In *English Hop Growers v Dering* (1928, CA) the defendant was a member of the plaintiff association. He agreed to deliver to the association all the hops grown on his land in 1926. He did not do so, and he was sued. He pleaded that the restraint was unreasonable. The restraint was upheld. He had joined the association voluntarily. It was a sensible attempt to spread the loss caused by excessive stocks of hops having been accumulated during the 1914–1918 war.

On the other side of the line of reasonableness lies *McEllistrim v Ballymacelligott Co-operative Agricultural and Dairy Society* (1919, HL). The society manufactured cheese and butter from milk supplied by members. The rules provided that no member should sell milk otherwise than to the society without consent of the committee; that no member could withdraw from the society unless his shares were transferred or cancelled; that there could be no transfer or cancellation of shares without consent of the committee; and that such consent could be refused without giving reasons. The restraint was held to be unreasonable.

It should be noted that trade unions are exempted from the doctrine of restraint of trade by s.11 of the Trade Union and Labour Relations (Consolidation) Act 1992.

"Solus" trading agreements

It is common for oil companies to enter into *"solus"* agreements with garage owners. An oil company advances money to help with the purchase or development of a garage, and/or offers a rebate on the price of the fuel, and the garage owner undertakes in return to sell only the company's products at the garage. A similar situation obtains in other trades.

In *Esso Petroleum Co Ltd v Harper's Garage (Stourport) Ltd* (1968, HL) the garage company owned two garages and had entered into a *solus* agreement with Esso in respect of each garage. The garage company agreed to buy all its motor fuel from Esso; to keep the garage open at all reasonable hours; and not to sell the garage without ensuring that the purchaser entered into a similar agreement with Esso. Esso agreed to allow a rebate on all fuels bought. The agreement in respect of one garage was to operate for four years and five months; that in respect of the other garage was to operate for 21 years. The latter garage was mortgaged to Esso in return for an advance of £7,000, and the mortgage was not redeemable before the end of the 21 years. The House of Lords held that both agreements were within the ambit of the doctrine of restraint of trade. In particular, the fact that one of the agreements was by way of covenant in a mortgage of land did not exclude the doctrine. The agreements were therefore prima facie void, and could only be enforced if they were reasonable. In the particular circumstances of the case, the crucial consideration in determining reasonableness was the duration of restraints. The agreement which was to last for four years and five months was reasonable; the agreement which was to last for 21 years was not.

In *Alec Lobb (Garages) Ltd v Total Oil (Great Britain) Ltd* (1985, CA), on the other hand, the Court of Appeal, in rather special circumstances, upheld as valid a restraint operating for 21 years.

In *Cleveland Petroleum Co Ltd v Dartstone Ltd* (1969, CA) the Court of Appeal held that the doctrine of restraint of trade does not apply where a person is let into possession of land on the express term that he "ties" himself; consequently, such a person cannot argue that the tie is void. This situation was sharply distinguished from the situation where a person who is already in possession of land ties himself. Whereas in the second case the person is giving up a freedom which he previously had, in the first case he is not; he never had freedom to trade in any manner at all from that land.

Agreements for exclusive services

It sometimes happens that a person enters into an agreement to provide services exclusively for someone else. Such agreements are found amongst professional sportsmen and entertainers, for example. It is not necessary for the person restricted to have a contract of employment, provided that he has agreed not to provide his services to anyone else.

In the field of professional sport, there are also agreements by which employers agree to regulate employment with the effect that one employer agrees not employ a person who has been employed by another party to the agreement. In *Eastham v Newcastle United Football Club* (1964), for example, it was held that the rules of the Football Association and Football League relating to the retention and transfer of professional footballers did not protect any interest of the employer which the law would recognise for this purpose, and consequently they were void. Similarly, in *Greig v Insole* (1978), the organisers of international and English county cricket tried to exclude from their matches players who took part in matches promoted by a private cricketing organisation. The plaintiff successfully challenged this ban.

In *A. Schroeder Music Publishing Co Ltd v Macaulay* (1974, HL) Macaulay, who at the time was an unknown song writer, entered into a standard form agreement with a publishing company, which was in favour of the publishers. He was to hand over all his musical compositions to the publishers, who were to have the full world copyright in the compositions in return for a fixed percentage of any royalties. The term of the agreement was five years, with automatic extension for another five years if the royalties payable to Macaulay within the first five years should exceed £5,000. The publishers could terminate the agreement or assign the benefit of it; Macaulay could not terminate the agreement and could only assign his rights under it with the publishers' consent. The agreement did not put the publishers under any obligation to publish or promote any of Macaulay's compositions. Macaulay sued for a declaration that the agreement was contrary to public policy, as being in unreasonable restraint of trade, and void. The trial judge granted the declaration sought, and this decision was affirmed by the Court of Appeal and the House of Lords.

The *Schroeder* case is important, because the ground on which the House of Lords decided the case was that where there is clear inequality of bargaining power between the parties, the courts can and should inquire into the circumstances to see whether the contract is fair. It follows that the restraint of trade doctrine can apply (as in the *Schroeder* case itself) to contracts for services as well as to contracts of service (contracts of employment strictly so called), and the courts can investigate the fairness of restraints operating during the currency of the employment as well as the restraints which are to operate after the termination of the employment. It follows also that any contract, whether it imposes a restraint or not, can be struck down by the courts for unfairness where there is inequality of bargaining power. But it should be noted that in *National Westminster Bank Plc v Morgan* (1985, HL, see p.138, above) Lord Scarman, in a speech concurred in by the other four Law Lords, said:

"In the field of contract I question whether there is any need in the modern law to erect a general principle of relief against inequality of bargaining power. Parliament has undertaken the task (and it is essentially a legislative task) of enacting such restrictions upon freedom of contract as are in its judgment necessary to relieve against the mischief ... I doubt whether the courts should assume the burden of formulating further restrictions."

General observations on restraint of trade

Three points should be made here. First, where a court holds that a restraint is valid it generally grants an injunction. This is one of the rare instances in the law of contract where an injunction, rather than damages, is the primary remedy.

Secondly, art.81 of the EC Treaty has the force of law in the United Kingdom by virtue of the European Communities Act 1972. Art.81 makes void (unless they are specifically exempted) agreements, decisions and concerted practices which have as their object or effect the prevention, restriction or distortion of competition within the Common Market. This article would clearly apply to a restrictive agreement between a body in the United Kingdom and a body in another Member State of the European Union and it could even apply to an agreement between two or more bodies within the United Kingdom if that agreement adversely affected competition within the European Union.

Thirdly, just as the doctrine of public policy does not apply only to contracts, so the doctrine of restraint of trade (which is an aspect of the public policy doctrine) does not apply only to contracts. This point was emphasised by the House of Lords in *Pharmaceutical Society of Great Britain v Dickson* (1970, HL). A motion passed by a majority of members of the society was held to be subject to the doctrine even though it was binding in honour only. It was further held to be in unreasonable restraint of trade and so void.

INCAPACITY

IN GENERAL all persons have full legal power to enter into any contract they wish and thus bind themselves; but a few groups of persons do not have this power in full, and they are said to be under incapacity. The groups concerned are minors, persons lacking mental capacity, drunkards and corporations. Different rules apply to these groups, which will be considered separately.

MINORS

Incapacity is imposed by law upon a minor in an attempt to protect him from the consequences of his inexperience. A minor is a person under the age of 18.

Minors' contracts are divisible into two groups: (1) some contracts are valid; and (2) some contracts are voidable in the sense that they are binding on the minor unless he repudiates them. Apart from these two groups, the general common law rule was that minors were not bound by contracts they entered into unless they ratified them after reaching majority.

Two points are common to all kinds of minors' contracts: (a) a parent is not liable on his child's contracts, unless the child was acting as the parent's agent; and (b) a minor's contracts cannot be validated by the consent or authorisation of his parent.

Valid contracts

Contract for necessaries

Contracts for necessaries are not affected by the Minors' Contracts Act 1987 and therefore remain subject to the common law rules. Necessaries may be goods or services. A minor is bound by a contract for necessaries only if it is, on the whole, for his benefit; if it is not, the minor is not bound by it, unless he ratifies it after reaching his majority. He is not bound by one entire contract comprising necessaries and non-necessaries.

So far as goods are concerned, necessaries are statutorily defined in s.3(3) of the Sale of Goods Act 1979 as "goods suitable to the condition in life of the minor ... and to his actual requirements at the time of the sale and delivery". Thus whether a particular article is a necessary or not depends upon two factors: the condition in life of the minor and his actual requirements at the time.

In the nineteenth century juries showed a marked tendency to find that luxuries supplied to young men of high social standing were necessaries. It was stated in the House of Commons that in one case an Oxford jury held that champagne and wild ducks were necessaries to an undergraduate minor. The courts gradually overcame this tendency by laying it down as a rule of law that "mere luxuries" could not be necessaries, and by holding that the question whether other goods were or were not necessaries was a question of mixed law and fact. Thus it was for the judge to rule whether a particular article in a particular case could be a necessary, and for the jury to say whether it was a necessary.

In considering this question, the jury had to consider not only the condition in life of the minor but also his actual requirements. In *Nash v Inman* (1908, CA) a Savile Row tailor sued a minor, a Cambridge undergraduate, for the price of clothes supplied, including 11 fancy waistcoats. The tailor failed in his action because he did not prove that the minor was not already adequately supplied with clothes. If it turns out that the minor was already adequately supplied, the plaintiff will fail even though he did not know this. See, however, s.3 of the Minors' Contracts Act 1987, considered below.

Necessary goods have been defined by statute. On the other

hand, necessary services have not been defined, but the tests are the same as for necessary goods. Necessary services include education (both liberal and vocational) and medical and legal advice. In *Chapple v Cooper* (1844) it was held that the provision of a funeral ordered by a minor widow for her deceased husband was a necessary.

If money is lent to a minor to buy necessaries, the loan as such is not recoverable, but the lender can sue for such part of the loans as represents a reasonable price for any necessaries that have in fact been bought by the minor.

A minor's contract for necessaries is a valid contract. There is no doubt that it is valid in the sense that the minor himself can sue on it, and there is no doubt that the other party can sue on it when he has performed his part. But there is some doubt whether the other party can sue on the contract where it is executory; that is, where the other party has not performed his part. Suppose a minor orders a (necessary) suit and then, before it has been delivered he says he does not want it. Can he be sued for non-acceptance?

There are three points in favour of the view that a minor is not liable on an executory contract for necessaries. (1) In *Nash v Inman* (above) Fletcher Moulton L.J. said that a minor was liable *re* (because he had been supplied with the thing), and not *consensu* (because he had contracted). In the same case, however, Buckley L.J. said that a minor is liable in contract. (2) The minor is liable to pay a reasonable price, not necessarily the price agreed in the contract. Section 3(2) of the Sale of Goods Act 1979 provides: "Where necessaries are sold and delivered to a minor ... he must pay a reasonable price for them." That does not look like a consensual contract. But it is not conclusive: a possible analysis would be that the law is interfering with one particular term—the price—without destroying the contract as such. (3) Section 3(3) of the Sale of Goods Act says: "'necessaries' means goods suitable to the condition in life of the minor ... and to his actual requirements at the time of the sale and delivery". It is arguable that this means that a minor can only be sued on a contract for necessary goods where they have been delivered. But the section does not say that in terms; it is dealing with the situation where necessaries have been sold and delivered, not with the situation where necessaries have been contracted for but not yet sold and delivered, which is the case with an executory contract.

There is one case in favour of the view that a minor can be liable on an executory contract for necessaries. In *Roberts v Gray* (1913, CA) the plaintiff was a famous billiards player, who agreed to take the infant defendant on a world billiards tour, and to pay for his board and lodging and travelling expenses. This was a contract for necessaries in the sense that its object was to teach the defendant the profession of a billiards player; a kind of education. Roberts expended time and trouble and incurred certain liabilities in making preparations. A dispute arose between the parties and, before the tour began, Gray repudiated the contract. He was held liable in damages. Hamilton L.J. said:

"I am unable to appreciate why a contract which is in itself binding, because it is a contract for necessaries not qualified by unreasonable terms, can cease to be binding merely because it is still executory."

The contract in the case was not wholly executory, but that point was not relied on in the decision.

It may be that one has to draw a distinction and say that contracts for necessary goods are not enforceable against the minor if executory, and that contracts for necessary services (which is what *Roberts v Gray* was about) are.

Contracts of employment

A contract of employment is binding on a minor if, viewed as a whole, it is for his benefit. Consequently, this type of contract is often referred to as a "beneficial contract of service". If a contract of service is not beneficial it will only be binding on the minor if he ratifies it on attaining his majority. The minor may be bound even though some of the clauses of the contract are to his disadvantage. In *Clements v London and N.W. Railway Co* (1894, CA) a minor porter agreed to join an insurance scheme, to which his employers contributed, and to give up his right to sue for personal injuries under the Employers' Liability Act 1880. Under the insurance scheme he could get compensation without proving negligence and without litigation; on the other hand, compensation under the scheme might be smaller than the amount recoverable under the Act. It was held that the contract was on the whole beneficial to him, and binding on him.

On the other hand, in *De Francesco v Barnum* (1890) a girl was apprenticed for stage dancing by a deed which provided that she should be entirely at the disposal of the master; that she should get no pay unless he actually employed her, which he was not bound to do; that he could send her abroad; that he could put an end to the contract if, after fair trial, he found her unsuitable; and that she should not accept any professional engagement or contract matrimony without his consent. It was held that the contract was unreasonably harsh and was invalid.

The same principles have been extended by analogy to contracts which are similar to employment contracts. In *Doyle v White City Stadium Ltd* (1935, CA) a minor professional boxer was engaged to fight for £3,000, win, draw or lose, subject to the Rules of the British Boxing Board of Control. Under these rules a boxer who was disqualified forfeited his "purse". Doyle was disqualified. He sued for the £3,000. He failed. It was held that his contract with the Board was on the whole beneficial to him. This was so, even though in the particular case it operated against him. In *Chaplin v Leslie Frewin (Publishers) Ltd* (1966, CA) the Court of Appeal unanimously held that a contract whereby a minor agreed to tell his life story to a publishing company in return for royalties on the resulting book was a contract analogous to a service contract. The majority of the court (Lord Denning dissenting) held that the particular contract was beneficial to the minor, and was therefore binding on him.

But these principles do not apply to a minor's trading contracts. It has long been settled that a minor is not bound by a trading contract, even if it is beneficial. He is not liable for the price of goods supplied to him for the purpose of trade; he is not liable for non-delivery of goods which he has sold as a trader; and he cannot be made bankrupt for trade debts. There is no precise definition of "trade" for this purpose. The principle seems to be that it is trade if the minor's capital is at risk.

Whatever may be the true position with regard to contracts for necessaries, there is no doubt that beneficial contracts of employment, and analogous contracts, are binding on the minor even when they are executory.

The issues that arise in minor's contracts received recent consideration in *Proform Sports Management v Proactive Sports Management Ltd* (2006). The footballer Wayne Rooney entered into an agreement at the age of 15 with a company that provided management and representation services for professional footballers. It was held that such a contract did not fall into the class of contracts analogous to contracts for necessaries, employment or education which are enforceable against a minor. The sort of work undertaken by players' representatives was not essential to the player's training or livelihood, nor did they enable him to earn a living or advance his skills. This case was also concerned with the issue of inducing a person to break a contract, which is itself a separate tort (see p.198 above). The decision makes clear that where, as in this case, a minor is entitled to avoid a contract there can be no action for the tort of wrongfully procuring a breach of contract.

Voidable contracts

The contracts in this group are voidable in the sense that the minor can repudiate them before majority or within a reasonable time afterwards. The other party cannot repudiate. The most common types of contract of this sort are contracts to buy or rent land and contracts to acquire shares in a company.

When a minor repudiates such a contract he is relieved of all liabilities (e.g. rent) that accrue after the repudiation, but he can be sued for liabilities (rent is a good example again) which have already accrued.

The minor can recover back money which he has paid under the contract only if there has been a total failure of consideration. In *Corpe v Overton* (1833) a minor agreed to enter into a partnership and paid a deposit of £100, the deposit to be forfeited if he failed to execute the partnership deed. He repudiated the contract, never did execute the partnership deed, and sued to recover back the £100. He won, as there had been a total failure of consideration. In *Steinberg v Scala (Leeds) Ltd* (1923, CA) a minor applied for shares in a company and then, after they had been allotted to her, repudiated the contract. She was freed from liability for future calls on the shares, but she failed in her action to recover back the money she had already paid. There was not total failure of consideration; she had got the very shares she had contracted for.

The possibility of recovering back money paid if there is a total failure of consideration is a feature of contract law generally, but the point that distinguishes minors' voidable contracts is that the minor can recover back even where the total failure of consideration is caused by his own act, as in *Corpe v Overton*.

The Minors' Contracts Act 1987

Until the Minors' Contracts Act 1987 was passed, contracts entered into by minors were affected by the Infants Relief Act 1874. Section 1(1)(a) of the 1987 Act repeals the 1874 Act. This means that the common law rules considered earlier in this chapter still prevail. There are two substantive provisions in the Act: s.2 affects guarantees and s.3 makes provision for restitution in certain circumstances. These are considered in turn below.

Guarantees

Section 2 makes a guarantee of a minor's contractual obligations enforceable against a guarantor irrespective of the fact that the main contractual obligation is not enforceable against the minor. This means that the guarantee of an unenforceable minor's contract is as effective as if the minor had been an adult. It does not affect contracts for necessaries, since, as was seen earlier, a minor is obliged to pay a reasonable price for them.

Restitution

Section 3 provides that where a contract is unenforceable against a minor, or he repudiates it, the court may require the minor to transfer to the other party any "property acquired" by him under the contract or any property "representing it"; but the court must consider that it is "just and equitable to do so". This means that in a case like *Nash v Inman* (where the minor was supplied with fancy waistcoats) the court would now have the power to order the minor to restore to the vendor the fancy waistcoats. If the minor has disposed of the property for value, he could still be ordered to give up the money or property representing the original property; if he has consumed or disposed of the goods and obtained nothing in return, he cannot be required to compensate the other person.

Quasi-contract and restitution

The doctrine of quasi-contract has grown up over the years to provide a remedy where one person has become unjustly enriched at the expense of another. One type of action in quasi-contract is an "action for money had and received by the defendant to the plaintiff's use". These rules are preserved by s.3(2) of the Minors' Contracts Act 1987.

The principles that govern a minor's liability in tort also govern his liability in quasi-contract. Just as an action in tort can be brought against a minor except where that would be an indirect way of enforcing a contract, so an action in quasi-contract can be brought against a minor except where that would be an indirect way of enforcing a contract against him. Thus in *Bristow v Eastman* (1794) a minor apprentice who had embezzled his master's property was held liable in quasi-contract.

That is the common law position, but equity has developed a principle which requires the minor to give up what he has got under the contract if the contract was fraudulently induced. This principle of restitution, however, operates on rather a narrow front. Where the minor is still in possession of the thing transferred to him under the contract, there is no doubt that an order for restitution can and will be made.

Where the minor obtains goods by fraud and then ceases to possess them, the position is more doubtful. In *Stocks v Wilson* (1913) the minor defendant, by fraudulently misrepresenting that he was of full age, induced the plaintiff to sell some goods to him. When he had obtained the goods, the defendant sold some of them. Lush J. held him liable to account to the plaintiff for the proceeds. But in *Leslie v Sheill* (1914, CA), *Stocks v Wilson* was criticised, though it was not formally overruled. In *Leslie v Sheill* a minor obtained a loan of £400 by fraudulently misrepresenting that he was of full age. It was held by the Court of Appeal that the equitable doctrine of restitution did not extend to the restoration of money borrowed. Lord Sumner said: "Restitution stopped where repayment began." It is difficult to reconcile *Stocks v Wilson* with *R. Leslie v Sheill*. One can say that the former case deals with goods sold to the minor and the latter with money lent to the minor; but that does not seem to be a difference in principle. It is probably better to go by *Leslie v Sheill* now, and say that where the goods have been resold or the money spent, restitution will not be granted. If the goods bought, or the actual notes or coins borrowed, are still in the hands of the minor, restitution will be granted.

PERSONS LACKING MENTAL CAPACITY

A person whose property is subject to the control of the court under Pt VII of the Mental Health Act 1983 appears to be incapable of entering into a contract. In the case of a person whose property is not subject to the control of the court under the Act, mental incapacity is not a ground for setting aside the contract unless the incapacity was known to the other party. Where the incapacity is not known to the other party and the affliction is not apparent, the validity of the contract must be judged by the same standards as a contract made by a person of sound mind and may only be set aside on the same principles. See *Hart v O'Connor* (1985, PC).

Section 3 of the Sale of Goods Act 1979 not only deals with minors, but also with "a person who by reason of mental incapacity ... is incompetent to contract". The section provides that, where necessaries are sold and delivered to such a person, "he must pay a reasonable price for them".

DRUNKEN PERSONS

If a person, when he enters into a contract, is in such a state of drunkenness as not to know what he is doing, and if this fact is appreciated by the other party, the contract is voidable at his instance. The question of having to prove the other party's knowledge of the drunkenness can hardly arise, because it is virtually impossible that a person could be so drunk as not to know what he is doing without that fact being obvious to the other party. In relation to necessaries, s.3 of the Sale of Goods Act applies to drunkenness in the same way as it does to mental incapacity.

CORPORATIONS

A corporation is, in law, a person; it is an artificial legal person. A corporation may be a "corporation sole", such as the vicar of a parish, or a "corporation aggregate", such as the mayor and corporation of a borough. Some corporations are created by Royal Charter from the Crown, such as universities. Some are created by special Act of Parliament, such as new universities, which were formerly polytechnics. Some corporations are set up under the provisions of a general Act of Parliament, notably trading companies set up under successive Companies Acts. The current statute is the Companies Act 2006.

A corporation created by charter has the same contractual

powers as a natural person of full age and capacity. The contractual capacity of a statutory corporation is subject to the doctrine of ultra vires.

The powers of a corporation set up by a special Act of Parliament are invariably set out in the creating Act. The powers of a corporation, such as a normal trading company, set up under the former Companies Act 1985, used to be limited by the objects as set forth in the memorandum of association. Any activity outside the objects clause in the memorandum of association was ultra vires (beyond its powers) and therefore void. The new Companies Act 2006 no longer requires a statement of objects and, unless a company includes a statement of objects in its articles, it will be taken to have unlimited capacity.

The doctrine of ultra vires was intended to protect investors in, and creditors of, the company, by enabling them to know that their money could only be spent on certain specified objects. In practice the doctrine's main effect had been to deny a remedy to outside persons dealing with the company by way of trade. The position is now covered by s.39(1) of the Companies Act 2006, which states:

"The validity of an act done by a company shall not be called into question on the ground of lack of capacity by reason of anything in the company's constitution."

The object of this section, like its predecessor in the 1985 Act, is to abolish the ultra vires rule as regards innocent third parties who deal in good faith with the company. Hence, contracts made by third parties who deal in good faith with the company remain valid and enforceable.

PART FOUR

WHO IS WITHIN THE AGREEMENT

CHAPTER TWELVE

PRIVITY OF CONTRACT

THE DOCTRINE of privity is to the effect that a person who is not a party to a contract cannot enjoy the benefits or suffer the burdens of that contract. It has been mentioned earlier in this book in Chapter 2, in connection with the rule that consideration must move from the promisee, and in Chapter 5, in connection with exemption clauses. It will thus be seen that the doctrine of privity has wide ramifications in the law of contract. But it is important to appreciate its limits.

WHAT THE DOCTRINE IS

The doctrine is often stated in this way: a contract cannot confer benefits on strangers, nor can it impose burdens on strangers. A "stranger" in this context simply means a person who is not a party to the contract.

In the case of *Tweddle v Atkinson* (1861) an agreement was made between William Guy and John Tweddle by which each promised to pay a sum of money to William Tweddle. William Tweddle was the son of John Tweddle, and he was about to marry the daughter of William Guy. William Guy died without having paid, and William Tweddle sued his executors. His action failed, on the ground

195

that William Tweddle was "a stranger to the consideration". See also Chapter 2, p.36 and p.206, below.

In *Dunlop Pneumatic Tyre Co Ltd v Selfridge* (1915, HL) the plaintiff company sold some tyres to Dew & Co, on the terms that Dew & Co would not resell them below certain prices and that when Dew & Co came to resell the tyres they would extract a similar undertaking from their purchaser. Dew & Co sold the tyres to Selfridge, who agreed to observe the restrictions and to pay to Dunlop the sum of £5 for each tyre sold in breach of the agreement. Selfridge sold some of the tyres below the fixed price, and Dunlop sued him. Dunlop were met by the defence that they were not parties to the agreement with Selfridge and had furnished no consideration. The House of Lords gave judgment for the defendant. Lord Haldane L.C. said:

> "My Lords, in the law of England certain principles are fundamental. One is that only a person who is a party to a contract can sue on it ... A second principle is that if a person with whom a contract not under seal has been made is to be able to enforce it consideration must have been given by him."

It will be noticed that Lord Haldane referred to two principles: that a stranger to a contract cannot sue on it, and that a stranger to the consideration cannot sue. The tendency nowadays is to regard these two statements as two aspects of the same principle. This is because of the notion of contract as bargain. Even if a person is mentioned in an agreement and stated to be the promisee, if he gives no consideration he will be not able to sue; though he is a party to the agreement, he is not a party to the bargain, and so is not a party to the contract. *Dunlop v Selfridge* put the stamp of House of Lords authority on the doctrine of privity. In *Scruttons Ltd v Midland Silicones Ltd* (1962) the House reaffirmed the doctrine in the context of exemption clauses: see p.92, above.

THE LIMITS OF THE DOCTRINE

1   The doctrine of privity does not forbid assignment of contractual rights. Assignment is a big subject, and the whole of the next chapter will be devoted to it.

2   The doctrine does not forbid agency. That is another big topic, which forms the subject-matter of Chapter 14.

3   There are many instances in land law where the doctrine does not apply. For example, a lease is a contract, but it also creates proprietary rights. Thus, if A grants a lease of land to B, the lease will contain a number of covenants (promises) by the tenant, e.g. to pay the rent, and a number of covenants by the landlord, e.g. to keep the premises in repair. As between A and B there is privity of contract, and so there is no difficulty about the enforcement of the covenants. But suppose A sells the freehold of the land to X, and B assigns the lease to Y. The law is that, although there is no privity of contract between X and Y, either may enforce a covenant in the original lease against the other. Similarly, when a freeholder sells his land, he can, subject to certain conditions, impose restrictions on its use which will be binding, not only on the immediate purchaser, but also on his successors in title. A restrictive covenant of this kind is a species of property and is said to "run with the land". Attempts have been made to extend the idea from land to goods, as will be seen.

4   In the law of trusts the doctrine of privity has no application. If A and B by contract create a trust for the benefit of C, C has a proprietary right in the trust property and can directly enforce his right, though he was not a party to the contract. Attempts have been made to extend this trust idea into the field of pure contract by arguing in various situations that a notional trust has been created: see p.199.

5   The legislature has intervened, in a rather piecemeal fashion, to provide some exceptions to the doctrine of privity. This has been notably so in the field of insurance. Most recently the Contracts (Rights of Third Parties) Act 1999 has created a device by which parties can give a third party the right to enforce a contract. In time this may make some of the case law which has sought to circumvent the doctrine of privity less important since it will become unnecessary. At the moment, however, many commercial agreements expressly include a clause making clear that there is no intention to create any legal rights under the Act. In these cases,

consideration of the pre-existing case law can still be relevant. The Act is considered below, p.205.

6   Where there is a contract between A and C to which B is not a party, there may also be another contract, between B and A. Where that is so, B will of course be able to sue on the A–B contract. That was the situation in *Shanklin Pier Ltd v Detel Products Ltd* (1951), which was looked in at Chapter 4 at p.65. In that case the pier company, although shut out by the doctrine of privity from suing the suppliers of the defective paint on the contract for the sale of the paint, were able to obtain a complete remedy by suing them on the collateral contract. Similarly, in *Charnock v Liverpool Corporation* (1968, CA) the plaintiff's car was damaged in a collision with another car, whose driver was solely to blame. The plaintiff took his car to a garage to be repaired. His insurance company's assessor attended. The insurance company later told the garage that it was in order for them to carry out the repair "as per your estimate". The garage took eight weeks to do the repairs, whereas a reasonable time would have been five weeks. The plaintiff sued the garage for £53, the cost of hiring another car for three weeks. The garage argued that there was only one contract, between them and the insurers, and that, as the plaintiff was not a party to that contract, he could not sue them. It was held by the Court of Appeal that that was not the only contract; although there was a contract between the insurers and the garage to pay for the repairs, there was also a contract between the garage and the plaintiff to carry out the repairs, and it was an implied term of that contract that the garage would carry out the repairs within a reasonable time—so the plaintiff won.

7.   Inducing a breach of contract is a tort. If C induces B to break his (B's) contract with A, A can sue C in tort. Thus, whilst the doctrine of privity ensures that no contractual duty can be imposed by the A–B contract on C, the law of tort does impose on C the negative duty of not interfering with the A–B contract.

ATTEMPTS TO EVADE THE DOCTRINE

The doctrine of privity often causes inconvenience in practice, and many attempts have been made to evade it. These attempts have centred on three ideas, which will be considered in turn.

The trust idea

In the first 30 years of the last century it looked as though the idea of the trust was going to provide a path round the doctrine of privity. In *Les Affreteurs Réunis S.A. v Walford* (1919, HL) Walford, a broker, negotiated a charter party between ship owners and charterers. By a clause in the charter party the owners promised the charterers to pay Walford a commission of three per cent on the estimated gross amount of hire. Walford sued the owners for his commission. The charterers were not made parties to the action. Walford applied to join them as parties, and the owners then agreed that the case should proceed as though the charterers were co-plaintiffs. Walford won. Lord Birkenhead said: "in such cases charterers can sue as trustees on behalf of the broker". The significant point is that, as the charterers were treated as trustees for the broker, the broker could ask them to sue the owners on his behalf, and, if they refused to sue, the broker could then join the charterers as co-defendants and proceed with the action as sole plaintiff. Thus, where the court is willing to find a trust, the beneficiary may himself enforce the contract by which that trust was set up, even though he was not a party to that contract.

In later cases, however, the courts have set their faces against this idea. One factor in this situation is that if it is held that a contract between A and B has created a trust in favour of C, then the terms of the A–B contract cannot be altered, however much A and B may want to alter them. This point was emphasised in *Re Schebsman* (1944, CA). Schebsman was employed by two companies. By a contract made between him and them, one of the companies agreed to pay £5,500 in six annual instalments. The money was to be paid to Schebsman, or, if he died, to his widow, or, if she died, to his daughter. During the instalment period, Schebsman first went bankrupt and then died. His trustee in bankruptcy claimed a declaration that all sums payable under the agreement formed part of the estate of the debtor (Schebsman). The trial judge dismissed the claim, and the Court of Appeal affirmed his decision. One of the arguments in the case was that Schebsman was a trustee of the company's promise, holding it on behalf of his wife and daughter. This argument was rejected. Du Parcq L.J. said:

"Unless an intention to create a trust is clearly to be collected from the language used and the circumstances of the case, I think that the court ought not to be astute to discover indications of such an intention. I have little doubt that in the present case both parties (and certainly the debtor) intended to keep alive their common law right to vary consensually the terms of the obligation undertaken by the company, and if circumstances had changed in the debtor's lifetime injustice might have been done by holding that a trust had been created and that those terms were accordingly unalterable.'

Lord Greene M.R. in the same case said:

"It is not legitimate to import into the contract the idea of a trust when the parties have given no indication that such was their intention. To interpret this contract as creating a trust would, in my judgment, be to disregard the dividing line between the case of a trust and the simple case of a contract made between two persons for the benefit of a third."

In *Re Schebsman* the company was quite willing to pay instalments to Mrs Schebsman and so it did not matter to her that there was held to be no trust in her favour; it was sufficient that, as the court held, payment by the company to her was due performance of the contract. That stopped the trustee in bankruptcy getting his hands on the money. But if the company had refused to pay her, that would have shown up the difference between a trust in favour of Mrs Schebsman and a mere contract for the benefit of Mrs Schebsman. In the former case she would have been able to sue; in the latter she would not.

It is also now the case that an agreement to pay an agent commission of the kind that begat the trust idea might now be covered by the Contracts (Rights of Third Parties) Act 1999 (see *Nisshin Shipping Co Ltd v Cleeves* (2003) p.242, below).

ATTEMPTS TO EVADE THE DOCTRINE

The restrictive covenant idea

Another attack on the doctrine of privity has taken the form of trying to carry over into the general law of contract the land law notion of covenants running with the land.

The land law case which has been most strongly relied on for this purpose is *Tulk v Moxhay* (1848). In that case the purchaser of the garden in the centre of Leicester Square entered into a covenant with the vendor promising not to build on the garden. The covenant was held to be binding in equity on a subsequent purchaser of the garden. At the time it was given, this decision was based on the fact that the subsequent purchaser had notice of the covenant. But in later years "the rule in *Tulk v Moxhay*" (as it came to be called) ceased to be based solely upon notice and became limited to situations where the original vendor or his successors retained a proprietary interest in other land in the neighbourhood which stood to benefit from the restrictive covenant.

This development made it very difficult to argue that the rule in *Tulk v Moxhay* could apply to contracts not concerned with land. In *Taddy v Sterious* (1904) the argument was tried. The plaintiffs were tobacco manufacturers, and they wanted to prevent retailers from selling the tobacco below a certain minimum price. They attached to each packet a printed notice stating that the tobacco was sold "on the express condition that retail dealers do not sell it below the prices above set forth". The plaintiffs sold some of the tobacco to a firm of wholesalers, and that firm resold it to the defendants, who were retailers. The defendants had notice of the condition, but they nevertheless sold the tobacco at a price below the minimum laid down. The plaintiffs sued for a declaration that the defendants were bound by the condition. They argued that the rule in *Tulk v Moxhay* should be applied. This argument was rejected by the judge. He said:

"Conditions of this kind do not run with goods and cannot be imposed upon them. Subsequent purchasers, therefore, do not take subject to any conditions which the court can enforce."

(Resale price maintenance is now governed by statute.)

Nevertheless, the argument from analogy with covenants running with the land found favour with the Privy Council in Lord *Strathcona Steamship Co v Dominion Coal Co* (1926, PC). The owners of the steamer Lord Strathcona chartered her to X. The contract provided that X should be free to use the ship on the St Lawrence River for each summer season and should surrender her to the owners in the November of each year. During the currency of the charter party, while the ship was in the possession of the owners, they sold her to Y, who in turn resold her to Z. Z knew of the charter party but refused to deliver the ship to X for the summer season. X obtained an injunction in the Canadian courts restraining Z from using the ship in any way inconsistent with the charter party; the Judicial Committee of the Privy Council affirmed this decision. They held in effect that Z was caught by the rule in *Tulk v Moxhay*. The Privy Council recognised that, for the rule to apply, the person seeking to enforce the restriction must have a proprietary interest in its subject-matter. They said that this condition was satisfied because X had an interest in the ship. But there are two difficulties in that reasoning. First, that interest was merely conferred on X by the very contract which he was seeking to enforce against a third party; it was nothing like the independent proprietary interest that the rule in *Tulk v Moxhay* requires. Secondly, there is clear authority for the proposition that a charter party does not give the charterer any right of property in the ship.

It is not surprising that Lord Wright M.R. said, in *Clore v Theatrical Properties Ltd* (1936), that the Strathcona principle must in any event be confined to "the very special case of a ship under a charter party". In *Port Line Ltd v Ben Line Steamers Ltd* (1958) Diplock J. went further; he declared that the *Strathcona* case was wrongly decided. Nevertheless, in the later case of *Swiss Bank Corporation v Lloyds Bank Ltd* (1979), the judge said that the *Strathcona* principle had continuing validity. More recently, in *Law Debenture Trust Corporation Plc v Ural Caspian Oil Corporation Ltd* (1993), Hoffmann J. proceeded on the basis that this was correct. Too much weight, however, should perhaps not be placed on this case since this was an interlocutory proceeding where ultimately the judge did not have to choose between the competing views, on which he clearly had doubts. In any event, he stated: "One thing is beyond doubt: it [the principle] does not provide a panacea for outflanking the doctrine of privity of contract."

The result of the cases therefore seems to be that, whilst restrictive covenants are not altogether unarguable in the case of charter parties, outside this area it seems unlikely that the doctrine has any application.

The section 56 idea

Section 56(1) of the Law of Property Act 1925 declares:

"A person may take an immediate or other interest in land or other property, or the benefit of any condition, right of entry, covenant or agreement over or respecting land or other property, although he may not be named as a party to the conveyance or other instrument."

This enactment has been used as a weapon with which to attack the doctrine of privity. It was argued in several cases that the subsection had destroyed the doctrine. The argument was that the phrase "other property" included a contractual right, and that the phrase "not ... named as a party" was equivalent to not being a party; therefore the subsection empowered a person to sue on a contract even though he was not a party to it. This argument gained the support of Lord Denning, but it was rejected by other judges in a number of cases and was finally killed off by the decision of the House of Lords in *Beswick v Beswick* (1968). Peter Beswick was a coal merchant. As he was getting on in years he contracted to sell the business to his nephew John. The consideration was a promise by John to pay Peter £6 and 10s. a week for as long as he lived, and, if Peter's wife survived him, to pay her £5 a week for as long as she lived. John did pay Peter's widow one sum of £5 and then refused to pay any more. The widow sued John for arrears and for specific performance of the contract. She sued in two capacities; as administratrix of Peter's estate and in her personal capacity. The House of Lords held that, as administratrix, the widow could obtain specific performance, but not in her personal capacity. The argument founded on s.56(1) was rejected. The majority in the House took the view that s.56(1) was confined in its application to covenants relating to land, and the whole House was of the opinion that it did not diminish the doctrine of privity in the field of general contract law.

THE PRESENT STATE OF THE LAW

Although the House of Lords, by their decision in *Beswick v Beswick*, decisively rejected the s.56(1) attack on the doctrine of privity, they cleared up one of the more objectionable features of the doc-trine. It was argued for the nephew that, though the widow might be entitled, in her capacity as administratrix, to damages for breach of the contract which the nephew made with her husband, she should not have substantial damages, but only nominal damages, and that she should not have specific performance. The basis of this argument was that, in her capacity as administratrix, the widow could only sue for loss which had been suffered by her husband's estate, and that the estate had not suffered any loss. The nephew's failure to make payment to the widow was no loss to the estate. The House of Lords rejected this argument. Granted that the estate had suffered no loss, the estate nevertheless had the right to enforce the contract. In the circumstances of the case the most just way of enforcing the contract was to order specific performance, and there was no impediment to the making of that order. The House also indicated that if, in other circumstances, justice required the making of an order for substantial damages, that order could be made.

An interesting application occurred in *Jackson v Horizon Holidays Ltd* (1975, CA). A man took his wife and children on a holiday, which turned out to be disastrous; he recovered damages not only for his own disappointment but also for the disappointment of his wife and children. But in *Woodar Investment Development Ltd v Wimpey Construction UK Ltd* (1980, HL) the House of Lords, though not overruling *Jackson*'s case, severely criticised some of its reasoning. It was said to be defensible because it related to a special category of situation, such as buying a meal in a restaurant or hiring transport for a group, where some modification of the general principle is conceded as an exception. Alternatively, it might be defended on the grounds that Mr Jackson's own distress was increased by his awareness of his family's discomfiture. This case nevertheless strongly endorsed the general principle that there was no general right for a third party to claim damages. Lord Scarman said:

"If the opportunity arises, I hope the House will reconsider *Tweddle v Atkinson* and the other cases which stand guard over this unjust rule."

Since that view was expressed, the law of privity of contract has developed in two ways. In *Linden Gardens Trust Ltd v Lenesta Sludge Disposals Ltd* (1993) the House of Lords seemed to move towards a more generous view of third-party rights. Here A

204

contracted with B for the construction of a large building and office development. Before the building work was completed A assigned its interest to C. A subsequently sued B for defective work that had taken place after the assignment. B's argument was that A had suffered no loss because, at the time, the property belonged to C. The House of Lords rejected this argument basing their decision on analogous principles in the carriage of goods. In this case B always knew that A was not going to occupy the premises itself and therefore it was perfectly foreseeable that any breaches by B would impact upon someone in the position of C. Part of the justification for such a principle is the "black hole" argument. If in this sort of situation the doctrine of privity prevents C from suing and A could only recover nominal damages, then B's liability would disappear altogether despite its breach of contract. Incidentally, Lord Browne-Wilkinson regarded it as "apparently established that, if a defective meal or holiday is supplied, the contracting party can recover damages not only for his own bad meal or unhappy holiday, but also for that of his guests or family". A similar approach was adopted by the Court of Appeal in the later case of *Darlington Borough Council v Wiltshier Northern Ltd* (1995), where Steyn L.J. took the opportunity to comment trenchantly on what he regarded as a technical and unjust rule. In *Alfred McAlpine Construction Ltd v Panatown Ltd* (2001) the House of Lords again considered these issues but, because the case to some extent turns upon the particular arrangements involved, it is difficult to be sure what broader principles can be extracted. In particular, it is not clear how broad the principle is to be deduced from the *Linden Gardens* case. The result of these cases currently appears to be that, whilst the third party has no independent right to bring an action, a contracting party who recovers damages may be under a duty to make restitution of those damages to the third party. The third party cannot, nevertheless, compel an action to be brought in the first place.

It would be surprising if there were to be no further case law in this area. On the one hand, the 1999 Act is meant to provide a mechanism by which parties can confer rights directly on third parties. There is then an argument that, if this is so, a restrictive view should be taken when the parties themselves have declined to articulate third-party rights. On the other hand, as noted earlier, many commercial agreements expressly exclude the operation of the Act. If this trend continues it is perhaps more likely that subsequent case law will have to explore the issue.

A second major development, as has been mentioned, is the enactment of the Contracts (Rights of Third Parties) Act 1999. Section 1(1)(a) provides that a third party can enforce a term of the contract if "the contract expressly provides." The result is that an arrangement such as that envisaged in *Tweddle v Atkinson*, above, p.195, could now be directly enforced by William Tweddle. Section 1(1)(b) deals with the situation where a term "purports to confer a benefit" on a third party. For example, in *Beswick v Beswick*, above, p.203, the contract between Peter Beswick and his nephew conferred a benefit on Mrs Beswick. She would now be able to sue the nephew directly under this provision rather than in her capacity as administratrix of her husband's estate, a status which in the actual case was entirely fortuitous. Section 1(2) makes clear that s.1(1)(b) does not apply if "the parties did not intend the term to be enforceable by the third party." This reflects the fact that the operation of the Act is essentially governed by the choice of the parties themselves. Many contracts expressly make clear that there is no intention to create rights under the Act. A failure to make this clear will mean that the court will have to decide, applying the objective approach, what is the proper construction of the contract. A recent example of a court doing this is to be found in *Prudential Assurance Co Ltd v Ayres* (2008). The Court of Appeal ultimately held that, having regard to the intentions of the parties and the commercial background, the Act had no place in the agreement concerned. Interestingly, in the lower court Lindsay J. expressed the view that the effect of s.1(1)(b) is that the benefit to be conferred on the third party does not have to be the predominant purpose or intent behind the term. It was also no objection that the term conferred a benefit on someone other than the third party. As regards both these points, this approach seems, with respect, entirely correct since otherwise the Act would be unlikely to have much practical application since both circumstances are likely to be very common. If the Act applies, s.1(5) allows the third party to enforce a term of the contract in just the same way as a party to the contract. One problem this throws up is what is to happen if the parties wish to cancel or vary the rights of the third party? This is covered by s.2(3) which allows the parties, if they wish, to include a term dispensing with the need for the third party to consent to a variation in the contract. In the absence of such a provision the third party's rights are protected, unless he consents to a variation, if one of three conditions is satisfied: (1) that the third party has communicated his assent to the relevant term; (2) that the third party has relied on the term and the promisor is aware of this; or (3) that the promisor could reasonably be expected to have foreseen that the third party would do so. Clearly without such a provision, the rights bestowed upon a third party would be ineffectual. There is also a residual power in s.2(5) to enable a court to dispense with any consent that the third party may be required to give for a variation. This might be helpful where, for example, the person's whereabouts are unknown or he was incapacitated.

By virtue of s.3 the third party will be subject to any defences or set-offs available to the parties. For example, A contracts to sell goods to B who is to pay the contract price to a third party, C. If A delivers defective goods and C sues for the price, B is entitled to reduce or extinguish the price by reason of the breach of contract. Provision is also made for the interaction of third parties and legislation such as the Unfair Contract Terms Act 1977. Section 7(2) states that a third party cannot rely on s.2(2) of the 1977 Act. This somewhat controversial provision means that, in this regard, a third party is disadvantaged as compared to a promisee who could challenge such an exclusion clause. Perhaps even more important s.7(4) is intended to mean that a third party cannot rely on s.3 of the 1977 Act, which deals with the significant area of parties where one is a consumer or is dealing on the other's written standard terms of business. Importantly, by virtue of s.6, the Act does not apply to certain contracts involving employment and carriage of goods.

Contract and Tort

There was a time in the early 1980s when the rule of privity appeared to lose some of its significance through a development in the law of tort. The doctrine of privity only matters where a remedy in contract is the only possible remedy. It used to be the law that a plaintiff could not obtain damages in the tort of negligence for pure economic loss. The House of Lords decision in *Junior Books Ltd v Veitchi Co Ltd* (1983, HL) appeared to change that. By a majority, they held that a building owner who was in close proximity to a subcontractor, but not in contractual relationship with him, could recover damages in tort for the economic loss caused by the subcontractor's negligence in laying a defective floor in the building owner's premises. Later cases, however, have indicated a reluctance to follow this approach. In *Simaan General Contracting Co v Pilkington Glass Ltd (No.2)* (1988, CA), for example, the plaintiffs were the main contractors for a building, whose plans and specifications stipulated that a particular type of glass manufactured by the defendants should be used in the curtain walling of the building. The supply and erection of the curtain walling was subcontracted to another company which, as required, ordered the glass from the defendants. The glass supplied was not right; so the building owner withheld payment from the plaintiffs who sued the defendants for economic loss caused by the withholding of payment. The Court of Appeal refused to allow the claim to proceed. They said that in the absence of a contract between the parties the plaintiffs could not bring a direct claim against the defendants for economic loss alone, because the defendants had not voluntarily assumed direct responsibility to the plaintiffs for the quality of the glass and the plaintiffs had not relied on the defendants. The Court of Appeal also pointed out that the plaintiffs had a remedy against the subcontractor who in turn could claim against the defendants; at each stage liability could be determined in the light of the exemption clause, if any, applying to each contract. (See also *Muirhead v Industrial Tank Specialities Ltd* (1985, CA) and *Greater Nottingham Co-operative Society v Cementation Piling & Foundations Ltd* (1988, CA).) In *D&F Estates Ltd v Church Commissioners for England* (1988, HL) the House of Lords stressed that where a defect in a chattel or structure makes the chattel or structure less valuable but is discovered before it causes personal injury or physical damage to other property, the remedy, if any, for the economic loss lies in contract not tort. It can be said for the present, then, that the courts have set their faces against pursuing the possibilities suggested by *Junior Books Ltd v Veitchi.*

ASSIGNMENT

ASSIGNMENT IS the transfer of the benefit of a contract, by the party entitled to that benefit, to a third party. The effect of the transfer is that the third party becomes entitled to sue the person bearing the burden of the contract. For example, if A makes a contract with B by which A undertakes to paint B's house for £1,000, A may assign to C the right to receive from B the £1,000. B's consent to the assignment is not necessary. If B declines to pay C, C can sue him. In this example, A is the "creditor" and the "assignor"; B is the "debtor"; C is the "assignee". In this context, "creditor" can mean the party who has any right (not necessarily a money right) under a contract and "debtor" can mean the party who owes any duty under a contract.

The right to receive the £1,000 is called a "chose in action". It is a right which can be enforced, if the need arises, only by action; that is, by suing for it. Assignment is concerned only with choses in action. Choses in action include shares, rights under a trust, legacies, policies of insurance, patents, copyrights, rights of action in tort, debts and other contractual rights. Only the benefit, not the burden, of a contract can be assigned (*Don King Productions v Warren* (1999)).

In the last chapter it was said that the doctrine of privity does not forbid assignment. In the example above, A gave C the right to sue B for the £1,000, by assignment to C of an existing contractual right. But if A had, in the original contract, stipulated that B should pay the £1,000 to C, the doctrine of privity (at least if the Contracts (Rights of Third Parties) Act 1999 does not apply) would prevent C from suing B. The explanation of this lies in history. The doctrine of privity is a common law doctrine; assignment is an invention of equity.

This chapter is mainly concerned with voluntary assignments. It should also be noted, however, that an involuntary assignment may take place where one of the parties to a contract dies or becomes bankrupt. Such assignments are called assignments by operation of law and are considered briefly at the end of the chapter.

METHODS OF ASSIGNMENT

An assignment usually takes the form of a deed or contract. Where the assignment is voluntary, the deed or contract will normally specify the terms on which the transfer of the benefit should take place. In *Explora Group Plc v Hesco Bastion Ltd* (2005), for example, T acts as a marketing agent for H. T had assigned its right to commission to its bank. The court found that the deed of assignment had expressly excluded the assignment of commission earned prior to the assignment but yet unpaid. Only the right to future commission had been assigned under the terms of the assignment. (See also *Ruttle Plant Hire v Secretary of State for the Environment and Rural Affairs* (2007)).

A deed of assignment is treated like a conventional contractual instrument and will thus be construed as such. Where the assignment operates in a commercial setting, it will be construed in that commercial context (*Abdul Ghani El Ajou v Stern* (2006, CA)). In *Angela Ngozi Onyeador v Miss World Ltd* (2005, CA), the assignment referred to "profits relating to the event" but the assignee claimed money given by sponsors of the Miss World event. The court held that profits relating to the event did not include sponsorship monies.

The assignee should consent to receiving the chose in action but he does not need to be aware of the full implications of the transfer. As long as he is aware of the main consequences, he would be said to have acquiesced to the assignment (*Scottish Widows Plc v Stewart* (2005)). At common law it was not possible for A to assign to C his contractual right against B. A could give C a "power of attorney" enabling C to sue B, but that was a very cumbrous and imperfect procedure. An exception was made in favour of the Crown; the Crown could make and take assignments. As a result of the common law rules, equity developed a doctrine of assignment. This is considered after statutory assignments, since it may still be important in a case where the statutory requirements are not satisfied.

Statutory assignments

Section 136(1) of the Law of Property Act 1925 provides:

"An absolute assignment by writing under the hand of the assignor (not purporting to be by way of charge only) of any debt or other legal thing in action, of which express notice in writing has been given to the debtor ... is effectual in law (subject to equities having priority over the right of the assignee) to pass and transfer from the date of such notice—

(a) the legal right to such debt or thing in action;
(b) all legal and other remedies for the same; and
(c) the power to give a good discharge for the same without the concurrence of the assignor."

The phrase "legal chose in action" includes an *equitable* chose in action. Most chose of actions would be a right to claim under a contract. A person who obtained by assignment such a contractual right could only enforce that right in accordance with the terms of the contract and subject to any restrictions or limitations which those terms might impose (*Through Transport Mutual Insurance Association (Eurasia) Ltd v New India Assurance Co Ltd* (2005)). The chose in action must be clearly ascertainable in the deed of assignment (*Technocrats International Inc v Fredic Ltd* (2004)).

It is not a necessary condition of a valid statutory assignment that there should be consideration. It has been held that an assignment that satisfies the requirement of the statute transfers the chose in action by virtue of the statute itself, so that consideration is irrelevant.

The statute does not destroy, or affect in any way, the possibility of equitable assignment. Thus an assignment which fails to meet the requirements of the statute—because it is non-absolute, or because it is oral, or because written notice is not given to the debtor—may yet be an equitable assignment: see below.

There are three conditions which must be satisfied to make an assignment valid under the statute: (1) it must be absolute; (2) it must be in "writing under the hand of the assignor" (not only must the assignment be in writing, it should also be signed (*Technocrats International Inc v Fredic Ltd* (2004)); and (3) written notice must be given to the debtor.

Absolute assignment

An absolute assignment is one by which the assignor divests himself of his whole interest in the thing assigned. In *Savva v Jaikaran* (2005), it was held that once an absolute assignment has been made, it cannot usually be repudiated. In that case, S agreed to buy a property from J. S then assigned his rights to N who agreed to complete the purchase contract. N did not complete the purchase contract. That was in breach of the underlying contract. S did and then tried to have the property transferred into his name. Isaacs J. rejected the claim stating that under s.136, the assignment was absolute and despite N's breach, S could not treat the assignment as having been brought to an end. S was only thus entitled to compensation for the purchase price.

An assignment may be absolute, however, even though it provides for the assignor to regain his interest at some time in the future. Thus it is well settled that a mortgage of a chose in action can be an absolute assignment. In *Tancred v Delagoa Bay and East Africa Railway Co* (1889) a debt was assigned as security for a loan of money, with the provision that if the assignor repaid the loan, the debt should be reassigned to him. This was held to be an absolute assignment.

An absolute assignment must be distinguished from: (a) a conditional assignment; (b) an assignment by way of charge; and (c) an assignment of part of a debt.

A conditional assignment is one which is to become operative or to cease to be operative upon the happening of some uncertain event. In *Durham Brothers v Robertson* (1898, CA) a firm of builders assigned a debt as security for a loan of money. The assignment was expressed to last "until the money with added interest be repaid to you". This was held to be a conditional, not an absolute, assignment. The difference between this case and *Tancred's* case, above, is that, whereas in *Tancred's* case the debtor could safely pay the assignee until he received notice of the reassignment, in *Durham Brothers v Robertson* the debtor would not know whether he ought to pay his debt to the assignee or to the assignor, because this would depend on whether or not the assignor had repaid the loan, and that the debtor could not know. It comes to this: where the assignment provides for automatic reversion to the assignor the assignment is not absolute; where the assignment provides for a reassignment it is absolute.

An assignment by way of charge is one which merely entitles the assignee to pay out of a fund, without transferring the fund itself. In *Jones v Humphreys* (1902) a schoolmaster assigned to a moneylender so much of his salary as should be necessary to repay a sum of £22. 10s. which he had borrowed and any further sums which he might borrow. This was held to be not an absolute assignment. Here again the debtor (schoolmaster's employer) would not know whom he ought to pay, because he would not know the state of accounts between the schoolmaster and the moneylender.

The assignment of part of a debt is not an absolute assignment. If A assigns to C £50 out of the £75 which B owes to A, that is not an absolute agreement: see *Forster v Baker* (1910).

Notice

Notice to the debtor is an essential part of the statutory transfer of the debt. But no very high standard of formality is required. In *Van Lynn Developments Ltd v Pelias Construction Co Ltd* (1969, CA) a notice of assignment was held to be good though it did not give the date of the assignment which was being referred to, and though it contained an incorrect statement. In *Barbados Trust Co Ltd v Bank of Zambia* (2006), the notice was defective because when it was given, consent had not been formally given. The assignment was incomplete. However, when consent was finally given, the notice need not be given a second time. The original defective notice had become good. Notice need not be given by the assignor.

Equitable assignments

The inability to transfer a chose in action, such as a contractual right, was a considerable inconvenience, and equity soon decided to recognise such transfers; that is, assignments. In equity, no particular formality is required to make an assignment valid, except that the assignment of an equitable interest (as distinct from a legal interest) must be in writing: see s.53(1)(c) of the Law of Property Act 1925. What is required is intention: there cannot be an assignment without an intention to assign. There must be clear evidence of this intention. In *John Michael Finlan v Winfield* (2007), Q had agreed to assign its right to sue E to F. In reliance on the agreement, F issued the claim form (issuing the claim form is the first step to institute legal action). Three hours later, the deed of assignment was completed. The court held that when F issued the claim form, he was not legally entitled to do so because the assignment had not taken place. Moreover there was also no equitable assignment because until the deed of assignment was completed, Q could not be said to have made an "outward expression of its intention to make an immediate disposition of the subject matter of the assignment".

Effect of an equitable assignment

The exact effect of an equitable assignment depends upon two factors: (1) whether the chose in action which is being assigned is legal or equitable; and (2) whether the assignment is absolute or non-absolute. The best example of a legal chose in action is a debt due under a contract; the best example of an equitable chose in action is a legacy or an interest in a trust fund. The nature of an absolute assignment has been considered above, in the context of statutory assignments.

The effect of an equitable assignment can be stated in three rules. First, where the chose in action assigned is legal the assignee can sue the debtor, but only if he joins the assignor as a party to the action. He must first ask the assignor to sue as a co-claimant with him. If the assignor refuses, the assignee may join him as a co-defendant with the debtor. This rule applies wherever a legal chose in action is assigned, whether the assignment is absolute or non-absolute. The reason for the rule is historical, arising from the different views of assignment taken by common law and equity.

Secondly, where the chose in action assigned is equitable and the assignment is non-absolute, again the assignee can only sue if he joins the assignor—either as co-claimant or co-defendant. There is a good practical reason for this rule. Since the assignment is not absolute—being conditional, or by way of charge, or of part of a debt—the court cannot safely adjudicate unless all three parties (assignor, assignee and debtor) are before the court.

Thirdly, where the chose in action assigned is equitable and the assignment is absolute, the assignee may sue by himself in his own name without making the assignor a party to the action. There is no reason why the assignor should be a party to the action: since the chose is equitable there is no historical reason for him to be present; and since the assignment is absolute, the assignor has given up all his rights in the chose.

Notice

In order to perfect the title of the equitable assignee as against the assignor, it is not necessary that notice should be given to the debtor. But if the case of *Warner Bros Records Inc v Rollgreen Ltd* (1976, CA) is rightly decided, it seems that such notice is necessary in order to give the assignee any rights against the debtor. The Court of Appeal held, on a preliminary issue, that the equitable assignee of a contractual option who has not given notice of the assignment to the grantor of the option cannot exercise the option in his own name so as to bind the grantor of the option. The principle of this case does not seem to be confined to options, but would apply to the equitable assignment of any kind of contractual right.

It is well settled that the assignee cannot sue the debtor if the debtor, not having had notice of the assignment, makes payment to the assignor. Notice is also important where there is more than one assignee, because they take priority in the order in which they give notice to the debtor. This is known as the rule in *Dearle v Hall* (1828). But the rule cannot benefit a person who takes an assignment knowing of a previous assignment.

Notice may be given by the assignor or by the assignee. It need not be in any particular form, but where an equitable chose in action is assigned notice will not give priority over later assignees unless it is in writing: see s.137(3) of the Law of Property Act 1925.

Consideration

The question arises whether consideration is necessary to an equitable assignment. This question arises only as between the assignor and assignee; the debtor cannot refuse to pay the assignee on the ground that the assignee gave no consideration to the assignor. The point most often arises when the assignor is dead or bankrupt; his personal representative or trustee in bankruptcy may wish to challenge the validity of the assignment. Bear in mind that an assignment for no consideration is a gift of a chose in action.

A gift of a chose in action is only irrevocable if it is completed, or perfected. If a gift is not perfected, the donor can change his mind and revoke it—so it is only an incomplete assignment that requires consideration to make it irrevocable. An assignment is incomplete if the assignor has not done all that he needs to do to transfer the right of action to the assignee. At first sight it looks as though the distinction between a complete and an incomplete assignment is the same as that between an absolute and a non-absolute assignment. But this is not so. It is true that an absolute assignment is necessarily complete, but it is not true that a non-absolute assignment is necessarily incomplete. In *Re McArdle* (1951, CA) the Court of Appeal indicated that the assignment of part of a debt can be a completed assignment. But assignments which are conditional or by way of charge are not completed assignments, and thus require consideration, because something remains to be done (such as settling the state of accounts between assignor and assignee) before the assignee can bring an action.

An assignment is the transfer of an existing right. Consequently, a promise to transfer a right which does not yet exist (sometimes called "future property") is not an assignment. For example, A may promise to transfer to B what he expects to get under the will of X, who is still living. That is not an assignment, it is an agreement to assign, and it requires consideration just like any ordinary contract. The same is true of a promise to transfer, in the future, an existing right.

<h2 style="text-align:center">"SUBJECT TO EQUITIES"</h2>

An assignee is said to take "subject to equities". (The word "equities" embraces legal and not merely equitable rights.) The effect of this rule is that the assignee cannot be in any better position than the assignor. So, the debtor can plead against the assignee any defences that he could have pleaded against the assignor. In *Roxburghe v Cox* (1881, CA), for example, Lord Charles Ker assigned to the Duke of Roxburghe the money that would accrue to him from the sale of his commission in the army. This money (£3,000) was paid, on December 18, to the credit of Lord Charles

Ker's account at his bank. On that date the account was overdrawn to the extent of £647. On December 19, the Duke gave notice of the assignment to the bank. It was held that the bank could set off the sum of £647 against the right of the Duke to the £3,000.

In *Roxburghe v Cox* the defence took the form of a set-off of a quantified sum; but a debtor can equally rely, by way of counter-claim, on an unliquidated amount. Suppose A, a builder, assigns to C money to become due to him from B at the conclusion of a building contract. C, the assignee, sues B, the debtor. B can defend the action by pleading, if it is the case, that he has suffered damage by reason of defective work by A. In this situation, because the debtor's claim arises out of the contract assigned, it does not matter whether the claim arises before or after notice of the assignment has been given. But where, as in *Roxburghe v Cox*, the debtor's claim arises out of some transaction other than the contract assigned, it can only be set up against the assignee if it arose before notice of the assignment. Thus, if Lord Charles Ker had drawn another £100 on December 20, the bank could not have increased their set-off; they would still have been limited to £647. A more recent (and more complicated) case in which these rules are expounded and applied is *Business Computers Ltd v Anglo-African Leasing Ltd* (1977).

The defence available to the debtor may be something much broader than a mere set-off or counter-claim. Any defect in the title of the assignor effects the title of the assignee. Thus mis-representation, mistake, illegality, incapacity and non-performance may all be pleaded by the debtor.

The question of priority may arise where there is more than assignment of a chose in action. If the chose in action is sufficient to satisfy the assignees' claims on it, there will be no problem. If, however, it is insufficient, the question of priority amongst the assignees will arise. In that case, the rule in *Dearle v Hall* (1823) will come into operation. The rule states that priority is determined according to the order in which notice of assignment is given. So, if there are two assignments and the second assignee gives notice first he will be given priority.

It is also important to remember that where the assignment is unconscionable, the court would not enforce the assignment (in *Hetul Navinchandra Patel v Ashwin Shah* (2004)).

RIGHTS WHICH CANNOT BE ASSIGNED

1   Public policy forbids the assignment of some contractual
    rights. In particular, a public officer cannot assign his sal-
    ary, and a wife cannot assign maintenance and similar
    payments to which she may become entitled in matrimonial
    proceedings.

2   Parties to a contract are free, if they so wish, to make it a
    term of the contract that the rights under it shall not be
    assignable. See, for example, *Linden Gardens Trust Ltd v
    Lenesta Sludge Disposals Ltd* (1993, HL), in which the
    House of Lords refused to hold void as being contrary to
    public policy a clause in the JCT Standard Form of Building
    Contract prohibiting the assignment of any benefit of the
    contract, including not only the assignment of the right to
    future performance but also the assignment of accrued
    rights of action. (See also *Ruttle Plant Hire v Secretary of
    State for the Environment & Rural Affairs* (2007)). It is a
    question of construction as to whether a particular con-
    tractual right is assignable and what extent the right can be
    assigned. In *Explora Group Plc v Hescon Bastion Ltd* (2005,
    CA), similarly, under a marketing agency contract H
    undertook to pay commission to T. T then fell into difficult
    times and agreed to assign its right to commission to its
    bank. The assignment had been done without H's consent.
    The court however found that there was nothing in the
    marketing agency contract prohibiting the assignment of the
    right to commission. Contractual terms prohibiting assign-
    ment may however be overridden by the force of statutory
    law. In *Co-operative Group Ltd v Stansell Ltd* (2006, CA),
    for example, the Court of Appeal held that the Industrial
    and Provident Societies Act 1965 (s.51(1)) overrode a pro-
    hibition against assignment in a building contract. Where
    the contract makes it plain that a benefit is wholly personal
    to the assignor, it cannot be assigned. In *Harbour Estates
    Ltd v HSBC Bank Plc* (2004), it was held that the break
    clause in the lease (a clause allowing termination of the
    lease) was not transferred even though the lease had been
    assigned. The assignee could not thus use the break clause.

3   A bare right of action is not assignable. This is because it savours of maintenance. Maintenance in this context is linked with champerty, and was considered in Chapter 10. A right of action is not bare if the assignee has a genuine commercial interest in the enforcement of the assignor's claim or if that claim is coupled with some other property which is assigned along with it. Thus if A sells his land to C, and assigns to him the right to sue for damages for breach of covenant committed by B (the tenant) before the sale, C gets a perfectly good right of action against B. But if A, whilst keeping the land, purported to assign to C the right to sue the tenant for breach of covenant, that would be the attempted assignment of a bare right of action and the assignment would be void. (See also *Ellis v Torrington* (1920)). In the past, the courts had been quite strict about the assignability of a cause of action in tort (as against one in contract). However, that trend was halted by the House of Lords in *Trendtex Trading Corporation v Crédit Suisse* (1982). Lord Roskill stressed in that case that any such assignment had to be considered in the light of the "totality of the transaction" and not be constrained simply by some policy against assignability. This was applied in *24 Seven Utility Services Ltd v Rosekey Ltd* (2004). There, L had assigned to C his right of action in negligence against D. The court did not accept the argument that the assignment was for a bare cause of action or was savouring of maintenance. It considered that L's right of action was a valuable right or interest within s.136 of the Law of Property Act 1925 and C had a "genuine commercial interest in taking the assignment and in enforcing it for its own benefit".

4   The benefit of a contract cannot be assigned if the "debtor" is reasonable in wishing to perform his contractual duty only in favour of one particular "creditor". If A, an author, contracts with B, a publisher, that A shall write a book for B to publish, B cannot assign to C the right to publish the book. A may reasonably have relied on B's skill and judgment as a publisher.

ASSIGNMENT DISTINGUISHED FROM NOVATION

Novation is a transaction by which a new contract is substituted for an existing contract. This can happen between the original parties but it can also happen (and this is where it becomes relevant to the present discussion) between the original parties and a new party. Suppose there is a contract between A and B under which A owes B £50, and a contract between B and C under which B owes C £50. By agreement between all three of them, the A–B contract and the B–C contract may be discharged and a new contract may be made under which A is to pay C £50. The essential point about novation is that it requires the agreement of all the parties concerned, whereas assignment does not require the agreement of the debtor. Novation can be used in connection with rights. In the example just given, B gives up his right to receive £50 from A—but he could more easily have done that by assignment to C, which would not have needed the consent of A. The real importance of novation is that it can be used in connection with duties, whereas assignment cannot. By novation (as in the example) B can get out of his duty to pay £50 to C. He could not have done that by assigning his duty to A. Duties cannot be assigned; only rights can.

ASSIGNMENT BY OPERATION OF LAW

Assignment is the transfer of a right by the voluntary act of the transferor. It is now necessary to consider the involuntary transfer of both rights and duties which may arise by operation of law on the death or bankruptcy of a party to a contract.

Death

If A and B have entered into a contract which is not of a personal nature, and A or B dies during the currency of the contract, his rights and duties pass automatically to his personal representatives. Where A has contracted to sell goods to B, and A dies before he has delivered the goods, his personal representatives acquire, by operation of law, the duty to deliver the goods and the right to sue for the price.

This does not apply, however, to a contract of a personal nature.

Thus, if A has entered into a contract of employment with B (the employer) and A dies during the term of employment, A's personal representatives do not acquire any rights or duties; they have no duty to perform the service and no right to (post-death) wages. If B, the employer, dies, B's personal representatives do not acquire any rights or duties; they have no right to A's service and no duty to pay A any (post-death) wages. In a personal contract, the death of either party puts an end to the contract. It is a form of frustration, as will be seen in Chapter 17.

Insolvency

When a person becomes insolvent, his trustee in bankruptcy must distribute all his property fairly amongst his creditors. The rule, therefore, is that any right of action relating to the property of the insolvent person passes automatically to the trustee in bankruptcy. If A (who becomes insolvent) has a contract with B under which B had to deliver goods or pay money to A, then C (the trustee) can sue B if he fails to deliver the goods or pay the money. Similarly with duties. If A had a contract with B under which it was A's duty to deliver goods, his trustee in bankruptcy must go on with the contract and deliver the goods (and then claim the price). There is a qualification to this rule; if an executory contract is onerous or unprofitable, the trustee is permitted to disclaim the contract. That means that he need not go on with the contract, but the bankrupt's estate will be liable for breach of it.

Personal contracts are not, as such, transferred. Thus, if an employee becomes insolvent, he will probably be able to go on serving, in which case there is no question of transferring his duties. If the insolvency makes it impossible for him to continue in his employment, the trustee in bankruptcy need not and cannot take up his duties. The contract is at an end. So far as rights are concerned, special rules apply. The right to sue for wages already earned, or for breach of contract already committed before insolvency, passes to the trustee. Post-insolvency wages, and damages for post-insolvency breach of contract, can be sued for by the insolvent person himself, but he must hand over to the trustee any part of such wages or damages that is not needed to support him and his family. The trustee's right to sue for pre-insolvency wrongs is limited to wrongs against the insolvent person's property in a narrow

JOHN MOORES UNIVERSITY
AVRIL ROBARTS LRC
TITHEBARN STREET
LIVERPOOL L2 2ER
TEL 0151 231 4022

sense. Thus a right of action for personal injury, or for injury to the feelings or reputation of the insolvent person, remains with him and does not pass to the trustee.

AGENCY

THE THIRD and last topic in this section of "Who is within the agreement" is agency. The law of agency is a major and important field of law in its own right. This chapter will examine only those aspects relevant to the subject-matter of this book—the personalities in the contractual agreement and their contracting capacity.

AGENCY

What agency is

Agency is the relationship which arises when one person is authorised to act as the representative of another person. The person authorised is the agent (A); the person authorising is the principal (P). Whether an agency contract is said to exist is a question of fact (*Waleed Aboualsaud v Aboukhater* (2007); *Ian Green Residential Ltd v Ayman Asfari* (2007); the type of agency relationship is also a matter of fact (*Proforce Recruit Ltd v Rugby Group Ltd* (2007)).

Usually, the agent is authorised to make a contract with a third party on behalf of the principal. In that situation, agency involves two contracts: the contract of agency between P and A, and the contract—of sale, or hire, or carriage, or whatever it may be—which A makes on behalf of P with X (a third party). In this book on the general principles of contract it is naturally the latter with which we are primarily concerned, though the contract of agency will also be considered, particularly as regards formation and termination.

A common form of agency is where A buys or sells goods (or land, or shares or anything else) on behalf of P. It is important to distinguish an agent of this kind from a person who buys goods on his own account and then resells them. Thus a shopkeeper is not usually an agent in the legal sense, though he may call himself "agent" of some well-known manufacturer. In *International Life Leisure Ltd v HM Revenue & Customs Commissioners* (2006), L produced a brochure featuring holiday accommodation. He took bookings from readers. It was found that as he had contractually warranted that the accommodation would be to the requisite standard and he was entitled to set his own rental rates, he was not acting as agent for the hotel owners. As the hotel owners did not know what the actual rental rates were, they could not be said to be principals.

COMMERCIAL AGENTS

The agent in the legal sense is entitled to certain rights and duties at common law. These rights and duties are usually subject to variation and limitation by the terms of the contract. Where the agent is classed a "commercial agent", special rules apply. The Commercial Agents (Council Directive) Regulations 1993 define the commercial agent as a self-employed intermediary who has continuing authority to negotiate the sale and purchase of goods on behalf of another person, or to negotiate and conclude such transactions on behalf of, and in the name of that principal.

In *Julian Smith v Reliance Water Controls Ltd* (2003, CA), the

Court of Appeal held that it was important for the purposes of the Regulations that a distinction be made between an agent who acts under a contract of service and one who acts under a contract for services. In that case, S was initially employed by R as a sales representative. He subsequently requested to continue working on a self-employed basis. A new contract was made. It set out a sales territory and sales targets for S and required R to pay commission on sales achieved. S was also liable for expenses, and had responsibility for his own car and mobile telephone which he used in relation to his work. The County Court concluded that S had remained an employee because each side's obligations were as close as possible to those that had existed before. That was rejected by the Court of Appeal. The Court of Appeal held that although there was some indication that the motive behind the making of the new agreement was not entirely wholesome, the details of the new contract could not be ignored. It was not a sham; as such, the natural conclusion was that S was a self-employed commercial agent fully entitled to claim under the Regulations.

Another important aspect of the definition is the requirement that the commercial agent negotiates the sale and purchase of goods on behalf of another person, or negotiates and concludes such transactions on behalf of and in the name of that principal. The word "negotiates" should be construed purposively so as not to exclude from protection of the Regulations agents who had been engaged to expand and develop the principal's business and commercial goodwill. This was the view taken in *PJ Pipe & Valve v Audco India Ltd* (2005). In that case, the agent did not have authority to negotiate the sale of valves, its business was to introduce customers to the principal's products. The court however considered that there was no good reason to exclude the agent from the definition of "commercial agents".

Where the agent buys and resells in his own name, he is not a commercial agent under the Regulations. In *Mercantile International Group Plc v Chuan Soon Huat Industrial Group Ltd* (2002), the court held that as the claimant in question was paid by mark-up not by commission and the terms on which the claimant subsequently sold the goods on were different to those on which he bought the goods from the defendant, there was a case for suggesting that he was not a commercial agent. That does not necessarily mean that he was not an agent, simply that he might not be a commercial agent; indeed, the documentation between the parties indicated that the claimant was an agent and such evidence could not be easily displaced by the mere fact that the claimant was paid by way of mark-up (*Ex p. White, re Nevill* (1871); *AMB Imballaggi Plastici SRL v Pacflex Ltd* (1999)).

Any consideration of the commercial agent's rights and duties must be made in the light of the fact that they are statutorily catered for. This does not mean that common law rules are to be totally displaced; in *Duffen v FRA BO SpA* (1998) the Court of Appeal stated that the commercial agent is entitled to plead common law remedies alongside relief afforded by the regulations. The common law rules, which will be examined later, must therefore be read in conjunction with the Regulations where the agent concerned is a commercial agent.

HOW AGENCY ARISES

Agency arises wherever one person acquires authority to act as the representative of another. An agent's authority may be "actual", or "apparent" (or "ostensible"), or "usual", or it may arise from "necessity", or it may be conferred retrospectively by "ratification". The issue of whether a contract made by an agent with a third party is valid depends on whether the agent had authority to bind the principal; it is immaterial whether or not any of the parties had acted unconscionably. This rejection of any element of good faith or conscience was sanctioned by the House of Lords in *Criterion Properties Plc v Stratford UK Properties LLC* (2004). In that case, A was P's managing director and had brought about the contract between P and X. The Court of Appeal held that it was necessary to decide whether the contract between P and X should be set aside on grounds of conscionability. The House of Lords rejected that approach stating that the agreement could only be set aside on the basis of authority; the allegation that X had acted unconscionably to assist A to act in breach of authority was immaterial.

Actual authority

Actual authority may be express or implied.

Express authority

This arises when express words are used, to the effect that P specifically appoints A as his agent. In general no formality is required (*Heard v Pilley* (1869)) but there must be clear evidence of agreement (*Pretty Pictures v Quixote Films Ltd* (2003)). An agent who has been appointed orally, not in writing, has the power to make a contract which the law requires to be in writing or to be evidenced in writing. An agent cannot execute a deed unless he has been appointed by deed. An exception to this rule is where the agent executes the deed in the presence of his principal (*Ball v Dunsterville* (1791)). Incidentally, the appointment of an agent by deed is called a "power of attorney".

Whether there is express authority is largely a matter of construction of the relevant stipulation in the agency agreement. As a matter of construction, the court will have regard to the general tenor of the agreement; it will not confine itself merely to the clause or stipulation in question. The "factual matrix" of the contract is important. In *Aylesford & Co (Estate Agents) Ltd v Rashid Khalaf Al-Habtoor* (2003), P had engaged the services of A to sell a property. The contract was made by P signing a pro forma sent to him by A. There was a leaflet accompanying the letter which contained A's terms of business which also required P's signature, required by the Estate Agents Act 1979. P did not sign the leaflet. A subsequently negotiated a sale of the property. The pro forma provided that the agents would act for P for a period of three months. However, the terms of business provided that the agency would continue after the three months until termination by either party. P relied on the pro forma to say that the agreement had lapsed when the sale was made and he, thus, owed the agents nothing. The court rejected P's submissions stating that it was clear to all concerned that the agency had subsisted regardless. P was required to pay the agent's fee. In general, though, where the agency contract required renewal or continuation of authority, that must be seen to in accordance with the contract (*DP Mann v Coutts & Co* (2003)).

Where a commercial agency exists as defined by the Commercial Agents (Council Directive) Regulations 1993, the principal and the commercial agent may request from the other a signed written statement of the terms of the contract of agency, including any terms agreed after the agency contract has commenced.

Implied authority

Authority may be implied from some other relationship. Thus, for example, a wife living with her husband has authority, implied by law, to "pledge his credit" for necessary household expenses. This means that she can order goods and services necessary and appropriate to the husband's lifestyle, and the supplier can sue the husband for the price. In *EC Gransden & Co Ltd v Ballard (Kent) Ltd* (2001), the court saw no objection in accepting the argument that the wife of a company's sole director had had the authority to give a guarantee on behalf of the company. That was notwithstanding the fact that she had no official capacity within the company because for all intents and purposes, she and her husband were effectively engaged in a joint venture through the medium of the company.

The authority derives from the family unit, that is, the cohabitation. It follows therefore that where there is a cohabitation and a family unit exists, the authority attaches to a mistress no less than to a wife. The matter is a question of fact rather than one of law.

The husband can prevent his wife from pledging his credit, and this is effective generally, except that he may be estopped (see "apparent" authority, below) as against a tradesman whose bills the husband has paid in the past. To such a tradesman the husband should give express notice that the authority has been withdrawn.

Another form of implied authority is that which is incidental to some larger agency where the terms of the agency are incomplete or where the agent has a discretion as to how he should act. An example of this is where P instructs A to insure goods but leaves A to select a suitable policy. Here A has implied authority to select a particular policy, and P will then be bound by its terms. Should that policy not cover the risk that arises, then (assuming the agent had acted in good faith) the principal bears the loss. In this connection, in *The Romina G* (2003), the Court of Appeal held that it was needful to have regard to commercial good sense and trade practice in construing whether there was intention by the parties to confer such implied authority on the agent. In that case, A, a shipping terminal owner, had made a contract with the owner of an oil tanker which provided, inter alia, for the liability of tugboats used. The court found that on the facts A had implied authority to make that contract not only on behalf of tugs owned by itself, but also any tug using its terminal (see *The Mahkutai* (1996); *Ocean Pride Maritime Ltd v Qingdao Ocean Shipping Co* (2007)).

Similarly, in *Hamer v Sharp* (1874) the agent who was instructed to "find a purchaser" was held as a matter of construction, not to have the "incidental authority to conclude a contract". The threshold as to whether there is incidental authority is generally high. In *Iveco Finance Ltd v Man Truck and Bus UK Ltd* (2003), the contract provided that X was to sell a number of trucks to Y who, in turn, was to lease them to Z. It was arranged by Z that X should deliver the trucks directly to Z. That was duly done but Y then purported to reject the goods on the basis that they did not meet their contractual description. X argued that as Z was acting as Y's agent, Y was bound by Z's acceptance of the goods. The Court of Appeal rejected the argument stating that the fact that Z had arranged the contract on behalf of Y and for the delivery of the trucks to itself did not create an agency agreement. More was required to prove the existence of agency.

Apparent or ostensible authority

Apparent authority arises where circumstances make it appear to others that a person has authority to act as agent of another person. In *Hely-Hutchinson v Brayhead Ltd* (1968) Lord Denning M.R. said:

"Ostensible or apparent authority is the authority of an agent as it appears to others ... [S]ometimes ostensible authority exceeds actual authority. For instance, when the board appoint the managing director, they may expressly limit his authority by saying he is not to order goods worth more than £500 without the sanction of the board. In that case his actual authority is subject to the £500 limitation, but his ostensible authority includes all the usual authority of a managing director. The company is bound by his ostensible authority in his dealings with those who do not know of the limitation."

If, therefore, the board appointed A to be managing director, but with an express limit on his authority (for example, that he is not to order goods worth more than £500 without approval of the board) and A nevertheless orders goods worth £1,000, he will have the apparent authority to make this contract if it can be shown that £1,000 is within the usual authority of a managing director of that type of company.

LIVERPOOL JOHN MOORES UNIVERSITY
LEARNING & INFORMATION SERVICES

In *Freeman & Lockyer v Buckhurst Park Properties (Mangal) Ltd* (1964) Diplock L.J. had this to say:

"An 'apparent' or 'ostensible' authority ... is the legal relationship between the principal and the contractor created by a representation, made by the principal to the contractor, intended to be and in fact acted upon by the contractor, that the agent has authority to enter on behalf of the principal into a contract of a kind within the scope of the 'apparent' authority, so as to render the principal liable to perform any obligations imposed upon him by such contract."

Apparent authority, therefore, is founded on a representation by P to X that A has authority. This representation more often arises from conduct than from some express words. In *Cunningham v Aryal and Rupack* (2002), C who had become infatuated with R agreed to transfer some £200,000 to Nepal for the benefit of R and/or his family. The evidence was that C had agreed for R to make all necessary arrangements for the transfer using a bank account in B's name. On that basis, the court found that R had been held out by C as having his ostensible authority to call for the transfer of the fund from B's bank account. It should be remembered that a question of apparent authority is primarily one of fact (*First Energy v Hungarian International Bank* (1993)). The question to ask is whether from the facts and circumstances of the case the principal had held out the agent as having authority to do the act on which the party relies.

The representation cannot emanate from the agent alone; there must be some act of the principal. In *ING Re (UK) Ltd v R&V Versicherung AG* (2006), A had entered into a contract with X without actual authority. X had relied on a document which showed that P had authorised A to act in the matter. That document had however been issued without P's authorisation. X claimed that there was ostensible authority. The court disagreed stating there had to be a representation from P that the person who issued the document held a senior position or had authority to issue it before a case of ostensible authority could be made out. Inaction or silence, on its own, could not constitute a representation (see also *GPN Ltd v O2 (UK) Ltd* (2004)). On the other hand, in *Racing UK Ltd v Doncaster Racecourse Ltd* (2005), where P, being aware of A's general activities, did not do anything to prevent A from representing himself as the "human face" of P and indeed, persisted in allowing A to represent them, such conduct would amount to representation. The fact that it was common knowledge in the racing world that P was the owner of the racecourse also made it plausible for X to assume that P had sanctioned and approved the contract signed by A.

Any purported representation will be considered from the perspective of the third party, that is to say, whether from the third party's point of view the agent appears to be properly authorised. The estoppel arises as soon as the third party acts in reliance on the representation made and prevents the principal from asserting that he is not bound by the contract (see, for example, *HSBC Bank USA v Securicor Cash Services Ltd* (2002)). It is totally irrelevant whether the agent had actual authority to enter into the contract. It is also immaterial that the agent had acted fraudulently (*Hopkins v T L Dallas Group Ltd* (2004)).

To the relationship between the principal and the third party, the agent is a stranger. He need not be (though generally he is) aware of the existence of the representation but he must not attempt to make the contract as principal himself (see the above example of the shopkeeper calling himself an agent but not in fact contracting as agent but, rather, on his own account).

Usual authority

The phrase "usual authority" denotes the authority which agents of the type concerned usually have in a particular trade or business. Usual authority arises where the agent is appointed by the principal to some position or office. There is an overlap with "implied" and "apparent" authority, as can be seen in Lord Denning's example above.

In *Watteau v Fenwick* (1893) the manager of a public house bought some cigars despite being instructed not to do so by the brewer who owned the house. The manager ordered the cigars in his own name, and the supplier believed that the manager was contracting on his own behalf. So this was not a case of apparent authority, because there was no representation from the owners that the manager was authorised to act on their behalf and, from the supplier's point of view, the manager was acting as principal. Nevertheless, the supplier successfully sued the owners on the basis that "the cigars ... were such as would usually be supplied to and dealt in at such an establishment". It was usual for public house managers to buy cigars for use and resale in these establishments. The principal, however, cannot be sued by the third party if the agent had acted on his own behalf and not for his principal (see in particular *Kinahan & Co Ltd v Parry* (1911)) and/or the third party knows or ought reasonably to know of the agent's limitations.

Whilst a bank manager does not have usual authority to bind his bank, in *First Energy v Hungarian International Bank* (1993) the bank was held to have authorised its manager to communicate the offer of finance made by others in the bank with authority to contract on its behalf. Thus this case distinguished between the making of an offer (or acceptance) and the communication of that offer (or acceptance) to a third party.

Authority of necessity

There is a limited class of cases in which a person may acquire authority to act for another even without his consent in circumstances of necessity. Thus the master of a ship, where it is necessary for the continuance of the voyage, may borrow money on the ship owner's credit, and so bind the ship owner. Or he may even bind the cargo owners where the cargo is in danger (e.g. of perishable goods perishing) by borrowing money on the security of the cargo, or by selling part of the cargo. The same power is possessed by a carrier by land in respect of perishable goods. The "principal" is bound in such cases only if:

(1) there is an unforeseen risk to the goods;

(2) the course adopted is reasonably necessary in the circumstances; and

(3) it was practically impossible to communicate with the owners.

Given the ease of international telecommunications, the third condition will often not be fulfilled, making authority of necessity extremely rare.

It might be observed that in carriage of goods cases, Lord Simon of Glaisdale said in *China-Pacific S.A. v Food Corp. of India*; *The Winson* (1982) that:

"For an agency of necessity to arise, the action taken must be necessary for the protection of the interests of the alleged principal, not of the agent; the alleged agent must have acted bona fide in the interests of the alleged principal".

Ratification

If A, without authority, purports to contract with X on behalf of P, P can subsequently adopt the contract. This subsequent adoption is called ratification. It relates back to the contract which A made with X. Ratification has a double effect; it sets up (retrospectively) a relation of agency between P and A, and it sets up (also retrospectively) a contractual relation between P and X. Ratification is usually express, but implied ratification is possible. In *Cornwall v Wilson* (1750) A, claiming to act on behalf of P, bought some hemp from X. A did not have authority to buy the hemp. P purported to repudiate the contract, but he then sold the hemp. It was held that his selling the hemp amounted to implied ratification of the purchase contract, since he could not sell the hemp unless he had first bought it.

In the context of the doctrine of privity of contract, the permissibility of ratification is somewhat puzzling, since by means of it P becomes entitled to the benefits of a contract which he had no intention of making. But equally he becomes liable on the contract, so that sometimes ratification is a positive gain to the third party. On that basis, the courts have always been slow to conclude that an unauthorised act by an agent had been ratified by the principal, especially, where the only evidence of ratification is silence and/or inactivity of the principal. In *Lass Salt Garvin v Pomeroy* (2003), however, it was held that the court must ask whether the principal's lack of action in the circumstances was clear to an objective observer that he had indeed ratified the agreement. In that case, L had provided legal advice to the defendants in relation to a financial transaction the latter were interested in. The contract with L had been negotiated by T, the husband of one of the defendants. T also had an interest in the financial transaction and was closely linked with the defendants' interest. The court held that although the defendants did not expressly ratify the contract with L, they must be said to have ratified it given the fact that they clearly knew about the law firm's involvement and that they had proceeded in reliance on the advice given by L, their inactivity could not rebut the finding that they had ratified the agreement. On the other hand, where the inaction or silence is because P is uncertain as to the true state of affairs, there is no ratification (ING Re (UK) *Ltd v R&V Versicherung AG* (2006)). Ratification depends on knowledge.

Ratification is subject to a number of conditions.

(1) The agent must purport to act on behalf of the principal. If A gives the impression that he is acting on his own behalf, then ratification is not open to P, so that even if P purports to ratify it will not be effective. In *Keighley, Maxsted & Co v Durrant* (1901, HL) A was authorised by P to buy wheat at 44s. 3d. a quarter on a joint account for A and P. A could not get wheat at that price, and (exceeding his authority) he bought from X at 44s. 6d. a quarter. A intended to purchase on the joint account, but he did not disclose this fact to X. X sued P. He failed on the ground that the purchase had not been professedly made on behalf of P. Indeed, for ratification to be possible not only must A expressly contract as agent, but the principal must be capable of being ascertained (i.e. identified). It is not necessary that the principal should be named. However, there must be such a description of him as shall amount to a reasonable designation of the person intended to be bound by the contract.

This is seen in the case of *Watson v Swann* (1862). There, an agent was instructed to take out a general policy of insurance on goods on behalf of his principal. The agent was unable to effect the policy. What he did instead was to declare the goods on the back of a general policy of insurance which he had taken out previously on his own account. Following the loss of the goods, the principal sued on the policy. It was held that the principal could not succeed because when the contract of insurance (policy of insurance) was not made on his behalf and that at the time of contracting, the agent had yet to make the acquaintance of the principal.

The rule is therefore that an undisclosed principal is unable to ratify a contract made without authority by the agent.

(2) The principal must have the legal capacity to do the act at the time the agent makes the contract with the third party. In *Ashbury Railway Carriage Company v Riche* (1875, HL), for example, the directors of a company entered into an

ultra vires contract on behalf of the company. That contract could not be ratified even by the unanimous vote of the shareholders since the principal did not have the necessary capacity at the time when the contract was made. Although the ultra vires rule no longer applies to third-party dealings with companies, this case remains important as an illustration of the principle. If a company has not been formally incorporated at the time a person purports to contract as its agent, ratification cannot be effected subsequently after the company has been incorporated: see *Kelner v Baxter* (1866). In such a case the agent becomes personally liable on the contract. This rule was subsequently enacted as s.36C of the Companies Act 1985. Section 36C has since been repealed by s.1295, Sch.16 Companies Act 2006.

The legal capacity to act can also be affected by the validity of the contract entered into by the agent. Where the agreement is void ab initio, it is trite law that it cannot be ratified. In *Brook v Hook* (1871) the agent had forged the principal's signature on a bill of exchange. That act was incapable of being ratified because the forged signature was to be treated as a nullity from the outset.

(3)   The principal must ratify in time. A contract cannot be ratified after the time fixed for its performance has passed. If no time is fixed for its ratification the contract must be ratified within a reasonable time.

RELATIONS OF THE PARTIES

Where A, on behalf of P, makes a contract with X, the transaction may set up a relation between P and X and/or a relation between A and X.

It is sometimes supposed that there can only be rights and liabilities between P and X or between A and X, and that these two contractual relationships are mutually exclusive. This is not correct. There may well arise a contract between P and X and between A and X. This is clear from *Teheran-Europe Co Ltd v S.T. Belton (Tractors) Ltd* (1968), more particularly in the judgment of Donaldson J. at first instance, and from *The Swan* (1968). In *Linpac Plastics Ltd v Europlast H Mudder GmbH* (2001) for example, X had failed to pay A for goods supplied to them by P. Under the contractual arrangements, despite the fact that X had failed to reimburse A, A was under a duty to pay P. It all depends on the words used, the conduct engaged in, and the surrounding circumstances.

Principal and third party

It is necessary to distinguish here between two situations: where the principal is disclosed, and where the principal is undisclosed. This distinction is important when considering the rights and liabilities arising from a contract made by an agent.

Where the principal is disclosed

A principal is called a disclosed principal when his existence is known to the third party at the time A enters into the contract with X. If the third party knew his name he is called a named principal. If the third party did not know his name, but knew that there was a principal, such a principal is called an unnamed principal.

The general rule is that a disclosed principal, whether named or unnamed, is liable and entitled on the contract, and the agent is not. Thus the principal, rather than the agent, can sue and be sued on the contract. The agent having made the contract on behalf of the principal is not liable on it and plays no further part in its performance. The agent effectively drops out of the transaction. However, words, conduct or surrounding circumstances may show that the agent is liable and entitled, either instead of, or as well as, the principal.

In *Universal Steam Navigation Co Ltd v James McKelvie & Co* (1923) a charter party was made between the ship owners and "James McKelvie & Co, Newcastle-on-Tyne, Charterers". The charter party was signed "For and on behalf of James McKelvie & Co (as agents)". McKelvie & Co were subsequently sued for breach of charter party. They claimed that they had acted as mere agents for an Italian company and were therefore not liable under the contract. The House of Lords held that the words were quite clear that McKelvie & Co were acting as agents although they were also described as charterers in charter party.

It should also be noted that it was once thought that there was a custom that an agent contracting on behalf of a foreign principal was personally liable. It is now settled that there is no such presumption (*Teheran-Europe Co Ltd v S.T. Belton Ltd* (1968)).

Where the principal is undisclosed

A principal is said to be undisclosed where his existence is not known to the third party at the time of contracting. Thus, if A makes a contract with X as though he were acting for himself and without saying anything about agency so that X is unaware that A is in fact acting for P, P is an undisclosed principal. Nevertheless, the undisclosed principal can sue and be sued on the contract.

The rationale for this is explained by Lord Lindley in *Keighley, Maxsted & Co v Durrant* (1901, HL):

"The explanation of the doctrine that an undisclosed principal can sue and be sued on a contract made in the name of another person with his authority is that the contract is in truth, although not in form, that of the undisclosed principal himself. Both the principal and the authority exist when the contract is made; and the person who makes it for him is only the instrument by which the principal acts. In allowing him to sue and be sued upon it, effect is given, so far as he is concerned, to what is true in fact, although that truth may not have been known to the other contracting party."

It is, however, difficult to reconcile the operation of the rule with the notion of consensus *ad idem* in contract. Indeed, there is an anomaly in holding one person bound to another of whom he knows nothing and with whom he did not, in fact, intend to contract. Nevertheless, in commercial transactions, the reliance on middlemen or agents is inevitable and, as Lord Lindley went on to say, "in the great mass of contracts it is a matter of indifference to either party whether there is an undisclosed principal or not". If he exists it is, to say the least, extremely convenient that he should be able to sue and be sued as a principal, and he is only allowed to do so on terms which markedly exclude injustice. Helpful though Lord Lindley's rationale may be, it has been rejected by some academics and other theories have been put forward. This is, however, not the place for a review of these theories.

Another anomaly generated by the rule is with regards to the doctrine of privity because the rule places rights and liabilities on the undisclosed principal although he was not privy to that contract. Diplock L.J. suggested in *Freeman & Lockyer v Buckhurst Park Properties* (1964) that the rule could be explained as being for the avoidance of circuity of action:

"The principal could in equity compel the agent to lend his name in an action to enforce the contract against the contractor, and would at common law be liable to indemnify the agent in respect of the performance of the obligations assumed by the agent under the contract".

P's right to come into the contract, however, is subject to several conditions.

(1) A must have had authority from P to make the contract when he did. This rule is vitally important. If it were not so, anyone could come in to any contract. The ratification rule and the "undisclosed principal" rule are the converse of each other. P may come in to a contract by ratification, though authority was absent, provided a disclosure of agency was present; P may come into a contract by the "undisclosed principal" rule, though disclosure of agency was absent, provided authority was present. These rules are, however, mutually exclusive; an undisclosed principal cannot ratify an agent's excess of authority.

(2) An undisclosed principal cannot intervene if this would be inconsistent with the terms of the contract. In *Humble v Hunter* (1848) a person signed a charter party as "owner of the good ship or vessel called The Ann". Clearly, acting in this manner was incompatible with the concept of agency. The undisclosed principal was not allowed to sue on the contract. It was held that the word "owner" implied that the person signing was the principal. Similarly, in *Ferryways NV v Associated British Ports* (2008), X's immediate contract of employment was expressed to be with A. A was in fact acting as an agent for P but P was not disclosed as a principal. The contract of employment contained the words "A as the employer". The court held that those words did not prevent P from intervening as an undisclosed principal. Those words did not mean that A was the only person with the rights and obligations of an employer. Indeed, the Court

of Appeal in *Asty Maritime Co Ltd and Panagiotis Strave-lakis v Rocco Giuseppe and Figli SNC; The Astyanax* (1985) stressed that in the main, unless the contract is absolutely clear, undisclosed principals should be entitled to intervene.

(3) An undisclosed principal cannot intervene if the third party can show that he wanted to deal with A and with no one else. Such a situation arises where the personality of the agent is of importance to the third party. In *Collins v Associated Greyhound Racecourses Ltd* (1930) A agreed to underwrite a new issue of shares to be made by a company. (To underwrite shares means to agree to take up any shares which are not subscribed for by the public.) P, the undisclosed principal of A, was not allowed to come into the contract. The contract was held to involve exclusive reliance by the other party on A's business reputation and integrity. Similarly in *Talbot Underwriting Ltd v Nausch Higan & Murray Inc* (2006), as the insurers (the third party) had made it clear that the insurance cover was extended only to A, P could not intervene as an undisclosed principal.

Another case of interest is *Said v Butt* (1920). In that case, X tried to get a ticket for the first performance of a play. Y, the theatre manager, refused to sell him the ticket. X then got his friend, Z, to buy a ticket. When X turned up with the ticket, Y refused him entry. On whether there was a breach of contract by Y, the court held that there existed no contract between X and Y because Y would not have sold the ticket to X's friend if he knew of the agency. The tickets in question were usually sold by favour only. That made the identity of the purchase extremely important. There is some disquiet as to whether this case was correctly decided because there was no term in the contract excluding the principal's intervention and the third party did not rely on the personal characteristics of the agent, unlike *Collins v Associated Greyhound Racecourses Ltd*, above. The only "personal" aspect of the case was that the tickets were sold by favour only, and X was not favoured.

A contrasting case is *Siu Yin Kwan v Eastern Insurance Co Ltd; The Osprey* (1994) where the Privy Council held that a contract for indemnity insurance was not a personal contract in the sense that the identity is central. Accordingly, the undisclosed principal was entitled to intervene and sue on a contract of insurance made by his agent. Similarly, in *Ferryways NV v Associated British Ports* (2008), Teare J. found that as far as the crew was concerned, it did not matter that the ship management company that "employed" them was in fact acting as agents for some undisclosed ship owners. The identity of the actual principal was not important to the crew.

Where an undisclosed principal is permitted to come in to the contract, the agent nevertheless remains liable and entitled along with the principal to the benefits under the contract.

Agent and third party

The general rule is that an agent is neither liable nor entitled under a contract which he makes on behalf of his principal. He just drops out of the picture. In *Simon Crook v James Keen* (2007), for example, A had sold X a car which had been parked in P's car park for a long time without having paid parking charges. It was subsequently ruled by a court that X did not acquire ownership since ownership had never passed from the original owner to P. The Court of Appeal held that A could not be held to be liable to X because A had merely acted as P's agent and this was known to X.

There are exceptions, however, to this general rule.

(1) An agent is liable on the contract if he shows an intention to undertake personal liability. In the case of a written contract, if there is no mention of agency in the body of the contract or in the signature, it is almost certain that a court will hold A to be a party to the contract. If A is referred to, both in the body of the contract and in the signature, as an agent, it is virtually certain that he will be held to be not a party. If agency is mentioned in the one place but not in the other, there is a presumption that he is not a contracting party, but the presumption may be rebutted from the circumstances. It is all a matter of words, conduct and circumstances. Where an agent is held liable on a contract, he is almost invariably held entitled as well.

In *Higgins v Senior* (1841) it was held that words in the written contract showing that the agent contracted personally cannot be contradicted by parol or other extrinsic evidence. This does not prevent the agent from establishing an extrinsic agreement between himself and the third party that he should not be made personally liable. This defence is one founded in equity.

(2) Trade usage or custom may lead to an agent becoming personally liable and entitled. In *Fleet v Murton* (1871) two brokers in the colonial fruit trade signed this contract: "We have this day sold for your account to our principal, etc. (signed) A and B, Brokers." The principal was not named, but he was clearly disclosed and the brokers clearly intended to contract as agents. The principal refused to accept some of the goods and the third party, the seller, sued the brokers. He won, on the basis of a custom in the fruit trade that a broker was personally liable if the name of his principal was not inserted in the written contract.

Incidentally, parol evidence of trade usage or custom could be introduced to show that the agent should be made personally liable when the written contract does not seem to indicate that personal liability. The only limitation is that the parol evidence as introduced must not contradict the contract.

(3) As has already been stated, where an undisclosed principal comes in to the contract the agent is liable and entitled along with the principal.

(4) Sometimes a person purports to act for a principal when he is in fact acting for himself. If he purports to act for an unnamed principal, he can enforce the contract for himself. If he purports to act for a named principal, he can only enforce the contract for himself if he notifies the other party that he was really acting for himself, and even then only if the other party would not be prejudiced.

(5) Where the principal is non-existent, as in *Kelner v Baxter*, it is easy to infer that the agent intended personal liability. However, the agent is not automatically liable; it will depend upon what the parties intended.

(6) Where the agent executes a deed he will be liable on it even when his principal is named. As already stated, an agent cannot execute a deed unless he has been appointed by deed. He could, of course, choose to execute the deed in the presence of his principal.

There is a another way which an agent may be made liable. In *Collen v Wright* (1857) A, describing himself as the agent of P, agreed in writing to lease to X a farm which belonged to P. Both A and X believed that A had P's authority to make the lease. This was not in fact so. X first sued P for specific performance and failed. He then sued A (or, rather, his executors) for the costs which he had incurred. He won. The court found a separate implied contract whereby A promised X that he had P's authority, in return for X's promise to enter into the lease. So here is a very early example of a "collateral contract" (see Chapter 4). This particular instance of collateral contract is sometimes called an "implied warrant of authority". This phrase is perhaps somewhat misleading: what is implied is not a warranty in the main contract, but a separate contract altogether.

In two situations, legislation has come to the agent's aid: (1) an agent under a power of attorney who acts after it has been revoked (either by actual revocation or by occurrence of any event, such as the death of the principal, which has the effect of revocation) incurs no liability to the donor or the third party if at the time of acting he did not know of the revocation: s.5 of the Powers of Attorney Act 1971; (2) a debt incurred after commencement of bankruptcy, which would otherwise be void, is deemed to have been incurred before the bankruptcy by s.284(5) of the Insolvency Act 1986, and accordingly is enforceable.

Agent as Third Party

Since *Nisshin Shipping Co Ltd v Cleaves* (2003) it has been confirmed that agents are entitled to rely on the Contracts (Rights of Third Parties) Act 1999 against the principal contracting parties. In that case, C acted as shipping brokers for N and had negotiated nine time charters on N's behalf. Those contracts provided that commission was payable by N. On whether C, as stranger to those contracts, was entitled to enforce the commission clauses, the court held that s.1(1)(b) of the Contracts (Rights of Third Parties) Act 1999 should extend to the agent. That section provides that where it is clear that the parties to the contract intended for the third party to benefit from the contract, the third party should be entitled to claim that benefit in his own right. There is in law no objection for an agent who is normally the *alter ego* of the principal to be treated as a "third party" under the Act. It is important that the benefit claimed should be properly ascertained (see also *Laemthong International Lines Co Ltd v Artis* (2005)).

Payments

As regards payment made to an agent, the law requires him to account to his principal for such payments (*Anangel Atlas Compania Naviera SA v Ishikawa-Harima Heavy Industroes Co Ltd* (1990)). The duty to account applies, a fortiori, where the agent is not authorised to handle money or payment on behalf of the principal. In *Allwood v Max Clifford & Max Clifford Associates Ltd* (2001), A became pregnant with octuplets and then engaged C to be her public relations consultants. C also negotiated a contract with a tabloid newspaper to advise the newspaper on the breaking of the story. The fee for that contract was £15,000. A's contention was that C was her agent when C agreed to perform services for the newspaper, as such, C was not entitled to keep the £15,000 fee for itself but was accountable for the sum to her, as C's principal. This was a case where the payment received by an agent from a third party might be one which the agent was not allowed to keep for itself, notwithstanding that the agent had no consciously improper motive in accepting it and notwithstanding that the agent might have believed, quite correctly, that there would be no damage to the interests of the principal from what he had agreed to do for the third party. There was an important exception to that principle—if the principal knew about the arrangement between the agent and the third party, including the fact that the third party would be making a payment to the agent and if the principal gave a fully informed consent to the agent receiving the payment, then the principal could not demand the agent should account to him for the payment. In that case, as C could not prove that A was aware of his dealings with the newspaper and that A had given consent, he had to account to A for the payment received.

Where A has made a contract on behalf of P with X, it may happen that either P or X makes a payment, in discharge of his contractual obligation, to A. Suppose A does not pass on the money, either because he is fraudulent or because he becomes bankrupt. Must the payer pay again?

In a contract of sale, for example, there are two situations to be considered: (1) A, on behalf of P, buys goods from X; P pays A; A does not pay X; and (2) A, on behalf of P, sells goods to X; X pays A; A does not pay P. We shall consider these in turn.

Agent for purchase

Here P is the purchaser, through the agency of A. X is the seller. P pays the purchase money to A. The money does not reach X. X now claims the purchase price from P.

Where the seller, X, knew that A was acting as an agent, the general rule is that the buyer, P, remains liable to X, and must pay again. But the circumstances may be such that X is estopped from denying that P's payment to A is a good discharge. This will be so if the seller's conduct shows that he looked to the agent alone for payment, thus inducing the principal to settle with the agent. But it takes strong circumstances to raise an estoppel. In *Irvine v Watson* (1880) P employed A, a broker, to buy some oil for him. A bought from X, disclosing the fact of agency but not his principal's name. It was a term of the contract that payment should be made "by cash on or before delivery". In fact X delivered the oil without waiting for payment. P, not aware that X had not been paid, paid A. A became insolvent. X sued P. It was proved in evidence that it was not an invariable custom in the oil trade to insist on prepayment even where the contract stipulated for cash on or before delivery. P argued that he was justified in paying A, because the terms of the contract made it reasonable for him to assume that, since the oil had been delivered, X must have been paid by A. This argument was rejected by the court. The clause about prepayment in the contract was not enough to raise an estoppel, because X was perfectly entitled if he wished, to deliver the oil without getting prepayment. This case shows that the general rule—that the buyer must pay again—is not easily displaced. In a case such as this, therefore, P would be wiser not to pay the purchase price to, or through, A, but to pay it direct to X.

The question arises whether the rule applies if the seller thought that the agent was acting for himself. Suppose A buys goods from X apparently on his own account, whereas in fact he has an undisclosed principal, P. P pays the purchase money to A, who does not pay X. X then discovers the existence of P. Can X compel P to pay the purchase price again? In *Heald v Kenworthy* (1855) it was held that he could. In other words, the general rule applies even though the principal is an undisclosed principal. It seems that only where X

244

has in some way induced P to act to his detriment will X be estopped from suing P.

Agents for sale

Here P is the seller, through the agency of A. X is the buyer. Suppose X pays the purchase money to A, and A does not pay P. Can P compel X to pay again? Where A is known to be an agent the answer turns on whether A is authorised to receive the purchase money. If A is so authorised, the buyer, by paying A, has discharged his contractual duty; if A is not authorised, the buyer must pay again. The general rule is that an agent authorised to sell is not authorised to receive the purchase money. But, of course, in a particular case the agent may have authority to receive the money. If he has been expressly authorised to receive it, the matter is clear. If not, then the buyer will only escape double payment if he can show that the agent had implied authority, or apparent authority, or usual authority to receive payment.

The foregoing, however, does not apply where A appears to be selling on his own account. If the buyer, in that situation, pays A, he can rely on that payment if he is sued by P, a formerly undisclosed principal. The question whether or not A has P's authority to receive payment is irrelevant.

A similar distinction between a disclosed agency and an undisclosed agency exists in connection with set-off. Suppose A, an agent for sale, owes a personal debt to the buyer X. The question arises, can X set off his debt against the purchase price? The answer is that if X knows A to be an agent he cannot set off A's debt. On the other hand, if X believed that A was acting on his own account, and then, later, an undisclosed principal is revealed, X can set-off what A owes against the purchase money.

In all matters of payment there is a general principle that the intervention of an undisclosed principal, P, should not put the other party, X, in a worse position than he would have been in had A really been (as X thought) acting for himself.

Election

It may happen that both the principal and the agent are liable on a contract. This does not mean that the other party can recover twice over. He has to "elect" whether he will hold the principal liable or the agent, and his election "releases" the other. What amounts to an election is a question of fact.

If X, the other party to the contract, obtains judgment against the principal or the agent, then, though the judgment debt is not paid, X cannot then sue the other. However, in *Clarkson Booker Ltd v Andjel* (1964) X was able to sue A successfully, even though he had earlier issued a writ against P. It was said that such was not a final election for P because X had also threatened to sue and had never withdrawn that threat, and because he had not proceeded with his action against P.

HOW AGENCY ENDS

The contract of agency may come to an end in any of the ways in which contracts generally may be discharged. Thus it may end by performance, agreement, frustration or breach. The reader may care to go over this topic again after reading Part Five of this book.

Modes of termination

Performance
When both principal and agent have performed their contractual obligations the contract of agency comes to an end. An agency of necessity ends when the circumstances giving rise to the necessity cease.

Notice
If the contract of agency provides that it may be determined by notice being given, then the giving of such notice as provided for in the contract will bring the agency to an end. As with other contracts, if no period is specified then reasonable notice must be given, and what is reasonable will depend on the facts. In *Alpha Lettings Ltd v Neptune Research & Development Inc* (2003), the Court of Appeal overruled the lower court's finding that a twelve-month notice was reasonable stating that in many comparable contracts, the notice period ranged between three and six months.

The notice period is on the high end of the bracket where there are restraint covenants in the contract against competition against the principal. The court found that on the facts (as there was no covenant against competition either during the agreement or after its conclusion) the right notice period should be at the lower end and was thus fixed at four months.

Unless the contract says so, the notice of termination does not need to be in a particular form. It thus does not have to be in writing, for example, but it does have to be effective (*Concourse Initiatives Ltd v Maiden Outdoor Advertising Ltd* (2005)).

An implied agency, no less than an express one, can be determined by notice. Thus, a wife's implied authority to pledge her husband's credit for necessary household expenses can be terminated by her husband's giving her notice to that effect.

It should be noted that under the Commercial Agents (Council Directive) Regulations 1993, reg.15(1)(2) states that where an agency contract is concluded for an indefinite period either party may terminate it by notice. The period of notice is fixed:

(1) one month for the first year of the contract;

(2) two months for the second year commenced; and

(3) three months for the third year commenced and for subsequent years.

The parties are not allowed to agree to any shorter periods of notice. Any such agreement will be null and of no effect.

Agreement

If the principal and agent agree to end their contract, that will be effective. The contract, normally through termination clauses, can also specify events which would bring the agency to an end (e.g. how long the agency is to last, events such as change in the law or procedure, etc.). Where this is the case, notice is still necessary unless it has been dispensed with (but note the statutory limitations on commercial agency contracts).

Termination clauses will be read and construed as conventional contract clauses. A wide enough termination clause will be given its full effect, there is no requirement to imply a term that the termination clauses could only be activated if the agency is not profitable (*HSS Hire Services Group Plc v BMB Builders Mecrhants Ltd* (2006)).

The Commercial Agents (Council Directive) Regulations 1993 provide in reg.14 that an agency contract for a fixed period which continues to be performed by both parties after that period has expired shall be deemed to be converted into an agency contract for an indefinite period.

Frustration

It is not practicable to go through all the events which might possibly frustrate a contract of agency, but three events in particular must be mentioned. Death of either party puts an end to the agency.

Insanity of either puts an end to the agency. The bankruptcy of the principal puts an end to the agency. The bankruptcy of the agent puts an end to the agency if it makes him unfit to perform his duties.

It should be noted, however, that courts are very slow to find frustration in any case. The judicial postulation that the contract must be strictly performed generally prevails. In *Turner v Goldsmith* (1891) the contract of agency was to carry on for five years. P was a shirt manufacturer. The contract provided that A was employed to sell "various goods manufactured or sold" by P. After two years, P's factory was burnt down and he closed down his business. A sued P for breach of the agency agreement. The Court of Appeal held that the contract was not rendered impossible because P could still supply goods manufactured by someone else or with other goods altogether.

Breach

As with any other contract, if either party commits a repudiatory breach of the contract, the other party is entitled to treat himself as discharged and to sue for damages for the breach. A non-contractual variation of the agency contract would amount to a repudiatory breach. However where the variation is in response to the other party's misconduct or poor performance, it could be justified. In *Tony Vick v Vogle-Gapes Ltd* (2006), P had reduced the territory and market in which A operated as sales agent because A was failing to maximise his sales opportunities. The court held that although the variation was not permitted under the contract, it was to be excused because it was induced by A's own breach.

Where a party commits an anticipatory breach, for example by declaring that he will no longer perform the terms of the contract, the other party can elect to accept the breach and bring an end to the contract, or to reject the breach and carry on with the agency in the hope that the other party might change his mind.

Effects on the agency

The agent may be entitled to remuneration when the contract of agency is discharged. Remuneration can only be paid if, and only if, the agency is contractual and there is an express or implied term conferring the payment of remuneration to the agent.

The agent may also be entitled to unpaid commission after termination of the agency contract. The rule of thumb is that unless the agent is able to demonstrate that he has substantially done what he was contractually bound to do to earn his commission, there is no right to commission. In *Toulmin v Millar* (1887, HL) Lord Watson stated that:

> "In order to found a legal claim for commission there must not only be causal, there must also be a contractual, relation between the introduction and the ultimate transaction of sale".

An illustration of the principle is seen in *Millar, Son & Co v Radford* (1903). A, a firm of estate agents, were engaged by P to find a purchaser or failing that, a tenant, for P's property. A introduced a tenant, X, to P. Fifteen months later, X decides to buy the property. A claims to be entitled to commission for the sale. Collins M.R. held that A could not succeed. They had not brought about the sale. That said, if it is the agent who brought about the contract between P and the third party, he would be entitled to his commission even though what he did was very minor and was not the sole cause (*Jennifer Jane Dashwood v Fleurets Ltd* (2007)). It is for the agent to establish that his actions actually brought about the relationship between the principal and the third party (*Pettigrew v George Wimpey UK Ltd* (2007); *Jacques Lichtenstein v Clube Atletico Mineiro* (2005)).

The agent's entitlement to commission is delineated by the contract. This makes it important that the terms of the contract be properly construed every time a claim for unpaid commission is made. In *County Homesearch Co v Cowham* (2008), for example, it is not unusual for the contract to specify clearly what constitutes an event giving rise to commission. There, P had engaged A to find him a property. The contract stated that A was deemed to have introduced a property if P received sales particulars from A or from any of the estate agents with whom A dealt. A had sent a long list of possible properties to P which included one that P ultimately bought. That was enough for A to succeed in a claim for commission. Similarly in *Foxtons Ltd v Thesleff* (2005), the Court of Appeal held that where the estate agency contract states that commission was payable by P to A when contracts are exchanged, P had to pay even though the sale fell through despite the exchange of contracts. It is important therefore to make clear in the contract what constitutes performance on which commission would be payable.

Generally, an agent is not entitled to commission on transactions which take place after termination of the agency, but this, too, is subject to what the terms of the contract are. Under the Commercial Agents (Council Directive) Regulations 1993, in particular reg.8, the commercial agent has a right to commission on business transacted after termination of the agency contract, so long as the business is mainly attributable to the work undertaken by the agent during the contractual period and was transacted within a reasonable time after termination of the agency relationship. The provisions of reg.8(a) are conjunctive and cumulative (*Tigana Ltd v Decoro Ltd* (2003))—that means an agent would be entitled to commission where the transaction concluded after the end of the agency contract was to be mainly attributable to the agent's efforts during the period of the agency contract and if the transaction was entered into within a reasonable period after the agency contract had terminated.

The agent loses his right to commission if:

(1)   he acts outside the scope of his actual authority;

(2)   he acts in a way which he knows or ought to have known to be unlawful; or

(3)   he commits a serious breach of his duties as agent.

Where the agent is liable in breach of contract or in tort in relation to his principal, the law allows the principal to set off the commission owed against a counter-claim which the latter has against the agent. In *John D Wood & Co (Residential and Agricultural) Ltd v Knatchbull* (2003), although the principal owed his estate agent unpaid commission, it was found that the agent had breached his duty of care towards the principal in failing to inform the principal of important new facts about the marketing of his property. As such, the principal was entitled to set off the commission against his counter-claim that the agent was in breach of contract or was negligent.

It would also appear that where the agent in question is a "sub-agent", he would have no claim under reg.8 against the principal. In *Light v TY Europe* (2003), S was designated in the contract as "sole authorised agent" for T. S had in turn engaged the claimants, a few self-employed agents, to assist the marketing of T's products. The Court of Appeal held that although the claimants were clearly self-employed commercial agents under the Regulations, they were not entitled to claim compensation under reg.8 because the Regulations only applied to a commercial agent who was contractually bound to the principal. The claimants were bound, not to T, but S (but note their possible rights under the Contracts (Rights of Third Parties) Act 1999).

Another right the agent might have against the principal following termination is a right to be indemnified against all losses and liabilities incurred by him as an agent. This, too, is a contractual right and could therefore be excluded by contract at common law (*Rhodes v Fielder, Jones and Harrison* (1919)).

The Commercial Agents (Council Directive) Regulations 1993 however make the presumption that the self-employed commercial agent is at a disadvantaged position. As such, no contracting out of the application of the Regulations is permitted, especially, the protective provisions in regs 17 and 18 on the agent's right to an indemnity and compensation (reg.19). The ECJ has also ruled that Directive 86/653/EEC on self-employed commercial agents must be applied where the commercial agent carried on his activity in a Member State even though the principal might be established in a non-member country and there exists a clause in the contract stipulating that the contract is to be governed by the law of that non-member country (Case C-381/98 *Ingmar GB Ltd v Eaton Leonard Technologies Inc* (2000)). As regards the Regulations which have implemented the Directive into English law, they too have mandatory effect—they cannot be opted out of by the insertion of a choice of foreign law clause in the agency agreement in a case where the English courts have jurisdiction.

Regulation 17(3) provides that the commercial agent shall be entitled to an indemnity if and to the extent that:

(1)   he has brought the principal new customers or has significantly increased the volume of business with existing

customers and the principal continues to derive substantial benefits from the business with such customers; and

(2) the payment of the indemnity is equitable, taking into account all the circumstances and, in particular, the commission lost by the commercial agent.

As far as compensation is concerned, reg.17(6) states that the commercial agent shall be entitled to compensation for the damage he suffers as a result of the termination of his relations with his principal. "Damage" is deemed to occur when termination takes place under the following circumstances, which:

(1) deprive the commercial agent of the commission which proper performance of the agency contract would have generated for him, whilst providing his principal with substantial benefits linked to the activities of the commercial agent (*Gulf Electrical Materials v Babcock Transformers* (2002)); and

(2) have not enabled the commercial agent to amortise the costs and expenses that he had incurred in the performance of the agency contract on the advice of the principal. ("Amortise" refers to the making of provisions to pay off a debt.)

The computation of the compensation due to the commercial agent should not lead to an unjustified windfall for the agent. The computation issue is highly fact-dependent, judges should thus be free to identify those matters which are relevant to the circumstances of the case (*PJ Pipe & Valves v Audco India Ltd* (2005)). Regard as to what is fair and equitable on the circumstances (*Ingmar GB Ltd v Eaton Leonard Inc* (2001)) instead of some reference to some tariff system as is the case in France and some other continental jurisdictions is needed (*Barrett McKenzie & Co Ltd v Escada (UK) Ltd* (2001)). The House of Lords has confirmed the correctness of this approach (*Lonsdale v Howard & Hallam Ltd* (2007, HL)). It held that the United Kingdom was not acting inconsistently with the directive by calculating compensation by reference to the value of the agency on the assumption that it continued (see examples below) rather than to adopt the largely technical French system of awarding twice the average annual gross commission over the previous three years. The directive had envisaged each Member

Loan Receipt
Liverpool John Moores University
Library and Student Support

rrower ID: 21111150047124

an Date: 12/01/2010

an Time: 11:39 am

vies on contract /
111012637870

e Date: 02/02/2010 23:59

Please keep your receipt
in case of dispute

State using their own method of calculation—the directive does not lay down any prescribed formula.

In *Moore v Piretta P.T. Ltd* (1998) it was held that the right to indemnity and compensation applies to the whole currency of the agency, including any period before the Regulations took effect. It is not open to the principal to argue that the right is confined to activities carried on after the Regulations had come into effect.

Similarly, that purposive approach to reg.17 must also mean that the compensatory provisions in it extend to contracts that had expired by effluxion of time. In *Tigana Ltd v Decoro Ltd* (2003), D, a furniture company, had engaged the services of a self-employed commercial agent T to penetrate the UK market. Following the termination of the agreement, D continued to take substantial orders from UK customers that had initially been introduced by T. D agreed to pay an agreed amount of the commission due to T under the sales agreement but T also sought compensation under the Regulations for indemnity or compensation for damage suffered as a result of the termination of the sales agreement. The court held that "damage" suffered by a commercial agent as a result of the termination of the agency was to be regarded as a punitive loss and not simply actual loss. In that case, damage had indeed occurred—D had also retained for itself without payment the substantial benefits of the customer connection introduced by T. T was thus entitled to claim under reg.17. The amount of compensation payable was to be assessed by reference to the net remuneration of T in the period of its agency.

Regulation 18 provides that indemnity and compensation shall not be paid where:

(1)　the principal has terminated the contract of agency because of default attributable to the commercial agent (in *John Harold Crane v Sky In-Home Service Ltd* (2007) as the agent had passed off his own products as his principal's, that was a serious breach warranting the loss of his right to indemnity and/or compensation; see also *Tony Vick v Vogle-Gapes Ltd* (2006));

(2)　the commercial agent himself has terminated the contract (unless he is forced to by circumstances attributable to the principal or incapacity); or

(3)   the commercial agent himself has terminated the contract by assigning his rights and duties under the agency contract to another person.

Effects on the third party

When the contract comes to an end, the actual authority of the agent terminates. But the ending of the contract does not necessarily terminate the agent's apparent or usual authority. For example, apparent or usual authority does not end by notice given by the principal to the agent; to end it, the principal must give notice to the third party. Whilst a principal's insanity terminates the agent's actual authority, he may still have apparent authority. In *Drew v Nunn* (1879), P, when sane, gave his wife, A, authority to act for him and held her out to X, a tradesman, as having that authority. P then became insane. His wife bought goods on credit from X, who did not know of P's insanity. Later P regained his reason. X successfully sued P for the price of the goods supplied. Although A's actual authority was terminated by P's insanity, her apparent authority continued.

In another case on insanity, *Yonge v Toynbee* (1910), X started an action against P. P instructed A, a solicitor, to defend the action for him. P then became insane. Not knowing of P's insanity, A entered an appearance and delivered a defence. X then learnt of P's insanity, and got the proceedings struck out. He sought an order against A for the costs of his abortive action against P, arguing that A had taken steps in that action without authority. X succeeded because an insane person could only defend proceedings by his guardian *ad litem* and because parties to proceedings are entitled to rely on an implied warrant of authority by a solicitor acting for a party to those proceedings.

Irrevocable agency

There are two situations in which an agency is irrevocable. That means that the purported revocation of the agent's authority is not of any effect, and the authority continues.

Authority coupled with an interest

If the agent's authority is given to him (for consideration or by deed) to secure some interest of his which exists independently of the agency, that authority cannot be revoked by the principal. In

Carmichael's case (1896) A promoted a company, with the idea that the company should buy from him a mine that he owned. P agreed to underwrite 1,000 shares in the company, and he authorised A to apply for the shares on his behalf. This authority was held to be irrevocable, because it was coupled with an interest—namely, the interest that A had in the shares being taken up, since if they were not taken up he would not get the purchase money for the mine.

This rule applied only where the authority is given for the protection of an interest which already exists. It does not apply where the interest arises after the giving of authority.

Irrevocable power of attorney

It is provided by s.4 of the Powers of Attorney Act 1971 that where a power of attorney is expressed to be irrevocable and is given to secure: (a) a proprietary interest of the donee of the power; or (b) to secure the performance of an obligation owed to the donee, then, so long as the donee has that interest or is owed that obligation, the power shall not be revoked by the donor without the consent of the donee, nor shall it be revoked by death, incapacity or bankruptcy of the donor, nor, if the donor is a body corporate, by its winding-up or dissolution.

Additionally, the Mental Capacity Act 2005, which repeals and replaces the Enduring Powers of Attorney Act 1985, sets up a new statutory scheme for the creation of "lasting powers of attorney". Since an object of the legislation is to ensure the welfare and care of those who, for example, grant a power of attorney to a close relative and then subsequently develop a mental disability, the power of attorney survives the subsequent mental incapacity of the donor.

PART FIVE

ENDING THE AGREEMENT

PERFORMANCE

THE LAST part of this book is called "Ending the Agreement". This will consider the four ways in which a contract may come to an end: performance, agreement, frustration and breach. In the final chapter remedies will be considered.

The most obvious way in which a contract may come to an end is by its being performed. If A and B make a contract under which A is to perform some service and B is to pay him for it, then when A has performed his service and B has paid the money, both parties have discharged their contractual obligations, and the contract is at an end.

The question arises: What amounts to performance?

THE GENERAL RULE

The general rule is that performance must exactly match what the party agreed to do, so that if he does something less than—or different from—what he agreed to do he has not discharged his contractual obligation, and consequently is not entitled to payment. In *The Kathleen* (1874) a ship was abandoned after a collision. It was later saved by third parties, who brought it to an intermediate port. It was held that the owners were not entitled to "freight" (that is, the charge for the carriage of goods) even though the contract of carriage exempted the ship owners from liability for loss caused by collisions, and even though the collision was entirely due to the fault of the other ship.

A party who has fallen short of complete performance cannot sue on the contract because his own complete performance is a "condition precedent" to his right to sue. This rule, requiring complete performance, sometimes leads to unjust results. In *Cutter v Powell* (1795) Cutter agreed to serve as second mate on a ship bound from Jamaica to Liverpool. He was to be paid 30 guineas "provided he proceeds, continues and does his duty ... from hence to the port of Liverpool." The ship sailed on August 2. It arrived at Liverpool on October 9. But Cutter had died at sea on September 20. It was held that his widow could not recover anything for the work he had done. The contract was said to be "entire"; nothing was to be paid unless Cutter had performed his entire duty under the contract. Although this was a hard case, it was not so unjust as at first sight appears. The ordinary rate for such a voyage at the time was about £8, or so the court appeared to believe, so the contract figure was almost four times the ordinary rate. Lord Kenyon C.J. said it was "a kind of insurance". It was a kind of insurance from the point of view of the ship owner; from Cutter's point of view it was a kind of gamble.

If the general rule, that performance to be effective must be complete performance, were maintained in all its rigorous logic, it would frequently lead to injustice. In practice it is subject to four exceptions, which will be looked at in turn. It is also subject to the doctrine of frustration, which will be considered in Chapter 17.

THE EXCEPTIONS

Severable contracts

Cutter v Powell, above, is an example of an entire contract. But not all contracts are entire; some are severable. Whether any particular contract is entire or severable depends upon the intention of the parties, which has to be determined by considering the express and implied terms of the contract. The problem is: Does the contract mean that the party in question is not to be entitled to payment unless and until he has completely performed his whole obligation, or does it mean that he can sue for payment when he has performed some part of what he undertook to do? In *Cutter v Powell* the contract was construed to be of the first kind (entire), as was the contract in *Vlierboom v Chapman* (1884). In that case a ship owner agreed to carry a cargo of rice from Batavia to Rotterdam. He in fact carried it only to Mauritius. It was held that he was not entitled to any freight. On the other hand, the contract in *Ritchie v Atkinson* (1808) was held to be severable. A ship owner agreed to carry a cargo of hemp, freight to be £5 a ton. He in fact only took part of the cargo. It was held that he could recover freight proportional to the quantity carried.

It is commonly said that a contract is entire or severable, but it would be more accurate to speak of a particular obligation within a contract as being entire or severable. Thus the obligation to carry to a particular destination is entire (*Vlierboom*'s case); the obligation to carry a particular quantity is severable (*Ritchie*'s case).

Prevention of performance

If a party to a contract performs part of the work that he has undertaken, and is then prevented by the fault of the other party from finishing the work, he can sue. This is so whether the contract (or his obligation) is severable or entire. He can either sue for damages for breach of contract, or he can sue on a quantum meruit and so obtain a reasonable remuneration for the work he has done. In *Planché v Colburn* (1831) the plaintiff agreed to write a book on costume and ancient armour, to be published by the defendants in a series called "The Juvenile Library". He was to be paid £100 on completion of the book. He collected material and wrote part of the book. The defendants then abandoned the series. On a quantum meruit claim ("as much as he has deserved") he was awarded £50. Alternatively, it seems that he could have regarded the publisher's action as an anticipatory breach of contract and, having completed the book, sued for the full contract price (see below, p.291)

Acceptance of partial performance

If one party partially performs his obligation and the other party accepts the work, it may be possible to infer that the parties have agreed to abandon the original contract (whether severable or entire) and to make a new one, under which the party making partial performance is entitled to a reasonable remuneration. In *Christy v Row* (1808) the plaintiff's ship was carrying the defendant's coal from Shields to Hamburg. The ship was prevented by "restraint of princes" from reaching Hamburg, and the master, at the request of the consignee, delivered some of the coal at Gluckstadt, a town on the Elbe below Hamburg. The plaintiff successfully sued for freight.

Such a new promise to pay will be inferred only where the beneficiary has a genuine choice whether to accept or reject the benefit of the work done. In *Sumpter v Hedges* (1898, CA) the plaintiff agreed to build two houses on the defendant's land for £565. He did work to the value of about £333 and then abandoned the contract. The defendant himself completed the buildings. The plaintiff's claim for a quantum meruit failed. No new implied promise to pay could arise from the mere fact that the defendant had reoccupied his own land and gone on with the building. He had no choice between accepting or rejecting the white elephant. But the plaintiff was awarded a reasonable sum in respect of the materials which he had left on the site and which the defendant had used in completing the buildings. A promise to pay a reasonable sum for these materials could be inferred from the defendant's choosing to use them.

Substantial performance

A party who performs his obligation defectively, but substantially, can enforce the contract. In *Boone v Eyre* (1779) the plaintiff conveyed to the defendant a plantation in the West Indies together with the slaves on it. He sued for the price. The defendant pleaded that the plaintiff was not lawfully possessed of the slaves. Lord Mansfield held that this was no defence. That case is perhaps the origin of the doctrine of substantial performance. It was given a revival in *Dakin v Lee* (1916, CA), which involved a contract for repairs to be done to a house. The work as done did not accord with the contract in certain respects. The Court of Appeal gave judgment for the plaintiff repairer, but with a deduction equal to the cost of putting right the defects. *Dakin v Lee* was followed in *Hoenig v Isaacs* (1952, CA). The plaintiff agreed to redecorate and furnish the defendant's flat for £750. The defendant complained of faulty design and bad workmanship, but he paid £400. The plaintiff sued for the balance,

£350. The court found that there were defects in the furniture, and assessed the cost of putting them right at £55. The defendant argued that, if the plaintiff was entitled to anything at all, it was certainly less than the contract price and should be assessed on a quantum meruit basis. The Court of Appeal held that the plaintiff had made substantial performance and that he was entitled to the contract price, less the cost of making good the defects.

Of course, there are limits to the doctrine of substantial performance, and these are well illustrated by the case of *Bolton v Mahadeva* (1972, CA). The plaintiff had contracted to install central heating in the defendant's house for £560. At the trial it was proved that the house was 10 per cent less warm than it should have been and that because of a defective flue there were fumes in the living rooms. It would have cost £174 to put right these defects. The Court of Appeal held that the plaintiff was not able to rely on the doctrine of substantial performance—so the plaintiff got nothing.

The doctrine of substantial performance can be applied to an entire contract, no less than to a severable one. In *Hoenig v Isaacs* (above) Somervell L.J. said that it could have been applied in *Cutter v Powell* if the sailor had served all the way to Liverpool but had "failed on some occasion in his duty as mate". This emphasises again that it is not a whole contract which is entire, but an obligation within a contract.

This discussion of the doctrine of substantial performance will no doubt recall to mind the distinction between conditions and warranties, considered in Chapter 4. That distinction does indeed come into the question of defective performance. If the defect in performance amounts only to a breach of warranty, the "defective performer" is a "substantial performer" and he can sue for his money, though he must submit to a deduction equal to the cost of making good the defect; if it amounts to a breach of condition he cannot sue. As Chapter 4 showed, not all contractual terms can be brought within the framework of conditions and warranties: see the *Hong Kong Fir* case (1962, CA) and the *Cehave* case (1976, CA). With "intermediate" or "innominate" terms, the test is whether B, the other party, has received substantially the whole benefit which it was the intention of the parties that he should obtain under the contract. If yes, then A, the "defective performer," is a "substantial performer" and he can sue for his money; if no, then he cannot sue.

Where a party performs only partially or defectively, although, as we have seen, he may be able to sue on the contract, he is not entirely discharged. If the incompleteness or defectiveness of his performance amounts to a breach of contract, he can be sued for that breach. Thus, in *Ritchie v Atkinson* (see p.261, above), a case decided in the context of severable contracts, although Ritchie won his action for proportional freight, he was later held liable in damages for failing to carry the rest of the cargo; see *Atkinson v Ritchie* (1809).

A tender of performance is an offer of performance. Tender of performance is equivalent to performance itself. The reason for this rule is that since one party often cannot complete performance without the concurrence of the other party, justice demands that if he makes an offer to perform which is rejected by the other party he should be treated as discharged. In *Startup v Macdonald* (1843) the plaintiff agreed to sell 10 tons of oil to the defendant and to deliver it to him "within the last 14 days of March". The plaintiff tried to deliver the oil at 8.30pm on March 31, a Saturday. The defendant refused to accept it, because of the lateness of the hour. The plaintiff was awarded damages for non-acceptance. This case would probably not be decided in the same way today. Section 29(5) of the Sale of Goods Act 1979 provides:

> "Demand or tender of delivery may be treated as ineffectual unless made at a reasonable hour; and what is a reasonable hour is a question of fact."

It is doubtful whether 8.30pm on a Saturday night is a reasonable hour to start examining and weighing 10 tons of oil. But the principle of *Startup v Macdonald* is unimpaired; a valid tender of goods discharges the tenderer from further liability and entitles him to damages for breach of contract.

The effect of a tender of money is not quite the same. Tender of a money payment does not discharge the tenderer from liability. He need not make any further tender, but his obligation to pay remains. If he is sued, he can pay the money into court, and if the other party goes on with his action he (the other party) will be ordered to pay the costs. For a tender of money to be valid it must be in "legal tender" and it must be of the exact amount due. The debtor is not entitled to ask for change. But, of course, he can always leave the surplus with the creditor.

If the contract states a definite time for performance, the question may arise whether the time is "of the essence" of the contract. That is the classic way of putting it. The broad answer is that at common law time is of the essence and in equity it is not. At common law, unless the contract provides otherwise, performance must be completed by the date specified. If it is not completed by that date, the other party can sue for repudiatory breach. But by s.10(1) of the Sale of Goods Act 1979, stipulations as to time of payment are not of the essence of a contract of sale, "unless a different intention appears from the terms of the contract". Section 10(2) says: "Whether any other stipulation as to time is or is not of the essence of the contract depends on the terms of the contract." Courts of equity have always rather leant against time being of the essence. Thus, in contracts for the sale of land, time is not necessarily of the essence, and specific performance may be decreed despite the failure of the plaintiff to keep to the time fixed for completion, if this can be done without injustice to the defendant. If the parties nevertheless make time "of the essence" then the impact can be dramatic. In *Union Eagle Ltd v Golden Achievement Ltd* (1997), the purchase price for a flat was to be tendered by 5pm. In fact, the buyer was 10 minutes late. The Privy Council agreed that this entitled the seller to repudiate the contract and retain the deposit. This reflected what the parties themselves had agreed and certainty was important in this transaction. But time is of the essence, even in equity, in some situations: (1) if that is expressed in, or can be inferred from, the terms of the contract; (2) if the circumstances are such that it is vital that the agreed date should be kept to, for example where the subject-matter of the contract is something which fluctuates in value, such as a block of highly speculative shares; and (3) where one party has already delayed, and the other party notifies him that unless performance is completed within some reasonable specified time he will treat the contract as broken. In such a case time becomes of the essence by virtue of the notice. In this last case, the party serving the notice may do so immediately the other party fails to carry out his obligation by the stipulated date, even though at that stage time was not of the essence of the contract; it is not necessary to wait until there has been unreasonable delay by the party in breach before serving the notice, though the notice has to give a reasonable period of time in which to perform the obligation: see *Behzadi v Shaftesbury Hotels Ltd* (1991). See also *Rickards (Charles) Ltd v Oppenheim* (1950, CA).

The rules of common law and equity on this matter were brought together by statute in 1873. The relevant enactment is now s.41 of the Law of Property Act 1925, which provides:

"Stipulations in a contract, as to time or otherwise, which according to rules of equity are not deemed to be or to have become of the essence of the contract, are also construed and have effect at law in accordance with the same rules."

Until recently many lawyers were under the impression that, in relation to a contractual term where time was not of the essence, failure to perform by the stipulated time was not a breach of contract at all. This was an error, as was made clear by the House of Lords in *Raineri v Miles, Wiejski (Third Party)* (1981, HL). The true position is this: if time is of the essence, late performance is a repudiatory breach; if time is not of the essence, late performance is not a repudiatory breach, but it is a breach, and it entitles the injured party to damages. (See also *Lombard North Central Plc v Butterworth* (1987, CA) and *Behzadi v Shaftesbury Hotels Ltd* (1991).) Section 41 of the Law of Property Act 1925 does not negative the existence of a breach of contract where one has occurred, but in certain circumstances it bars any assertion that the breach has amounted to a repudiation of the contract.

VICARIOUS PERFORMANCE

Vicarious performance arises where A engages B, by contract, to perform some service and then B gets C to perform the service in fact. If this is done with the knowledge and consent of A, no difficulty is likely to arise. But if it is done without A's consent, what then? The answer is that the "creditor" (that is, the party to whom something, not necessarily money, is due under a contract) cannot object to vicarious performance unless it really matters to him that B should perform the service personally. To take an obvious example, if B's duty under the contract is to pay a sum of money to A, A cannot refuse to accept the money because in fact C, not B, pays it to him. And the same principle has been applied to performances other than the payment of money. In *British Waggon Co v Lea* (1880) B contracted to let out railway wagons to A and keep them in repair for seven years. It was held that the contract could be performed by C; it did not matter to A who kept the wagons in repair, so long as the work was properly done.

If the work were not properly done it would be B, not C, who would be liable to A. For this reason it is misleading to speak of vicarious performance as being an "assignment of liabilities". The phrase is sometimes used, but it is not really correct. The liability is not transferred. The original contractor remains liable—for bad work, for example—and the sub-contractor does not become directly liable on the original contract. Of course, if the contractor is sued he may in turn sue the sub-contractor who did the defective work for breach of contract and so recover his loss. In *Stewart v Reavell's Garage* (1952) the plaintiff took a 1929 Bentley to the defendants' garage to have the brakes relined. With the plaintiff's consent, they arranged for the work to be done by a sub-contractor. The work was done badly, the brakes failed and the car crashed into a tree. The defendants were held liable for the sub-contractor's bad workmanship. Since the plaintiff had agreed, the defendants were obviously entitled to perform vicariously, but that did not lead to any transfer of liability.

Whenever a contracting party performs his obligation vicariously he remains liable to the other party for any bad workmanship or other breach which may occur. This is so, even in a quite "impersonal" contract. In a "personal" contract a still stricter rule applies; the contractor is not permitted to delegate performance at all. This is true of such obviously personal contracts as a contract to paint a portrait, and it is also true of less obvious cases. For instance, in *Edwards v Newland* (1950, CA) the principle was applied to a contract to store goods. It was said that the owner of the goods relies on the skill and integrity of the contractor. In such a case, vicarious performance does not count as performance at all. The person originally contracted to do the work is not discharged and the person for whom the service was meant to be provided is not obliged to pay.

CHAPTER SIXTEEN

AGREEMENT TO DISCHARGE OR VARY A CONTRACT

THE CONTRACTUAL bond is founded on the agreement of the parties. The parties may, by agreement, untie the bond.

In its simplest form, discharge by agreement occurs where A promises to give up his rights under the contract in return for a promise by B to give up his rights. In that case the contract is at an end; or the parties may add to this discharge of the old contract new promises which constitute a new contract. For example, B has agreed to sell to A a television. Before it is delivered, they may agree that B is to sell to A a video recorder, not a television. Where this happens it is usually by means of express agreement, but it can happen by implied agreement. B may agree to sell to A a dozen bottles of red wine. In the event, B delivers a dozen bottles of wine, of which six are red and six are white. A, if he wishes, can accept the dozen bottles delivered. If he does so, the first contract is discharged by agreement and a new contract comes into existence. The first contract is not discharged by performance, because there has not been performance, but it is discharged by implied agreement.

Discharge by agreement may arise out of a term in the contract itself. The most important instance of this is where the contract contains a provision for notice. This is commonly the case in a contract of employment. If the provisions as to notice are complied with, the contract is discharged by agreement. If one or other party purports to end the contract without complying with the provisions as to notice, that is a breach. Breach will be considered in Chapter 18.

Just as the parties may agree to discharge a contract, so they may agree to vary a contract. Indeed, it is sometimes not easy to say whether they are varying a contract or discharging one contract and making a new one. To substitute a video recorder for a television is undoubtedly to discharge the first contract and make a second. On the other hand, to change the date on which the television is to be delivered is merely to vary the contract. But there is a more debatable borderland in between. Although the distinction is often not important, sometimes it is, as will be seen.

Two points arise in connection with discharge and variation which require some discussion. These are formality and consideration.

As a general proposition, it can be said that contracts can be discharged or varied by an agreement in any form the parties wish—by deed, in writing, by word of mouth, or by conduct. For example, in *Berry v Berry* (1929) a husband entered into a deed of separation, in which he covenanted to pay his wife £18 a month. Some years later, by a written contract not under seal, he agreed to pay her £9 a month plus (if his earnings were in excess of £350 a year) 30 per cent of the excess. The wife brought an action claiming arrears on the basis that £18 a month was due. It was held that that claim was not open to her; the second agreement had validly replaced the original deed, and the second agreement had been complied with.

It might seem, at first sight, that the discharge or variation of a written contract by word of mouth would conflict with the parol evidence rule. But this is not so. Chapter 4 said that that rule "does not prevent extrinsic evidence being given to prove that the contract does not yet operate or has ceased to operate"; so a party can give evidence of an oral agreement to end the contract. The parol evidence rule also does not apply "where the written agreement is not the whole agreement". A party can give evidence to prove that the original written agreement has been varied by a subsequent (as distinct from an antecedent) oral agreement.

Some contracts, however, although they can be discharged by subsequent oral agreement, cannot be varied in that manner. This is particularly true of contracts which were required to be evidenced in writing by the Statute of Frauds, of which one remains: contracts of guarantee (see also Chapter 6). (For a recent example of a failure by the parties to comply with this provision see *Actionstrength Ltd v*

International Glass Engineering (2003)). (The same principle applies to contracts required by other rules of law to be made in a particular manner.) The position can be stated in three rules.

(1) If the discharge is total it will be effective even though it is not evidenced in writing.

(2) If the discharge is only a partial discharge, so that in effect it is a variation, that discharge must be evidenced by writing, and if it is not it is of no effect. In *Goss v Nugent* (1833) there was a written contract for the sale of land, which, among other terms, bound the vendor to make good title. Later the purchaser agreed orally not to insist on title being made to part of the land. Then the purchaser changed his mind and declined to go on with the contract. The vendor sued. He failed; he was unable to deliver the title that he had agreed to deliver by the original contract; that contract still stood, the oral variation being of no effect. (It should be noted that, at the time when this case was decided contracts for the sale of an interest in land were required to be evidenced in writing. Now they must be in writing, to comply with the requirements of the Law of Property (Miscellaneous Provisions) Act 1989.)

(3) If the oral discharge is a total discharge coupled with the making of a new contract in substitution, it is effective to put an end to the original contract and the new contract is not enforceable.

It is sometimes difficult to decide whether the parties intended variation or whether they intended total discharge plus substitution. If they intended variation then the original contract is enforceable in its unvaried form; if they intended total discharge plus substitution then nothing is enforceable, since the original contract is gone and the new one is not evidenced in writing.

CONSIDERATION

In cases of discharge

Just as a contract is formed by agreement plus consideration, so discharge by agreement requires consideration. Where the contract is executory, in the sense that neither party has completely performed his obligation, no difficulty arises. If A promises to give up his rights and B promises to give up his, that is a good discharge.

Consideration moves from both A and B. But if A has completely performed his obligation under the contract, and he releases B from his obligation, there is no consideration moving from B. The consequence is that A could go back on his promise to release B. It is similar to the situation looked at in Chapter 2, involving part payment of a debt and *Pinnel's* case and *Foakes v Beer*. If the doctrine of promissory estoppel (see pp.45–49, above) is strong enough to overthrow *Foakes v Beer*, consideration will not be necessary for discharge by agreement.

The difficulty can be overcome by B giving to A some new consideration in return for A giving up his rights under the contract. What is required is "accord and satisfaction". Accord is agreement and satisfaction is consideration. A has painted B's house, for which service the contractual price is £2,500. B cannot pay this sum. He offers, instead of paying £2,500, to rewire A's house. A agrees. There is accord and satisfaction. It should be noted, however, that the requirement of consideration seems to have been modified by the Court of Appeal's decision in *Williams v Roffey Bros & Nicholls (Contractors) Ltd* (1990): see Chapter 2.

At one time it was thought that the satisfaction could only become effective when it was executed. But the modern law is that an executory promise may constitute effective satisfaction, if that is what the parties have agreed. In *Elton Cop Dyeing Co v Broadbent & Son Ltd* (1919, CA) A bought some machinery from B which turned out to be defective, and A claimed damages for breach of warranty. By a compromise agreement, A agreed to withdraw his action and B agreed to make good the machinery, bearing half the cost of so doing. A then sued on the original contract. He failed. B successfully pleaded accord and satisfaction. It was held that the compromise agreement, properly construed, meant that A accepted as satisfaction, discharging his original cause of action, B's promise to make good the machinery. If B did not eventually carry out that promise, A could sue him on that.

A more recent illustration is *British Russian Gazette Ltd v Associated Newspapers Ltd* (1933). A Mr Talbot agreed to compromise (i.e. to settle) a libel action for a sum of money. His letter stated:

"I accept the sum of one thousand guineas ... in full discharge and settlement of my claims ... and I will forthwith instruct my solicitors to end the proceedings now pending."

Before he had actually received the money Mr Talbot disregarded his agreement and continued with the action arguing that until the payment had actually been made there was no effective discharge. The Court of Appeal rejected this view. There was accord and satisfaction; a promise had been exchanged for a promise and Mr Talbot was bound by the terms of the compromise. He had promised to discontinue the action; the newspaper had promised to pay him the money.

In cases of variation

If a variation is for the benefit of both parties, then it contains within itself its own consideration. Suppose A has agreed to buy from B a car to be delivered and paid for on October 31. It turns out to be convenient to both A and B that delivery should be postponed until November 30, and they agree to that new date. That is an effective variation. Consideration moves from A and from B; A gives up his right to receive delivery on October 31 and B gives up his right to make delivery and take payment on October 31.

If, however, a variation is made for the benefit of only one of the parties, the situation is different. If B (the seller) agrees, for the sole benefit of A (the buyer), that delivery of the car shall be postponed from October 31 to November 30, A has given no consideration. Does this mean, then, that the indulgence granted by B has no effect? If this were so it would lead to some unjust results. B would be able to make a claim on November 1 for non-acceptance by A, and (even more unjustly) A would be able, if sued by B for non-acceptance on November 30, to plead that he was excused because B was in breach of his contractual duty to deliver on October 31.

Even the common law did not go to this length. The party for whose benefit the indulgence had been granted was not allowed to repudiate it. Thus, in the example, A could not refuse acceptance on November 30 by arguing that B was in breach of his contractual obligation to deliver on October 31. The common law evolved a doctrine of "waiver", under which, in many cases, the party who had granted the indulgence was not allowed to go back on his word.

Thus, in the example, B might not be permitted to insist on his contractual right to make delivery and take payment on October 31. The doctrine of "waiver", however, was dependent upon the mysterious distinction between waiver and variation. If the court found that an indulgence was a waiver (or forbearance), it would give effect to it; if it found that an indulgence was a variation, it would not. It is not possible to find in the cases a rational line of distinction between the two.

Courts of equity were free to take a more consistent view, and hold that a party who had granted an indulgence to the other was bound by it. This view now prevails in all courts. It is an application of the doctrine of "promissory estoppel", and since it does not conflict with *Foakes v Beer*, it has received general acceptance.

In *Alan (W.J.) & Co v El Nasr Export & Import Co* (1972, CA) a contract for the sale of coffee provided for the price expressed in Kenyan shillings to be paid by irrevocable letter of credit. The buyers obtained a confirmed letter of credit expressed to be for payment in sterling. The sellers raised no complaint about the terms of the letter of credit, and they drew on the credit in part payment of the contract price. While shipment of the coffee was in progress, sterling was devalued. The sellers claimed such amount in Kenyan shillings as would make up for the devaluation. The Court of Appeal held that the sellers, by their conduct in accepting the letter of credit and/or in drawing on it, had waived the right to be paid in Kenyan currency. In accordance with the principle of *Hughes v Metropolitan Railway Co* the sellers' claim must fail. (See also p.44, above.) Another example of equity's more elegant solution is well illustrated by *Charles Rickards Ltd v Oppenheim* (1950). The defendant ordered a body to be built on a car chassis he had purchased, the work to be completed within "six or seven months." At the end of this time the work was not finished but he agreed to wait a further three months. The work was still by then unfinished so he gave final notice that unless it was completed within another four weeks the order would be cancelled. At the end of this period the body was still not complete and the car was only offered to him three months later when he refused to accept it. The plaintiffs thereupon sued him for his failure to accept the car. The Court of Appeal decided that, although originally time had been of the essence, the agreement to extend the performance time by three months operated as a waiver. If the car had been delivered within that time the defendant would have been bound to accept it.

However, the defendant, by giving reasonable notice that time was once again of the essence, rendered the plaintiffs in breach of contract by their failure to complete the work. Accordingly, their action against the defendant failed. The result is satisfactory and in accordance with the principles enunciated on a case such as *Hughes v Metropolitan Railway Co* (1877).

FRUSTRATION

IN EARLY days the law took the view that contractual obligations were "absolute". As expounded in *Paradine v Jane* (1647), this meant that if a person undertook by contract to do something he was absolutely bound to do it. If subsequent events made it impossible for him to do it, he was in breach of his contract and was liable in damages to the other party. In 1863, however, in the case of *Taylor v Caldwell*, a major dent in this rule of absoluteness was made. Caldwell had agreed to give Taylor the use of The Surrey Gardens and Music Hall on four named days for the purpose of holding concerts there. Just before the first of these days the hall was destroyed by fire. Taylor sued for damages for breach of the agreement. The court gave judgment for the defendant. Blackburn J. said:

> "We think ... that the Music Hall having ceased to exist, without fault of either party, both parties are excused, the plaintiffs from taking the gardens and paying the money, the defendants from performing their promise to give the use of the Hall and Gardens and other things."

THE EXTENT OF THE DOCTRINE

From this case there developed the doctrine of frustration, under which the parties to a contract are excused further performance of their obligations if some event occurs during the currency of the contract, without the fault of either party, which makes further performance impossible or illegal, or which makes it something radically different from what was originally undertaken. The present extent of the doctrine will be considered under those three heads.

Impossible

A contract may become impossible in three ways.

Subject-matter destroyed

This point is well illustrated by *Taylor v Caldwell* itself. The contract related to "The Surrey Gardens and Music Hall", and though only the music hall was destroyed that was enough to frustrate the contract, because the object of the contract was rendered impossible. So the total destruction of the subject-matter is not necessary.

Death

A "personal contract" is ended by frustration if either party dies. The contracts covered by this rule include contracts of employment and agency.

Subject-matter unavailable

A contract is frustrated if a thing or person required for its performance ceases, through some extraneous cause, to be available for that purpose. Thus a charter party may be discharged if the ship is damaged; a contract for the sale of goods may be discharged if the goods are requisitioned; a contract of service may be discharged if one of the parties becomes ill, or is imprisoned. See, for example, *Marshall v Harland & Wolff Ltd* (1972), *Egg Stores (Stamford Hill) Ltd v Leibovici* (1977) and *F.C. Shepherd & Co Ltd v Jerrom* (1986).

Even temporary unavailability may discharge a contract, if the interruption is such as to make performance after it substantially different from what was originally undertaken. In *Jackson v Union Marine Insurance Co Ltd* (1874) a ship was chartered to carry rails from Newport to San Francisco in January. It went aground in Caernarvon Bay on its way to the port of loading, and was not fully repaired until August. It was held that the delay frustrated the contract.

An important factor in deciding whether or not there has been frustration is to consider the ratio of the likely length of the interruption to the contract period as a whole. In *Morgan v Manser* (1948) a music hall artiste, known professionally as "Cheerful Charlie Chester", was called up for war service in 1940. His 10-year contract with a manager (made in 1938) was held to be frustrated by the call-up, since it was likely that Cheerful Charlie would be in the army for a very long time.

On the other hand, in *Nordman v Rayner and Sturgess* (1916) an agent, engaged under a long-term contract, was interned during the First World War. He was from Alsace and was anti-German in his sympathies. It was held that the agency contract was not frustrated, since his internment was not likely to last long. In this type of case, though the trial may be held years later, the court has to consider what the prospects must have looked like at the time the event in question happened.

Illegal

A contract is discharged by frustration if, during the currency of the contract, further performance becomes illegal. A clear example of this principle is that a contract is frustrated if legislation (including delegated legislation) is passed after the contract was made, which renders it illegal. Another example is where the outbreak of war means that further performance of a contract would amount to "trading with the enemy". See *Fibrosa Spolka Akcyjna v Fairbairn Lawson Combe Barbour Ltd* (1943, HL).

As with destruction of the subject-matter, so with illegality: it is sufficient if the "object of the exercise" is defeated. The fact that some minor part of the contract could still be performed does not save it from frustration.

Radically different

The highwater mark of the doctrine of frustration was reached in a series of cases, usually called "the coronation cases", which arose out of the postponement of the coronation of King Edward VII.

These cases establish that a contract may be frustrated, though it does not become impossible or illegal, if it becomes futile. In *Krell v Henry* (1903, CA) Henry hired a room in Pall Mall for the days on which the coronation processions of King Edward VII were due to take place. Both parties understood that the object of the letting was to watch the processions from the windows of the room, although this was not stated in the contract. The king's illness caused the processions to be postponed. Henry could still have come and sat in the room, although it would have been futile. The Court of Appeal held that the contract was frustrated. The doctrine of frustration, it was held, can apply where a "state of things", essential to the contract, "fails to be in existence". This decision has been doubted but never overruled.

In *Davis Contractors Ltd v Fareham UDC* (1956, HL) a building company had agreed to build 78 houses for a local authority in eight months for the sum of £92,425. Owing to shortages of skilled labour and building materials the work took 22 months, and the builders incurred additional expenses of £17,651. The builders claimed that the contract was frustrated. The builders wanted to claim a sum in excess of the contract price, on a quantum meruit basis. To be able to do so, they had first to get rid of the original contract, because a quantum meruit claim was not open so long as that contract stood. Hence their argument for frustration. The House of Lords held that there was no frustration. Lord Radcliffe said:

> "[I]t is not hardship or inconvenience or material loss itself which calls the principle of frustration into play. There must be as well such a change in the significance of the obligation that the thing undertaken would, if performed, be a different thing from that contracted for."

In another passage Lord Radcliffe used the phrase "radically different". This case shows that the principle of *Krell v Henry* is narrowly confined.

FRUSTRATION IN THEORY AND PRACTICE

In Chapter 9 the similarity between "possibility mistake" and frustration was pointed out. In spite of this similarity, theorising about frustration has tended to proceed quite independently of any discussion about mistake. There are numerous theories as to the basis of frustration, but the broad issue lies between two. One theory is that frustration is based on the supposed intention of the parties, in the sense that if the parties, at the time of contracting, had contemplated the catastrophic event that later occurred, they would have said: "If that happens, all will be over between us". This may have been an approach attractive to adherents of nineteenth-century laissez-faire individualism but it now rings as somewhat artificial. As Lord Radcliffe said in *Davis v Fareham U.D.C.* (1956) there is "a logical difficulty in seeing how the parties could even impliedly have provided for something which *ex hypothesi* they neither expected nor foresaw." There is more to be said, and this is the prevalent theory now, for the view that the law is intervening to impose a fair solution when events have happened that render the whole situation radically different from that originally envisaged by the parties. As Lord Radcliffe went on the say, "*Non haec in foedera veni*. It was not this that I promised to do."

It really comes down to a question of risk. Is it reasonable to put the risk of some catastrophic event upon either A or B, the parties to the contract? Or should A (and/or B) be excused for not performing?

The important point about frustration is that it excuses the parties. If a ship is delayed, will the court say that the delay is a breach by the ship owner (or, in other circumstances, by the charterer) making him liable in damages? Or will the court say that it is not a breach by either party, but is a frustration, which excuses both parties?

Whatever the theoretical basis of the doctrine, a court faced with the question "Frustration or not?" has to consider the whole terms of the contract, the whole circumstances surrounding its formation, and the whole circumstances that are alleged to constitute frustration.

There are four points which may arise and which require discussion.

Self-induced frustration

The doctrine only applies where the frustrating event comes about without the fault of either party. This is sometimes put by saying that a party cannot rely on self-induced frustration. In *Maritime*

National Fish Ltd v Ocean Trawlers Ltd (1935, PC) A chartered to B a trawler, the St Cuthbert, which was no good unless fitted with an otter trawl. Both parties knew that it was not lawful to use an otter trawl without a licence. B applied for five licences, but was only granted three. He was asked to name the ships to which the three licences should apply, and he named three ships other than the St Cuthbert. A sued for the hire money, and B argued that the charter was frustrated. This argument was rejected by the Privy Council on the ground that "it was the act and election of the [charterers] which prevented the St Cuthbert from being licensed for fishing with an otter trawl". This case was purportedly followed by the Court of Appeal in *The Super Servant Two* (1990). The defendants had contracted to carry drilling machinery from Japan to Rotterdam on either of their two vessels. When one of them unexpectedly sank, they found they had insufficient capacity to carry all the cargos they had contracted for and chose not to perform the contract for carriage of the drilling machinery. The court held that their exercise of a choice not to carry that cargo was fatal to the plea of frustration. A difficulty with this reasoning is that the *Maritime National Fish* case could surely be distinguished on the basis that in that case it was perfectly foreseeable that the Minister would not issue enough licences. The charterers took a commercial gamble. In *The Super Servant Two* nobody considered the possibility that the ship would sink and it seems artificial to say that the carriers had much of a choice or election in the matter. They were unable to perform their contract in unforeseen circumstances for which they may not have been responsible. That is surely just when frustration should come into play.

Where there is an allegation that the frustration was self-induced the onus of proving this rests upon the party who alleges it (see *Joseph Constantine Steamship Line Ltd v Imperial Smelting Corp Ltd* (1942)).

Events provided for

Sometimes a contract lays down what are to be the rights and duties of the parties if some misfortune, such as unavoidable delay, happens. A difficult question may then arise as to whether the provision in the contract covers the event which has in fact happened. If the contractual provision does cover the event, then that provision governs the rights and duties of the parties, and the general law of frustration is excluded. (There is one exception to this, founded on public policy; if illegality supervenes, the contract is frustrated whatever the parties may have agreed between themselves.) If the contractual provision does not cover the event, then the law of frustration may apply. The courts tend to construe the contractual provision narrowly, so as to allow the doctrine of frustration to apply.

In *Metropolitan Water Board v Dick, Kerr & Co* (1918, HL) contractors agreed to construct a reservoir in six years. The contract provided that in the event of delays "howsoever occasioned" the contractors were to have an extension of time. The Minister of Munitions made a wartime order that the contractors were to stop work and sell their plant. Although that event was literally within the delay clause, the contract was held to be frustrated. The delay clause, it was held, did not "cover the case in which the interruption is of such a character and duration that it vitally and fundamentally changes the conditions of the contract ... ".

The contractual provision may be held not to apply, not because it is too narrow in scope, but because it is only designed to protect a party from liability and not to exclude the possibility of frustration. This (rather difficult) point is illustrated by *Jackson v Union Marine Insurance Co Ltd* (1874) (considered on p.276). The charter party provided that the ship should proceed with all possible dispatch (dangers and accidents of navigation excepted) to Newport, to load. It went aground before it ever got to Newport, and was not fully repaired for eight months. The charter party was held to be frustrated. At first sight, one might think that the provision "dangers and accidents of navigation excepted" would mean that the charter was not frustrated, and that the charterer would remain bound by the contract. But the court held that the exception of "dangers and accidents of navigation" only served to save the ship owner from liability for not proceeding "with all possible dispatch". It did not follow from the fact that the ship owner was excused for the delay that the charterer was shut out from relying on the delay as a frustration.

It is common for contracts these days to contain what are called "force majeure" clauses, the effect of which is to release both parties from their obligations under the contract on the occurrence of certain stipulated events. For example, in *Channel Island Ferries Ltd v Sealink U.K. Ltd* (1988), the clause stated:

"A Party shall not be liable in the event of non-fulfilment of any obligation arising under this contract by reason of Act of God, disease, strikes, lock-outs, fire, and any accident or incident of any nature beyond the control of the relevant party."

Since the courts tend to be slow to invoke the doctrine of frustration, there are considerable advantages in including a force majeure clause in a contract. An appropriately drafted clause will enable the parties to agree upon the allocation of risk in specified circumstances.

Events foreseen

If the event which is alleged to have frustrated the contract was foreseen, or should have been, by one party but not by the other, that party cannot rely on frustration. (Here again illegality is an exception.) In *Walton Harvey Ltd v Walker & Homfrays Ltd* (1931, CA) A granted to B the right to display an advertisement on the outside of A's hotel for seven years. Within the seven years, the local authority compulsorily acquired, and then demolished, the hotel. The contract was held not to be frustrated; A knew, and B did not, that there was a risk of compulsory acquisition. A was held liable in damages.

Where the event was foreseen, or should have been, by both parties the position is not so clear. There are dicta in two cases that in such a situation frustration is possible. The cases are *WJ Tatem v Gamboa* (1939) and *The Eugenia* (1964, CA). But those dicta seem to be inconsistent with the following passage in the speech of Lord Radcliffe in the *Davis Contractors'* case (1956, HL):

"Two things seem to me to prevent the application of the principle of frustration to this case. One is that the cause of the delay was not any new state of things which the parties could not reasonably be thought to have foreseen. On the contrary, the possibility of enough labour and materials not being available was before their eyes and could have been the subject of special contractual stipulation. It was not made so."

The result, therefore, is that where both parties foresee the alleged frustrating event, the doctrine does not apply. It will normally be assumed that the contract has taken account of the possibility and allocated the risk accordingly. Frustration may, nevertheless, be available when some type of event was foreseen but not on the scale that the parties had envisaged. An example is *Pacific Phosphate Co Ltd v Empire Transport Co Ltd* (1920). An agreement to provide ships contained a clause suspending the agreement in the event of war. This was nevertheless held not sufficient to cover the catastrophic dislocating effects of the First World War which was outside the ambit of anything which the parties had contemplated when they made the agreement. Consequently the contract was frustrated.

Leases

It had been held in many cases that the doctrine of frustration did not apply to a lease. The idea is that a lease is more than a contract in that it creates an interest in land. Whatever happens, the land will always be there, and so the interest in the land will always be there. Thus, where a building was very seriously damaged by a bomb, the tenant remained liable on his covenant to pay rent and on his covenant to repair the property: see *Redmond v Dainton* (1920).

For many years the point was left open in the House of Lords. Then in 1981 in *National Carriers Ltd v Panalpina (Northern) Ltd* the House of Lords stated that there was nothing in principle to prevent the ordinary contractual doctrine of frustration from applying to a lease. This decision does show that the courts are prepared to extend the doctrine of frustration in appropriate circumstances. Nevertheless, since many leases are for long periods, such as 99 years, it will be infrequently that the doctrine applies. In any time scale that long it will normally be assumed that the parties have assumed the risk of some dramatic supervening events. The significance of the decision is much more likely to be felt when, for example, a building is rendered unusable for a large proportion of, say, a five-year lease.

EFFECTS OF FRUSTRATION

Where frustration occurs, the contract comes to an end at the moment of the frustrating event. Neither party has any choice whether or not to treat the contract as discharged; it is automatically discharged. The rights and liabilities of the parties become crystallised, as it were, at the moment of frustration. In the classic phrase, "the loss lies where it falls". That is the common law position. That will be looked at first; the effect of statute will then be considered.

In *Chandler v Webster* (1904, CA) the plaintiff hired a room overlooking the coronation procession route for £141.15s., payable immediately. In fact he paid only £100 at the time, and still owed the balance when the announcement of cancellation was made. He sued to recover back his £100. It was held that his claim failed, and also that he remained liable to pay the balance, £41.15s. The contract was frustrated, but the loss lay where it fell. The reasoning was that, since the frustrating event only terminated the contract from that time, and the money was payable before this, then he was still liable on what was at that stage a valid contract.

In *Krell v Henry* (above, at p.278) the practical result was different, though stemming from the same basic idea. The contract is that case was in different terms. The agreed price for the room was £75. The hirer paid £25 on June 20, and agreed to pay the balance, £50, on June 24. It was on that very day that the announcement of cancellation was made. The owner of the room sued for the £50. He failed. There is a rule of law that if a debt is due on a named day the debtor has until the last moment of the day in which to pay. Therefore at the moment of frustration the owner did not have an accrued right to the £50. (The hirer put in a counter-claim to recover back his £25, but he withdrew this in the Court of Appeal.)

Forty years later *Chandler v Webster* was overruled by the case of *Fibrosa Spolka Akcyjna v Fairbairn Lawson Combe Barbour Ltd* (1943, HL). Fairbairn agreed, in July 1939, to make machinery for Fibrosa (a Polish company) for £4,800 of which £1,600 was payable in advance. In fact Fibrosa paid only £1,000. On September 3 war was declared, and on September 23 Gdynia (the place of delivery) was occupied by the Germans. The contract was thus frustrated. Fibrosa sued to recover back the £1,000. They won. The House of Lords held that there had been a total failure of consideration. Lord Simon said that, whereas in the formation of a contract consideration may be a promise, when one is considering "failure of consideration" it is actual performance that one is thinking of as being the consideration. If there is no performance there is a total failure of consideration.

But the law was still far from perfect. The payment could only be recovered back where the failure of consideration was total. In

Whincup v Hughes (1871) the plaintiff apprenticed his son to a watchmaker for six years at a premium of £25. After one year the watchmaker died. The plaintiff failed to recover back any part of the premium; the failure of consideration was not total. Also, where a party was allowed to recover back an advance payment this might cause injustice to the other party. In the *Fibrosa* case itself, the English company had gone to considerable expense for which it got nothing.

Then came the Law Reform (Frustrated Contracts) Act 1943, which is only concerned with the effects of frustration; it has nothing to say on the earlier question whether the contract has been frustrated or not. There are four main points in the Act.

(1) The Act extends the decision in the *Fibrosa* case by providing that money paid before the frustrating event ("the time of discharge") can be recovered back, even though the failure of consideration is only partial.

(2) Money due (payable), but not in fact paid, before the frustrating event, ceases to be payable.

(3) A party who has incurred expenses may be awarded his expenses, up to the limit of the sums paid or payable to him before the frustrating event. Notice that if nothing was paid or payable before the frustrating event, he will not be able to get any expenses at all.

(4) A party who has gained a valuable benefit under the contract before the frustrating event may be required to pay a just sum for it. This is so whether or not anything was paid or payable before the frustrating event.

There are three contracts to which the Act is expressed not to apply. These are: (1) any charter party (except a time charter or a charter by way of demise) and any non-charter contract for the carriage of goods by sea; (2) a contract of insurance; and (3) certain contracts for the sale of goods. The provision concerning sales of goods is couched in rather obscure language, but it seems that the contracts which are excluded are contracts for the sale of specific goods which are frustrated by the perishing of the goods. If the goods are not specific or if frustration occurs by some cause other than the perishing of the goods, the Act does apply. Why this distinction should be made is not clear.

The purpose of the 1943 Act is to escape from the arbitrary common law rules that "the loss lies where it falls" and to apportion the loss, in a fair way, between the parties. To this end, the court is given a wide discretion as to how much to award for expenses or for a valuable benefit.

It is useful to reconsider in the light of the 1943 Act some of the cases considered in this chapter, such as *Chandler v Webster*, the counter-claim in *Krell v Henry*, the *Fibrosa* case, and *Whincup v Hughes*, and see how they would have been decided if the Act had been in operation at the time.

A case not so far considered is *Appleby v Myers* (1867). The plaintiff agreed to erect some machinery in the defendant's factory and then to keep it in running order for two years. The price was to be £459. When the erecting of the machinery was nearly complete, an accidental fire destroyed the factory and all that it contained. The plaintiff sued for £419 in respect of work done and materials supplied. He failed; the contract was frustrated and no money was due at the moment of frustration. The question arises whether Appleby should have been any better off if his case had arisen after the passing of the 1943 Act. Appleby would not get any expenses under the Act, because nothing was paid or payable before the moment of frustration. Did Myers "obtain a valuable benefit"? The Act refers to the obtaining of a valuable benefit "before the time of discharge". There was some nearly completed machinery in Myer's factory before the time of discharge, so in a sense he did obtain a valuable benefit, unless one takes the view that incomplete machinery is not a benefit. But viewing the events as a whole, in the long run Myers did not obtain any benefit, so probably Appleby would get nothing. This conclusion is supported by s.1(3) of the Act, which is helpfully considered in the judgment of Goff J. in *BP Exploration Co (Libya) Ltd v Hunt (No.2)* (1979). The court is required to award for "valuable benefit" such sum as it considers just, having regard to all the circumstances, including "the effect, in relation to the said benefit, of the circumstances giving rise to the frustration". In *Appleby v Myers* the circumstance giving rise to the frustration was the fire, and the effect of that on the benefit (if any) constituted by the partially installed machinery was to destroy it.

BREACH

A BREACH of contract occurs where a party fails to perform, or evinces an intention not to perform, one or more of the obligations laid upon him by the contract.

FORMS OF BREACH

Where a party fails to perform one of his obligations, that may be called actual breach; where he shows an intention not to perform, that may be called anticipatory breach.

Actual breach may take one of three forms. Non-performance is one form of breach. If A, a ship owner, charters his ship to B, undertaking to have the ship at Liverpool for loading by a certain date and then never takes his ship to Liverpool, that is a breach of contract by non-performance. Another form of actual breach is defective performance. If A attempts to get his ship to Liverpool, but arrives late, that is a breach of contract by defective performance. A third form of actual breach is the non-truth of a statement that is a term of the contract. If it is written into the contract that the ship is suitable for carrying cars, and in fact it is not, that is a breach of contract.

Anticipatory breach means a breach which occurs before the date of performance laid down in the contract. There are two forms of it: explicit repudiation and implicit repudiation. If A, in June, contracts to charter his ship to B from August 1, and then in July A notifies B that he has no intention of putting the ship at B's disposal, that is explicit repudiation. If C contracts, in September, to charter his ship to D from November 1, and then in October C sells the ship ("free from any charter arrangements") to E, that is implicit repudiation.

Any breach of contract entitles the innocent party to sue for damages. In some circumstances, but not all, a breach gives the innocent party the additional right to treat himself as discharged (or excused) from further performance of the contract (which includes the right to refuse to accept any attempted further performance by the party at fault). This right has often been described as "the right to treat the contract as discharged" and sometimes (though less commonly) as "the right to rescind the contract". It should have been clear since 1942, when the case of *Heyman v Darwins Ltd* was decided by the House of Lords (see below), that these expressions are incorrect. But in fact it has taken two further decisions of the House of Lords finally to eliminate them. The first in time was *Johnson v Agnew* (1980, HL). Lord Wilberforce said:

"In the case of an accepted repudiatory breach the contract has come into existence but has been put an end to or discharged. Whatever contrary indications may be disinterred from old authorities, it is now quite clear, under the general law of contract, that acceptance of a repudiatory breach does not bring about 'rescission ab initio'."

I need only quote one passage to establish these propositions. In *Heyman v Darwins Ltd*, Lord Porter said:

"To say that the contract is rescinded or has come to an end or has ceased to exist may in individual cases convey the truth with sufficient accuracy, but the fuller expression that the injured party is thereby absolved from future performance of his obligations under the contract is a more exact description of the position. Strictly speaking, to say that, upon acceptance of the renunciation of a contract, the contract is rescinded is incorrect. In such a case the injured party may accept the renunciation as a breach going to the root of the whole of the consideration. By that acceptance he is discharged from further performance and may bring an action for damages, but the contract itself is not rescinded."

Then in *Photo Productions Ltd v Securicor Transport Ltd* (1980, HL) Lord Wilberforce cited the same passage from *Heyman v Darwins Ltd* to make the point that it is incorrect to "pass ... from saying that a party, victim of a breach of contract, is entitled to refuse further performance, to saying that he may treat the contract as at an end ...". It may be understandable shorthand to say that the contract is ended or discharged, but it is not correct; the victim is discharged but the contract itself is not discharged.

Some breaches of contract merely entitle the innocent party to sue for damages; that is so, for example, in the case of breach of warranty. Some breaches (which may be described as repudiatory breaches) entitle the innocent party, in addition to suing for damages, to treat himself as excused from further performance. This is the case with breach of condition and also with "fundamental breach" in the sense of a breach which has the effect of depriving the innocent party of substantially the whole benefit that it was intended that he should get from the contract. (See in Chapter 4 above, under the heading "Express Terms".) So in all cases the test is whether the breach is of vital, as distinct from minor, importance.

A point which needs emphasis is that even where the breach is such as to give the injured party the right to treat himself as discharged, he need not treat himself as discharged. He has a choice (or election). The choice can be described as a choice either to accept or not to accept the wrongdoer's conduct as being a repudiation of the contract. More briefly, one can say that the injured party has a choice whether or not to accept the repudiation. There is nothing automatic about it. If the injured party decides to affirm the contract and to continue his obligations, he may still sue the wrongdoer for damages for any loss he has suffered as a result of the breach. But, as Lord Simon L.C. said in *Heyman v Darwins Ltd*, above, the innocent party must act in such a way "as to make plain that, in view of the wrongful action of the party who has repudiated, he claims to treat the contract as at an end".

Anticipatory breach

Some special features of anticipatory breach need to be pointed out. It used to be thought that anticipatory breach always entitles the innocent party to treat the contract as discharged, (or, to put it in modern terms, to treat himself as discharged) and that the test of "vital or minor importance" does not arise. But, since *Decro-Wall v Practitioners in Marketing Ltd* (1971, CA), this is no longer so; in cases of anticipatory breach the same test applies as in cases of actual breach. Thus, the innocent party must act so as to make plain that he claims to treat the contract as at an end. There is no reason why the acceptance of an anticipatory repudiation should not take the form of words or conduct which makes it plain that the innocent party is responding to the repudiation by treating the contract as at an end. Thus, a failure to perform contractual obligations is capable of amounting to an acceptance of an anticipatory repudiation of a contract: see *Vitol S.A. v Norelf Ltd*; *The Santa Clara* (1996).

Where one party commits an act of repudiatory anticipatory breach, the other innocent party, can sue at once, and need not wait for the contract date of performance to come round. If he does sue at once, he can win even though at the time of action his right is contingent. In *Frost v Knight* (1872) Mr Knight promised Miss Frost that when his father died he would marry her. While his father was still alive, Mr Knight broke off the engagement. Miss Frost sued him. She won, even though it was not certain that the contingency on which Mr Knight's promise was founded would ever be fulfilled. After all, Mr Knight or Miss Frost might have died before Mr Knight senior. A promise to marry is no longer enforceable at law, but that does not invalidate the principle of *Frost v Knight*. That principle is, however, very much qualified by *The Mihalis Angelos* (1971, CA), which shows that if the rights lost to the plaintiff by reason of the anticipatory breach are certain to be rendered valueless, the plaintiff is entitled at most to nominal damages. A charter party contained an expected readiness to load clause (cl.1): "expected ready to load Haiphong under this charter about 1st July 1965". By cl.11 it was provided: "Should the vessel not be ready to load ... on or before the 20th July 65 charterers have the option of cancelling this contract". By July 17 it had become clear that the vessel would not be ready to load by July 20. On July 17 the charterers cancelled the charter. The Court of

Appeal held that they were entitled to "terminate the charter" forthwith (see p.71, above). The Court of Appeal further held that even if the charterers had not been so entitled under cl.11, so that the purported cancellation was a wrongful repudiation, the owners would have been awarded only nominal damages because the charterers would on July 21 have become entitled to cancel under cl.11 and would undoubtedly have done so.

The innocent party, faced with anticipatory breach, need not sue at once. He may go on treating the contract as still alive, hoping that the other party will change his mind. If he takes this course, however, he is taking a risk, because events may happen to destroy his right of action. In *Avery v Bowden* (1855) Bowden chartered Avery's ship, The Lebanon, and agreed to load it with a cargo at Odessa within 45 days. During this period Bowden repeatedly advised Avery to sail his ship away, as it would be impossible to provide him with a cargo. Avery, however, refused to accept this advice, and kept his ship at Odessa, hoping that Bowden would after all fulfil his obligation to load a cargo. Before the 45 days were up, the Crimean War broke out. That frustrated the contract, since Odessa became an enemy port. Assuming that Bowden's repeated statements amounted to a breach, Avery could have accepted the breach and sued at once. By choosing to keep the contract alive, he lost forever his right to sue, because the contract became frustrated before the loading days had expired. See also *Fercometal SARL v Mediterranean Shipping Co S.A.*; *The Simona* (1988, HL), in which the House of Lords emphasised that if an innocent party elects to affirm a contract he is not absolved from further performance of his own obligations under the contract. They also pointed out that if a repudiation by anticipatory breach is followed by affirmation of the contract, the repudiating party can escape liability if the affirming party is subsequently in breach of the contract.

Where a party, faced with anticipatory breach, chooses to keep the contract alive, all he usually does is to wait, as the ship owner did in *Avery v Bowden*. Avery could not go on with his own contractual duty to receive cargo into the ship, because that required Bowden's co-operation. But occasionally circumstances arise in which the innocent party can go on with his contractual duties without the other party's co-operation. This was so in *White and Carter (Councils) Ltd v McGregor* (1962, HL). The plaintiffs were advertising agents who supplied local authorities with litter bins on which they attached plates carrying advertisements. The defendant engaged the plaintiffs to advertise his garage in this way for three years. Later the same day the defendant cancelled his order. The plaintiffs refused to accept his repudiation. Although they knew that the defendant did not wish it, they prepared advertisement plates, attached them to litter bins, and displayed them. The plaintiffs sued for the full contract price for the three-year period. The House of Lords, by a majority of three to two, upheld their claim. This is a rather startling result, but it is a logical conclusion from the principle that a party has an election whether to accept a repudiation or not. Lord Reid qualified his decision (that the plaintiff should have the agreed sum) by saying that if a plaintiff had "no substantial or legitimate interest" in completing performance, he could only claim damages. This qualification was applied in *Clea Shipping Corporation v Bulk Oil International* (1984). In this case the charterers of an elderly ship announced they had no further use for it and were thereby clearly guilty of an anticipatory breach. Nevertheless, the owners spent £800,000 on having the vessel repaired, maintained it at anchor with a full crew for the remaining period of the charter party and then sold it for scrap. On these rather extreme facts the court was unwilling to disturb the arbitrator's finding that the owners had no legitimate interest in continuing to perform the contract. This case therefore suggests that a court may be unwilling to grant a remedy to a claimant when the effect of the innocent party's election is commercially quite futile and simply inflates the damages.

REMEDIES

SEVEN REMEDIES will be discussed in this last chapter of the book. Rectification will not be considered again, as it was mentioned in Chapter 4; nor will the special code of adjustment remedies laid down by the Law Reform (Frustrated Contracts) Act 1943, which were looked at in Chapter 17, be considered further.

Rescission was considered at some length in Chapter 7 in connection with misrepresentation, and was touched on in connection with duress and undue influence in Chapter 8. Chapter 18 (on breach) made it clear that it is incorrect to use the word rescission in reference to acceptance of a repudiatory breach of contract. Rescission (e.g. for misrepresentation) is rescission ab initio. That means that the contract is treated as though it had never existed. Acceptance by the innocent party of a repudiatory breach of contract by the wrong-doing party does not have that effect. The contract is recognised as having existed and, indeed, as still being in existence. It seems to follow from this distinction that, whereas the right to rescind for misrepresentation is lost if the injured party cannot provide restitution of what he has received under the contract, no such principle should apply to acceptance of repudiatory breach. There is at least one case to the contrary— *Thorpe v Fasey* (1949)—but that case must be regarded as impliedly overruled by *Johnson v Agnew* (1980, HL). It can be said with confidence that inability to make restoration does not debar the innocent party from accepting repudiatory breach.

A related, but separate, question arises: If the innocent party is able to make restoration, will the court require him to do so? The answer seems to be "Yes". The clearest illustration of the point is that where a buyer of goods rightfully rejects the goods for breach of a condition as to quality, the ownership of the goods vests (or revests) in the seller: see per Bankes L.J. in *Hardy v Hillerns & Fowler* (1923, CA). (Of course, the buyer may have a right to damages.) The principle is the same where it is money, as distinct from other property, that the innocent party has received under the contract. Thus, a seller of goods who accepts the buyer's default must return any part of the purchase price that has been prepaid. (But, of course, the seller may have a right to damages.) There is one qualification to this principle, namely that where the buyer makes a prepayment, not simply as a "part payment" of the total price, but as a "deposit" (that is, an "earnest" of the buyer's intention to perform the contract), the seller who accepts the buyer's default may keep the deposit. The danger in this rule is that it could circumvent the law relating to penalty clauses (see below, p.306). The only real difference between a deposit and a penalty is that the former is paid before the contract is performed and the latter becomes due when something has gone wrong later with performance of the contract. A similar rule therefore applies to both deposits and penalties. In *Workers Trust and Merchant Bank Ltd v Dojap Investments Ltd* (1993) the Privy Council decided that a 25 per cent deposit on a contract for the sale of land was not a reasonable pre-estimate of the vendor's loss, was therefore penal and had to be repaid to the purchaser. It was accepted that the standard 10 per cent deposit common in contracts for the sale of land was lawful even though it may bear little relation to the vendor's loss. When a court does decide that a deposit is unreasonable that provision fails altogether. A court will not substitute a reasonable deposit. The practical consequence is that, as with liquidated damages clauses, it is better to fix a deposit that errs on the side of caution than risk having the whole clause struck down. Whilst the law relating to deposits and penalties is now therefore very similar, it is not quite identical. The crucial question in deciding between a liquidated damages and a penalty clause is whether the clause represents a "genuine pre-estimate of the loss"; in the case of a deposit, the issue is, is it reasonable? As Lord Browne-Wilkinson noted in the *Worker's Trust* case, at least in contracts for the sale of land, a deposit might be reasonable even though it does not represent a genuine pre-estimate of loss. In principle, however, it is difficult to see why the same rules should not apply to both deposits and penalty clauses.

DAMAGES

Damages can be claimed by the party injured by breach, whether or not the breach is repudiatory. It is outside the scope of this book to deal with the differences between damages in contract and damages in tort. Only contract damages are considered here.

General principle

The object of awarding damages for breach of contract is to put the injured party, so far as money can do it, in the same position as if the contract had been performed: see *Robinson v Harman* (1848). In upholding this principle, the courts have stressed that the object is to compensate the injured party for his loss not to transfer to him, if he has suffered no loss, the benefit which the wrongdoer has gained by his breach of contract. The injured party is not to be put in the same position as if the contract had never been made, but in the same position as if the contract had been performed. That is the key to the fact that damages often yields a higher sum than an indemnity in connection with misrepresentation.

The injured party can never obtain more in damages than the loss which he has suffered. Therefore if he has suffered no loss, he may win his action (because breach of contract is actionable per se) but he will get only nominal damages and may not get his costs.

Whilst these principles generally hold true, the Court of Appeal in *Attorney General v Blake* (1998) has signalled that, in exceptional circumstances, a restitutionary claim might be entertained when compensatory damages would be inadequate. For example, the court had in mind the situation where a contractor wrongly skimps on performance, thereby increasing his profits, but by chance does not cause any loss to the plaintiff. In this situation a restitutionary claim for loss of profits might now succeed. Another possibility, which arose in the *Blake* case itself, is that a defendant makes a profit by doing the very thing he contracted not to do, in this case breaching a duty of confidence. Here again a restitutionary claim might be possible. These innovative suggestions received little support when the case eventually reached the House of Lords. The decision of the Court of Appeal was affirmed on the basis that there was no reason in principle why an account of profits should not be a remedy for a breach of contract. This was such a case in that the spy George Blake had written his memoirs in breach of his contractual undertaking not to reveal details of his work as a member of the intelligence services. Consequently the Crown was entitled to all the royalty monies owed by the publishers to Blake for his memoirs. Clearly the decision breaks new ground but Lord Nicholls stressed that the remedy of an account of profits would only be available "in exceptional circumstances." Unfortunately the decision itself offers little guidance on when this will be. The statement that a relevant question is "whether the [claimant] had a legitimate interest in preventing the defendant's profit-making activity, and, hence, in depriving him of his profit" is a remarkably inexact test. In *Blake*, at least, the exceptional circumstances were that the Crown had a legitimate interest in preventing the spy Blake from profiting from the disclosure of official information gained from his work as a member of the security services. It was also relevant that the obligation broken was said to be closely akin to a fiduciary obligation where an account of profits is a standard remedy.

It is probably too early to assess whether *Blake*'s case represents the start of a new development in contractual damages or whether, as Lord Hobhouse dissenting considered, it simply reflects the court's distaste, on rather unusual facts, for allowing a convicted spy to benefit from his criminal conduct. Some guidance has, however, now been given by the Court of Appeal in *Experience Hendrix LLC v PPX Enterprises Inc* (2003). In this case the claimant sought an account of profits on the basis that the defendant, in breach of contract, had licensed various recordings of the musician Jimi Hendrix. Part of the difficulty of this type of claim is that it is very difficult to assess the loss to the claimant, although it was quite clear that the defendant had made a profit from a deliberate breach. The issue in the case was whether the facts revealed the "exceptional" circumstances required in *Blake* for an account of profits, and the Court of Appeal held that it did not. The case was not concerned with the special and sensitive area of national security; there was nothing analogous to a fiduciary relationship; there was nothing inherently unusual in commercial parties choosing to break a contract. Significantly, however, the court went on to award the claimant such sum as could have been demanded from the defendant for permission to licence the recordings, even though the claimant would probably never, if asked, have given such permission. The importance of the decision is, therefore, that the claimant still recovered substantial damages on facts which, before *Blake*, might only have yielded nominal damages.

These cases also cast doubt on the correctness of some earlier decisions such as *Surrey CC v Bredero Homes Ltd* (1993). In that case, in breach of contract, Brodero Homes built more houses on the land sold to them than the contractual stipulations allowed, thereby increasing their profit. On the other hand, this did not actually cause a loss to Surrey County Council who had sold them the land. The Court of Appeal accordingly rejected the Council's claim for damages. It seems probable that, if the facts were to recur today, the Council might well have a strong argument for entitlement to such sum as could have been demanded for granting permission to build the extra houses.

Remoteness of damage

The injured party may sometimes get less than the loss that he has suffered. There is a general principle of exclusion called the principle of "remoteness of damage". The idea is that it is not just or practicable to award damages for every consequence, however unusual, which may flow from a breach of contract. When a court is awarding damages, two questions face it: (1) what consequences should be compensated for? and (2) how should the damages be quantified?

The dividing line between damage which should be compensated for and damage which is too remote to be compensated for was laid down in *Hadley v Baxendale* (1854). The plaintiffs, mill owners at Gloucester, engaged the defendant carrier to take a broken mill shaft to Greenwich as a pattern for a new one. The defendant promised to deliver it at Greenwich the next day. Owing to his neglect, the mill shaft was delayed in transit. The plaintiffs claimed damages for loss of profit arising from the fact that the mill was stopped for longer that it need have been, which in turn arose from the delay in transit. All that the carrier knew was "that the article to be carried was the broken shaft of a mill and that the plaintiffs were the millers of that mill". In delivering the judgment of the court, Alderson B. said:

"Where two parties have made a contract which one of them has broken, the damages which the other party ought to receive in respect of such breach of contract should be such as may fairly and reasonably be considered either arising naturally, i.e. according to the usual course of things, from such breach of contract itself, or such as may reasonably be supposed to have been in the contemplation of both parties, at the time they made the contract, as the probable result of the breach of it."

This statement has come to be known as "the rule in *Hadley v Baxendale*".

Applying that principle to the facts of the case, the court held that the carrier was not liable for loss of profit. The loss did not arise "according to the usual course of things"; "in the great multitude of cases" the absence of a shaft would not cause a stoppage at the mill, because, for example, the mill owner might have another shaft in reserve. And the special circumstances that the mill could not restart until the shaft came back was not known to the defendant and so could not "reasonably be supposed to have been in the contemplation of both parties".

The rule in *Hadley v Baxendale* has been considered in many cases since 1854, for example *Victoria Laundry (Windsor) Ltd v Newman Industries* (1949). The plaintiffs, who were launderers and dyers, wanted a large boiler to expand their business. The defendants agreed to install a boiler on June 5, 1946 but owing to their breach of contract it was not delivered until November 8, 1946. The plaintiffs claimed under two heads: (1) £16 a week damages for loss of profits for the extra custom they could have taken on; and (2) £262 a week which they could have obtained under certain especially lucrative contracts with the Ministry of Supply. It was found that the defendants knew that the plaintiffs were anxious to have the boiler installed as soon as possible but not that they were aware of the lucrative supply contract. Accordingly, they were liable for the loss of profits arising from the failure to enlarge the business and carry out normal contracts but not for the much greater loss of profits obtainable from contracts with the Ministry. The rule was also considered by the House of Lords, in *Koufos v C. Czarnikow Ltd*; *The Heron II* (1969). The defendant ship owner agreed to carry a cargo of sugar belonging to the plaintiffs from Constanza to Basrah. He knew that there was a sugar market at Basrah and that the plaintiffs were sugar merchants, but he did not know that they intended to sell the cargo immediately on its arrival. Because of a breach of contract by the defendants, the sugar reached Basrah nine days later than it should have done. The plaintiffs sold the sugar (3,000 tons) at £31. 2s. 9d. per ton. If there had been no delay they could have sold it at £32. 10s. per ton. They claimed something over £4,000 as loss of profit. The House of Lords unanimously upheld the plaintiff's claim, on the footing that the loss should be regarded as arising in the usual course of things and so as being within the contemplation of the parties.

Whereas the Court of Exchequer in *Hadley v Baxendale* gave only one judgment, the House of Lords in *The Heron II* gave five, and it is not easy to bring together all that was said. The present state of the law may be put in this way: the rule in *Hadley v Baxendale* stands; it is not two rules, but one rule with (possibly) two branches, dealing with usual and non-usual consequences respectively; usual consequences are presumed to be in the contemplation of both parties; non-usual consequences may be held to have been in the contemplation of both parties if the evidence shows that a reasonable man, knowing what the defendant knew or ought to have known of the special circumstances, would have thought them liable to result; and a consequence may be liable to result though it is considerably less than a 50:50 chance.

The working of the rule in *Hadley v Baxendale* may be illustrated by two further cases. In *Diamond v Campbell-Jones* (1961) the defendants contracted to sell some premises in Mayfair to the plaintiff for £6,000. The defendants wrongfully repudiated the contract. They knew that the plaintiff was a dealer in real estate, but they did not know that he intended to convert the premises himself. The defendants were held liable for loss of the profit which the plaintiff would have made by resale, but not for loss of the much larger profit which he might have made by converting the premises. On the other hand, in *Cottrill v Steyningand Littlehampton Building Society* (1966) the vendor of land knew that the purchaser intended to develop it himself. On breach of the contract to sell, the vendor was held liable in damages for the loss of the profit which the purchaser would have made by developing the property.

Quantification

After deciding which consequences should be compensated for, the court then has to consider how to quantify the loss, and how to translate the loss into a monetary sum.

The market value

This rule, which applies particularly to the sale of goods, is that if there is a market for the goods, then prima facie the loss is quantified by reference to the market. If a seller fails to deliver the goods, the buyer can go into the market and buy similar goods at the market price. His loss (if any) will be the amount by which the market price, at the time the goods ought to have been delivered, exceeds the contract price. Conversely, if a buyer refuses to take delivery, the seller can go into the market and sell the goods at the prevailing price. He will recover in damages the amount by which the market price, at the time the goods ought to have been accepted, is below the contract price. In *Shearson Lehman Hutton Inc v Maclaine Watson & Co Ltd* (1990) Webster J. said in respect of a buyer's breach a market would exist where either, if the seller actually offers the goods for sale, there is one actual buyer on that day at a fair price or, if there is no actual offer for sale, there are sufficient traders potentially in touch with each other to evidence a market in which the actual or notional seller could if he wished sell the goods. The market price of the goods is then either the "fair price" obtained by the actual sale or, in the absence of an actual sale, a fair price for the total quantity of goods sold on the market on the relevant day, or such price as might be negotiated "within a few days with persons who were members of the market on that day and who could not be taken into account as potential buyers on the day in question only because of difficulties of communication". These principles also apply in the case of a seller's breach. This definition of "market" is limited.

Where there is no market the loss must be calculated in some other way. If it is the seller who defaults, and the buyer has contracted to resell the goods, it is generally accepted that the resale price may be taken as representing the value of the goods, and the damages will be the difference between the sale and resale prices. For this purpose, it does not matter that the seller had no notice of the resale contract.

Where there is no market and it is the buyer who defaults (by refusing to accept delivery), the extent of the damages will depend on the supply position. In *W.L. Thompson Ltd v Robinson Gunmakers Ltd* (1955) the defendants bought a Vanguard car from the plaintiffs, and then refused to accept it. The plaintiff's profit would have been £61. The defendants argued that the plaintiffs could have sold the car to another customer, or (as they in fact did) returned it to their supplier. The court rejected this argument, because it was proved that the supply of Vanguards exceeded the demand. The plaintiffs had therefore sold one Vanguard less than they otherwise would, so that their loss was the whole loss of the bargain. In *Charter v Sullivan* (1957, CA) the defendant bought a Hillman Minx car from the plaintiff and then refused to accept it. The plaintiff's profit would have been £97. 15s., but he was awarded only nominal damages. It was proved that he could sell as many Minx cars as he could get from the makers, so that he could resell this car without loss. Both these cases were decided at a time when cars could be sold only at fixed list prices, so that in that sense there was no market. A market involves freedom for prices to fluctuate in response to the pressures of supply and demand.

Factual damages

Whatever rules are developed in the law of damages, the object should be to compensate the plaintiff for what, in fact, has been his loss. The principle is sometimes easier to state than apply, an example being *Ruxley Electronics Ltd v Forsyth* (1995). Here a swimming pool had been constructed, in breach of contract, at a lower depth than that which had been specified. The issue of damages was whether the owner of the property was entitled to the cost of remedying the defect, which was enormous, or the very modest cost representing the amount by which the property was rendered less valuable or amenable. The House of Lords, reversing the Court of Appeal, awarded only the more modest sum. In reality the owner had not suffered a significant loss. The court might have taken a different view if the owner had intended to carry out the works, which he apparently did not. Then the cost of repair would, in fact, have reflected his real loss.

Speculative damages

In some cases the quantification of damages is extremely difficult, and may involve the court in speculating on what might have happened if there had been no breach of contract. But in a proper case the court will not be deterred, by the difficulty or by the need to speculate, from making an award of damages. In *Chaplin v Hicks* (1911, CA) the defendant, an actor and theatrical manager, agreed with the plaintiff that if she would attend an interview with 49 other actresses she would have a chance of being selected as one of 12 to whom he would give employment. The defendant broke his contract by failing to give the plaintiff a reasonable opportunity to attend the interview. When sued, he argued that the plaintiff should have only nominal damages, since she would have had only a one in four chance of being selected. At the trial the jury awarded the plaintiff £100 damages. The Court of Appeal held that the award should stand. Of course, in 1911 damages of £100 was far more than nominal.

But though the court will speculate if that is unavoidable, it will not speculate where the plaintiff could have produced evidence of his actual loss and has not done so. In *Clark v Kirby-Smith* (1964) a solicitor negligently failed to acquire for his clients a new tenancy of business premises, and they sued him for damages for loss of the new tenancy. It was held that as no evidence of the value of the new tenancy had been given, though it could have been, they should have only nominal damages of £2. It would be different if it were not just difficult, but quite impossible, to estimate the damages. In *McRae v Commonwealth Disposals Commission* (1951) (above, p.150) the plaintiffs failed in their claim for damages based upon loss of bargain. It was impossible to calculate the value of salvaging a non-existent tanker on a non-existent reef. In these circumstances, as in *McRae*, a claimant can only recover his reliance loss, i.e. the expenditure thrown away as a result of the defendant's breach of contract. This is likely to be less valuable than a claim for loss of bargain but at least offers some compensation (see also *Anglia Television v Reed* (1972)).

Non-pecuniary loss

Generally damages in contract will be to compensate purely for economic loss. In the older cases it is said that one cannot get damages merely for the mental distress associated with a breach of contract. Even so, it was long held that damages were available for physical inconvenience. In *Hobbs v L. & S.W. Ry* (1875) the defendant set down the plaintiff at the wrong station, at night, requiring them to walk five miles in the rain with no other transport available. As a result the defendant was found liable for the physical inconvenience caused. Whilst the line between physical and mental distress can be fine, it was drawn at the former. Then in *Jarvis v Swan Tours* (1973) the Court of Appeal awarded a plaintiff twice the cost of a disappointing holiday and recognised that non-pecuniary damages are available where, as in booking a holiday, the object of the contract was pleasure and enjoyment. Subsequent case law expanded this to include a contract which was intended to provide peace of mind or freedom from distress. Development in this area has been somewhat uneven. In *Watts v Morrow* (1991) the court of Appeal declined to extend the ambit of these cases to the negligence of a surveyor whose breach of contract led to the plaintiffs suffering many months of anguish whilst remedial building work took place. An ordinary contract of survey was held simply not to be in the exceptional class where damages for injured feelings could be recovered. Nevertheless, recently there does appear to be the start of a trend towards a more generous approach to non-pecuniary loss. In *Farley v Skinner* (2001) the claimant instructed a surveyor to inspect a property, particularly asking him to investigate if the property was affected by aircraft noise. The surveyor erroneously reported that it was unlikely that the property would be so affected. Having purchased the property for his retirement, and spending substantial sums of money on it, the claimant discovered the truth. The House of Lords affirmed the correctness of the award of £10,000 for non-pecuniary loss. Significantly, it was said to be sufficient that a major or important element of the contract was to give pleasure, relaxation or peace of mind. Lord Steyn noted that awards in this area should be restrained and modest and clearly the amount awarded in this case was regarded as being at the top end of the scale.

Most recently in *Hamilton Jones v David & Snape* (2004) a firm of solicitors negligently failed to take steps which resulted in a father removing the claimant's children from England to Tunisia. The court held that, as a result, she had suffered serious distress and continuing loss of company. A significant reason for employing the defendant had been to ensure her peace of mind in retaining custody of the children. As a result she was awarded the significant sum of £20,000 for non-pecuniary loss.

Taxation

In some cases the incidence of taxation has to be taken into account in quantifying the damages. In *British Transport Commission v Gourley* (1956, HL) the plaintiff was injured in a railway accident and he sued in negligence, claiming damages for, amongst other things, loss of earnings. It was estimated that if the plaintiff had not been injured his earnings over the rest of his working life would have come to £37,000. But the defendants argued that since the plaintiff's earnings would have been taxed, the damages should be reduced to take account of this factor. It was estimated that Gourley's earnings after tax would have been only £6,000. So the issue was whether his damages should be £37,000 or £6,000. The House of Lords decided for £6,000.

Gourley's case was brought in tort, but the same principle applies in contract. The reasoning of the principle is that the plaintiff ought not to make a profit out of the tort or breach of contract. In the case of an ordinary individual, damages for loss of earnings are not themselves taxable, whereas the earnings which the damages represent would have been taxable had they come to him as earnings. The principle of *Gourley's* case only applies where both these factors are present—non-taxable damages representing taxable earnings. Thus, since a trader is taxed on damages which come to him for breach of a trading contract, no deduction is made by the court from his damages. Where damages represent some non-taxable item those damages are not reduced by the court.

Mitigation

Where a breach has occurred, the injured party, if he accepts the breach as discharging the contract, must take all reasonable steps to mitigate the loss occasioned by the breach. So a buyer, faced with the seller's refusal to deliver the goods due on March 15, must go in to the market at once to buy replacement goods. If he waits unreasonably until, say, April 15, and the market price has risen, he will not receive in damages the difference between the contract price and the April 15 price, but only between the contract price and the March 15 price. Similarly, an employee wrongfully dismissed must mitigate his loss by accepting a reasonable offer of other employment.

Reasonableness is at the heart of this principle. The injured party is not required to act with lightning speed, or to accept any old offer of other employment that comes along, or to embark on some difficult course. For example, in *Pilkington v Wood* (1953) the plaintiff instructed the defendant, a solicitor, to act for him in the purchase of a house. The defendant negligently advised the plaintiff that the title to the house was good. This breach of contract led to all sorts of unfortunate results, and the case is interesting on remoteness of damage. But we are concerned with it in reference to mitigation. The defendant argued that the plaintiff should have mitigated his loss by taking legal proceedings against the vendor for having conveyed a defective title. The judge rejected this argument, holding that the duty to mitigate does not oblige the plaintiff to "embark on a complicated and difficult piece of litigation against a third party ... to protect his solicitor from the consequences of his own carelessness".

The burden lies on the defendant to prove, if he can, that an opportunity of mitigation has been neglected.

Agreed damages

Sometimes the parties to a contract provide, in the contract itself, that a specified sum is to be payable in the event of breach. Such clauses are called "agreed damages clauses" or "liquidated damages clauses".

This kind of clause is perfectly permissible, because the quantification of damages in court can be a difficult, long and expensive process. So, in a building contract it is frequently provided that if the builder is late in completing he will pay damages of £x per day. A demurrage clause, common in charter parties, is of this nature. Where there is an agreed damages clause in the contract, the plaintiff can recover the specified sum although his actual loss may be less. If his actual loss is more than the specified sum he can still only recover the specified sum.

But a clause of this kind may be challenged on the ground that it is a "penalty", a threat held over the head of a party, to try to force him to perform the contract. If the court holds that the clause is a penalty clause it is disregarded, and the plaintiff cannot recover more than his actual loss. If the actual loss turns out to be more than the sum mentioned in the penalty clause (an unlikely but possible event), the plaintiff is permitted to ignore the clause and recover damages in full: see *Wall v Rederiaktiebolaget Luggude* (1915). There is a Canadian case to the contrary, *Elsley v Collins Insurance Agencies Ltd* (1978), and the point may one day have to be reconsidered in England.

In deciding whether a clause is or is not a penalty, the following rules have evolved:

(1) The fact that the payment is described in the contract as a "penalty" or as "liquidated damages" (or any similar phrase) is relevant but not decisive.

(2) It will be held to be a penalty if the sum stipulated for is extravagantly greater than the damage which could conceivably follow from breach.

(3) It will be held to be a penalty if the breach consisted only in not paying a sum of money, and the sum stipulated is greater than the sum which ought to have been paid.

(4) There is a presumption (but no more) that it is a penalty when "a single lump sum is made payable ... on the occurrence of one or more or all of several events, some of which may occasion serious, and others but trifling, damage".

(5) "It is no obstacle to the sum stipulated being a genuine pre-estimate of damage, that the consequences of the breach are

such as to make precise pre-estimation almost an impossibility. On the contrary, that is just the situation when it is probable that pre-estimated damage was the true bargain between the parties."

These rules are set out in *Dunlop Pneumatic Tyre Co Ltd v New Garage and Motor Co Ltd* (1915, HL).

ACTION FOR AN AGREED SUM

There is a distinction between an action for damages and an action for an agreed sum. In the old terminology an action for an agreed sum is an action in debt. This is exemplified by an action to recover the contract price of goods sold and by an action to recover the contract remuneration for work done.

In an action for an agreed sum, questions of remoteness and quantification do not arise. In addition, as the law stands at present, the question of mitigation also does not arise. In *White and Carter (Councils) Ltd v McGregor* (1962, HL), which was looked at in Chapter 18, the defendant argued that the plaintiffs ought to have mitigated their loss by re-letting the advertising space. The majority of the House of Lords held that no question of mitigation arose because there had been no operative breach (as the plaintiffs had not accepted the defendant's "anticipatory breach"); mitigation means mitigation of damages, and it was not damages that was being sued for.

SPECIFIC PERFORMANCE

Specific performance is an order issued by the court to a defendant to perform a promise that he has made. Where a plaintiff claims specific performance (or an injunction) the court has power to award damages either instead of, or as well as, ordering specific performance (or an injunction). In English contract law damages is by far the most usual remedy, and specific performance is comparatively rare. Any movement towards a more generous approach to the granting of specific performance has been checked by the House of Lords decision in *Co-operative Insurance Society Ltd v*

Argyll Stores (Holdings) Ltd (1997), which affirms damages as the standard remedy for breach of contract.

As was pointed out in the Introduction to this book, to say that a contract is "an agreement enforceable at law" does not mean that every contract can be made the subject of specific performance. In lawyers' language, damages is as much "enforcement" as is an order for specific performance.

There are a number of principles that limit the scope of specific performance.

Not where damages adequate

If the court takes the view that damages will adequately compensate the plaintiff, it will not order specific performance. Thus specific performance is very rarely ordered on a contract for sale of goods. There is no absolute bar against it and, indeed, it is expressly provided for in s.52 of the Sale of Goods Act 1979. But in practice it is very rarely granted. In *Cohen v Roche* (1927) the court refused to grant specific performance to a buyer of a set of Hepplewhite chairs.

There is no bar against granting a decree of specific performance of an obligation to pay money. If damages would not be an adequate remedy, the decree will be made. This was done in *Beswick v Beswick* (1968, HL), which was considered in Chapter 12 at p.203.

The law takes the view that a buyer of a particular piece of land, including the most ordinary suburban house, is not adequately compensated by damages if the vendor breaks his contract; hence he can obtain specific performance. The vendor can also obtain specific performance, on the principle that, as it could be ordered against him, it is just to allow it to him.

The court's discretion

Specific performance is an equitable remedy and, along with other equitable remedies, it is discretionary. It is not obtainable, as damages is, as of right. An example of this difference is to be found in Chapter 9, in connection with mistake. In *Wood v Scarth* (1855 and 1858) the plaintiff first sued for specific performance and failed and then sued for damages on the same facts and won.

The court's discretion is not an arbitrary discretion. It is exercised in accordance with settled principles. It may be summarised by saying that the court will only grant specific performance where to do so would be just and equitable.

Some contracts not specifically enforceable

There are some contracts of which specific performance will not be granted.

Personal service contracts

Specific performance will not be ordered of a contract of personal service. It is considered as undue interference with a person's personal liberty that he should be compelled to serve an employer if he does not wish to do so. Similarly, an employer cannot be compelled to continue to employ a person whom he does not wish to have as an employee. This rule only applies where the contract involves services of a personal nature. The mere fact that work of some kind is involved in a contract is not a bar to specific performance.

Contracts that require constant supervision

Specific performance will not be ordered of a contract of such a nature that constant supervision by the court would be required. In *Ryan v Mutual Tontine Association* (1893, CA) the lease of a service flat required that the lessors should provide a porter who would be "constantly in attendance". A lessee who applied for specific performance of that obligation failed. Supervision was also a factor in *Co-operative Insurance Society Ltd v Argyll Stores (Holdings) Ltd* (1997) (above, p.307), which led the House of Lords to decline specific performance. Such an order would have involved keeping a supermarket open.

Contracts which lack mutuality

Specific performance will not generally be ordered in favour of a party unless the court could order it, if the facts so required, against him.

INJUNCTION

An injunction is a decree by the court ordering a person to do or not to do a certain act. In the law of contract it can be used to restrain a party from committing a breach of contract. It will not be granted if its effect would be to compel the defendant to do something which he could not have been ordered to do by a decree of specific performance. In a case concerning The Troggs pop group, Page One Records Ltd v Britton (1968), the plaintiffs moved for an interlocutory injunction to restrain The Troggs from engaging as their manager anyone other than the first plaintiff. The injunction was refused, on the ground that to grant it would in effect compel The Troggs to continue to employ the first plaintiff. Despite this principle, the Court of Appeal (Stamp L.J. dissenting) in Hill v CA Parsons & Co Ltd (1972, CA) granted an interlocutory injunction to the plaintiff, restraining his employer from treating the employment as at an end. It was emphasised that the circumstances were very exceptional.

An injunction may be granted, restraining the breach of a negative undertaking in a personal service contract, if its effect is merely to encourage, and not compel, the defendant to perform a positive service. In Warner Bros Pictures Inc v Nelson (1937) a film actress, professionally known as Bette Davis, agreed to act for the plaintiffs for a fixed period, during which she undertook not to act for any third party, nor to engage in any other occupation, without the plaintiffs' written consent. The court granted an injunction, but only to the extent of restraining her from acting for third parties. This would not compel her to act for the plaintiffs, because she could earn a living by doing other work.

These cases were considered in the later case of Warren v Mendy (1989), where a boxer agreed to employ the plaintiff as his sole manager for three years. The Court of Appeal declined to grant an injunction to enforce the agreement. To do so would have been indirectly to compel performance of the contract. It was said that a realistic approach had to be taken and that a court would be less ready to grant an injunction where there was a contract involving maintenance of a skill or talent and there had been a breakdown in confidence between the parties. This seems undoubtedly a more practical approach and Warner Bros v Nelson is best regarded as a case turning upon its rather peculiar facts, for example that Bette Davis failed to give evidence in the case.

QUANTUM MERUIT

A party can claim on a quantum meruit ("as much as he has deserved") where the contract makes no express provision for remuneration. Thus, if a contract for the sale of goods does not fix the price, the buyer must pay a reasonable price. This is stated in s.8(2) of the Sale of Goods Act 1979, but that is merely declaratory of the common law.

Where there is an express contractual provision for remuneration, the general principle is that a plaintiff cannot succeed on a quantum meruit unless he can show that the contract was really void or that it has been discharged in some way. See the discussion of this point in reference to *Davis Contractors Ltd v Fareham UDC* (1956, HL) at p.278 in Chapter 17.

There are exceptions, however. For example, where one party prevents the innocent party from completing his performance, the innocent party can sue on a quantum meruit; see p.261, above. Also, a party may sue on a quantum meruit where he partially performs his contractual obligation and the other party voluntarily accepts that partial performance: see pp.261–262, above.

CLAIMS IN QUASI-CONTRACT AND RESTITUTION

It is outside the scope of this book to discuss the whole wide field of quasi-contract and restitution. But two restitutionary principles must be mentioned because they provide remedies to a person in a contractual situation.

(1) Money paid under a contract which is void can generally be recovered back: see, for example, *Strickland v Turner* (1852) at p.150, above.

(2) Money paid under a contract where there is a total failure of consideration can be recovered back. An example is *Rowland v Divall* (1923, CA). Rowland, who was a car dealer, bought an "Albert" car from Divall for £334. He repainted the car and sold it to Colonel Railsdon for £400. Later the car was seized by the police as (unknown to Rowland, Divall and Railsdon) it was stolen property. Rowland repaid the £400 to Railsdon, and brought an action in quasi-

contract to recover back his payment to Divall of £334, on the ground that there had been a total failure of consideration. Rowland succeeded. The Court of Appeal held that he had not "received any portion of what he agreed to buy ... He did not get what he paid for—namely a car to which he would have title."

EXTINCTION OF REMEDIES

A right of action for breach of contract may become extinguished by effluxion of time. The Limitation Act 1980 provides that an action founded on a "simple contract" (that is, not a contract by deed), or an action for an account, cannot be brought after the expiration of six years from the date on which the cause of action accrued. An action on a "specialty" (that is, a contract by deed) cannot be brought after the expiration of 12 years. Where damages are claimed for personal injuries the period is, in general, three years.

Where there is fraud or mistake, the period of limitation does not begin to run until the claimant has discovered the fraud or mistake or could with reasonable diligence have discovered it.

In the case of a minor, or other person under a disability, time does not begin to run until the disability is removed; for example, when the minor comes of age.

If the person liable makes a written acknowledgment of a debt or makes any payment in respect of it, time begins to run again.

The statutory provisions do not apply to claims for specific performance or an injunction or other equitable relief. But this does not set equity so far apart from the common law as at first sight appears. Where a court is exercising an equity jurisdiction it will apply the statutory rules "by analogy" or it will apply the equitable doctrine of "laches". Laches may, for example, defeat a claim founded on undue influence, as was seen in Chapter 8.

These rules, for the extinction of remedies, both statutory and equitable, are founded on a principle of policy in our law that it is in the general interest that there should be "an end to litigation".

INDEX

Penalty clauses
generally, 306–307
Performance
see also **Frustration**
agency
termination of, 246
defective performance, 287
exceptions to rule
acceptance of part performance,
261–262
prevention of performance, 261
severable contracts, 260–261
substantial performance, 262, 263,
264
existing duty as consideration
duty imposed by contract with
promisor, 39–40
duty imposed by contract with
third party, 40–41
duty imposed by the general law,
38–39
generally, 37–38
general rule, 259, 260
non–performance, 287
tender of performance, 264–265
time of performance, 265–266
vicarious performance, 266–267
Personal service contracts
specific performance, 309
Pinnel's **case, rule in**
accord and satisfaction, 42–44, 46
Possibility mistake
existence, as to, 150–151
generally, 148–150
ownership, as to, 151
quality, as to, 151–155
Postal services
communication of acceptance, 17–18
revocation of offer, 23
withdrawal of acceptance, 18
Powers of attorney
generally, 227, 242
irrevocable powers of attorney, 255
Presumed undue influence
generally, 131–133
rebutting the presumption, 135
relationships giving rise to the
presumption as a matter of law,
133
trust and confidence, 133–134
Prevention of performance
generally, 261
Principals and agents
see **Agency**

Privity of contract
see also **Agency; Assignment**
economic loss, 207, 208
generally, 37, 195–196, 202–207
limits, 196–198
restrictive covenants, 201–202
trusts, 199–200
Public policy
contracts contrary to
see also **Restraint of trade**
administration of justice, contracts
damaging to, 163–166
commission of crime, tort or fraud,
162–163
country's foreign relations,
contracts damaging to, 163
country's safety, contracts
damaging to, 163
defrauding the revenue authorities,
167
generally, 162
institution of marriage, contracts
damaging to, 167–168
ousting jurisdiction of courts, 166
promoting corruption in public
life, 166–167
promoting sexual immorality, 168
Quantification of damages
factual damages, 302
market value, 300–301
non–pecuniary loss, 303–304
speculative damages, 302–303
tax, 304–305
Quantum meruit
remedies, 311
Quasi–contract
minors, 188–189
remedies, 311–312
Ratification
agent's authority, 233–235
Rectification
parol evidence, 62–63
Remedies
see also **Rescission**
account of profits, 296, 297
action for an agreed sum, 307
damages
agreed damages, 305–307
generally, 295–297
mitigation, 305
quantification, 300–305
remoteness of damage, 298–300
extinction of, 312
injunctions, 181, 310

Index

322